THOMAS CHARLES OF BALA

Y PARCH. THOMAS CHARLES, B.A., BALA.

THOMAS CHARLES

OF

BALA

John Aaron

THE BANNER OF TRUTH TRUST

THE BANNER OF TRUTH TRUST

Head Office
3 Murrayfield Road
Edinburgh, EH12 6EL
UK

North America Office
PO Box 621
Carlisle, PA 17013
USA

banneroftruth.org

First published 2022
© John Aaron 2022

*

ISBN
Print: 978 1 80040 095 5
Epub: 978 1 80040 096 2
Kindle: 978 1 80040 111 2

*

Typeset in 11/14 Adobe Garamond Pro
at The Banner of Truth Trust, Edinburgh

Printed in the USA by
Versa Press Inc.,
East Peoria, IL

I Gwyn,
am ei garedigrwydd di-ffael

To Jenny,
for her loving support and faithfulness

CONTENTS

LIST OF ILLUSTRATIONS

PREFACE AND ACKNOWLEDGEMENTS

Thomas Jones, Denbigh, and Thomas Charles were the two most discerning theologians of the last [19th] century; indeed they were the greatest [Welsh] theologians from 1790 to the present day.[1]

Perhaps no man was the means of bringing more blessing to his native land [than Thomas Charles], and yet no books on his life have been available for a long time.[2]

Only four biographies of Thomas Charles have ever been published, and none, in English or Welsh, since 1908. Not one is currently in print and this has been the situation for over a hundred years. The 1908 *Life* by D. E. Jenkins is a massive three-volume work of 1,927 pages: it is a gold-mine of letters, documents, and facts but is utterly unreadable as a biography. In all its pages there is not one discussion of Charles's theological position.

No substantial volume on any aspect of Charles's life has been published for over a century, except for the collected papers of a symposium held during Easter 2013. Edited by Prof. D. Densil Morgan, *Thomas Charles o'r Bala* (University of Wales Press, 2014) is a valuable book, but it contains only limited mention of the numerous and important links that Charles maintained with English evangelicals — connections which were vital for the financing of his work, especially in the early days. Also, of course, its readership is limited to those who can read Welsh.

My aim in this book has been to write an accurate and readable account of Charles's life, presented against the backcloth of his day

---

[1] R. M. Jones, *Llên Cymru a Chrefydd* (Swansea: Christopher Davies, 1977), 462.

[2] Iain H. Murray, *Heroes* (Edinburgh: Banner of Truth Trust, 2009), 134.

and age, and in the light of his extensive network of correspondents, both Welsh and English. I have tried to describe and gauge his strengths and weaknesses, and to discuss briefly his scholarship and theology, particularly as expressed in his very popular catechism, *Yr Hyfforddwr* (*The Instructor*), published in 1807 and going through eighty editions before 1900, and his *magnum opus*, the 944-page *Geiriadur Ysgrythyrol* (*Scriptural Dictionary*), published in parts from 1805 to 1811.

My main sources for this Life have been the two volumes mentioned above, especially the biography by D. E. Jenkins. Of much value also have been two Welsh works by the late R. Tudur Jones: *Thomas Charles o'r Bala: Gwas y Gair a Chyfaill Cenedl* (Cardiff: University of Wales Press, 1979) and 'Diwylliant Thomas Charles o'r Bala,' in J. E. Caerwyn Williams (ed.), *Ysgrifau Beirniadol* IV (Cardiff: University of Wales Press, 1969), 98-115. Other printed sources are mentioned in the Abbreviations and Bibliography sections. The spelling and punctuation of eighteenth and nineteenth century letters have, in general, been modernized; in a few cases, some of the Welsh expressions in Thomas and Sally Charles's letters for example, the original has been retained.

This book would not have been written without the substantial help of two individuals. I am deeply grateful to Dr Gwyn Davies, Aberystwyth, for his careful, detailed and far-sighted comments on the complete manuscript. He has saved me from innumerable mistakes. To my wife, Jenny, I owe an incalculable debt, not only for her careful correcting of grammar and style, but even more for her unfailing love, support and encouragement. It is to these two therefore that I dedicate the book.

It is a pleasure to thank three kind friends, Gwydion and Catrin Lewis, and Gareth Williams, for providing some of the photographs of Bala.

I am very grateful also to the Revs Dr Eryl Davies, Cardiff, Philip Eveson, Wrexham, and Mark Thomas, Wrexham, who read the work and provided many valuable suggestions, and to the Revs Iain Murray and Jonathan Watson, along with their colleagues at the Banner of Truth Trust, who helped extensively in its preparation for publication.

JOHN AARON
July, 2021

ABBREVIATIONS

DDM (2014)   Morgan, D. Densil, (ed.), *Thomas Charles o'r Bala*
               (Cardiff: University of Wales Press, 2014).

DEJ   Jenkins, D. E., *The Life of the Rev. Thomas Charles
               B.A. of Bala*, Vols I-III (Denbigh: 1908). Thus,
               for example, DEJ, II, 412, stands for Volume II,
               page 412.

DWB   Jenkins, R. T. (ed.), *The Dictionary of Welsh Biography
               down to 1940* (Oxford: The Honourable Society
               of Cymmrodorion, 1959).

HMGC1   Roberts, Gomer M. (ed.), *Hanes Methodistiaeth Gal-
               finaidd Cymru, Cyf. 1, Y Deffroad Mawr* (Caer-
               narfon: Llyfrfa'r Methodistiaid Calfinaidd, 1973).

HMGC2   Roberts, Gomer M. (ed.), *Hanes Methodistiaeth Gal-
               finaidd Cymru, Cyf. 2, Cynnydd y Corff* (Caer-
               narfon: Llyfrfa'r Methodistiaid Calfinaidd, 1978).

HMGC3   Jones, John Gwynfor (ed.), *Hanes Methodistiaeth
               Galfinaidd Cymru, Cyf. 3, Y Twf a'r Cadarnhau*
               (Caernarfon: Gwasg Pantycelyn, 2011).

JHS   *Journal of the Historical Society of the Presbyterian
               Church of Wales*. The Journal runs in two series:
               Volumes 1-60 (1916 to 1976) and Volumes 1 on-
               wards (1977 onwards). They are given by the vol-
               ume and year, thus, for example, JHS, 37 (1952);
               JHS, 28 (2004).

Memoir   Morgan, Edward, *A Brief Memoir of the Life and
               Labours of the Rev. T. Charles, A.B.* (London: 1831).

RTJ (1979)   Jones, R. Tudur, *Thomas Charles o'r Bala: Gwas y
               Gair a Chyfaill Cenedl* (Cardiff: University of
               Wales Press, 1979).

THOMAS CHARLES TIMELINE

Life of Thomas Charles	Related Matters	Other Dates
	1684 Birth of Griffith Jones	
		1688 The 'Glorious Revolution'
		1689 Accession of William and Mary
		1689 Toleration Act passed
		1689 SPCK formed
		1702 Accession of Anne
		1703 Birth of John Wesley
	1713 Birth of Daniel Rowland	
	1714 Birth of Howel Harris	1714 Accession of George I
		1714 Birth of George Whitefield
	1717 Birth of William Williams, Pantycelyn	
	1723 Birth of John Evans, Bala	
		1725 Birth of John Newton
		1727 Accession of George II
	1731 Birth of Thomas Foulks, Bala and Machynlleth	
	1734/5 Griffith Jones commences circulating schools	

Life of Thomas Charles	Related Matters	Other Dates
	1738 First circulating school, Bala	
	1740 First visits of Howel Harris to Bala	
	1745 Methodist Society formed at Bala	
		1747 Birth of Thomas Scott
	1750 First CM chapel built in north Wales, Adwy'r Clawdd	
	1750 'The Disruption' – Howel Harris and Daniel Rowland separate	
	1752 Birth of Thomas Jones, Creaton	
1753 Birth of Sally Jones, 12 November		
1755 Birth of Thomas Charles, 14 October		
	1756 Birth of Simon Lloyd, Bala	
	1756 Birth of Thomas Jones, Denbigh	
	1757 First CM chapel at Bala	
1758 Birth of Jane Ellis, 'Shani,' the maid		
		1759 Birth of William Wilberforce
	1760 First Association to be held at Bala	1760 Accession of George III
		1760s Beginnings of Industrial Revolution
	1761 Death of Griffith Jones	
	1762 Birth of David Charles	
	1762 The Llangeitho Revival	

Life of Thomas Charles	Related Matters	Other Dates
1763 Grandfather, David Bowen, Sheriff of Carmarthen		
1769 Enters Carmarthen Academy		
		1770 Death of George Whitefield
		1770–79 James Cook discovers Pacific Islands
	1772 Birth of John Davies, Tahiti	
1773 Converted during sermon from Daniel Rowland		
1773 Hears of Sally Jones of Bala	1773 Death of Howel Harris	
	1774 Birth of John Elias	
	1774 Birth of John Hughes, Pontrobert	
1775 Enters Jesus College, Oxford		1775–63 American War of Independence
	1776 Birth of Ann Griffiths	
1778 Ordained Deacon		
1778 First meting with Sally Jones, August		
1778–83 Curacies in Somerset		
1779 B.A.	1779 Death of Madam Bevan and end of circulating schools	1779 Newton and Cowper's *Olney Hymns*
1779 First letter to Sally Jones, 28 December		
1780 Ordained Priest, 21 May		1780 Newton's *Cardiphonia*
	1781 The 'Great Revival' at Llangeitho	
1781 Revival at Bala		

Life of Thomas Charles	Related Matters	Other Dates
1782 CM chapel at Bala enlarged		
1783 Marries Sally, 20 August	1783 Birth of Edward Morgan, Syston	
1783–4 Curacies in North Wales		
1784 First meeting with Thomas Jones, Denbigh	1784 Birth of Mary Jones, Llanfihangel-y-Pennant	
1784 Joins Bala society, 2 July		
Mid 1780s Re-establishes circulating schools		
1785 Death of Mrs Foulks, Sally's mother		
1785 Birth of first child, Thomas Rice Charles, 6 June		
1787 First Sunday school established	1787 Pall Mall, first CM chapel in Liverpool built	
1787 Birth of second child, Sarah, 17 February, who died before her first birthday		
1789 Appointed one of the Countess of Hunting-don's preachers		1789 French Revolution
	1790 Death of Daniel Rowland	
1791 Expulsion of Peter Williams	1791 Death of William Williams	1791 Death of John Wesley
1791 onwards Leadership of the CM Connexion		
1791–93 Revival at Bala		
1792 Bala chapel enlarged again		1792 Baptist Missionary Society formed

Life of Thomas Charles	Related Matters	Other Dates
1793 Birth of third child, David Jones Charles, October		1793–1815 Napoleonic Wars
	1795 London Missionary Society formed	1795 Wesleyan Methodist denomination
1798 Account of maiden voyage of *The Duff* to South Seas published		
1799 Commences *Trysorfa Ysbrydol* with Thomas Jones	1799 Religious Tract Society formed	1799 Church Missionary Society formed
1799 Left hand frostbitten when crossing Migneint in winter		
1800 Mary Jones walks to Bala		
1800 Assumes directorship of Philip Oliver's connexion of chapels		
1800 Thumb amputated, severe illness, November		
1801 *Rules for the Private Societies*	1801 John Davies sails on *The Royal Admiral* to Tahiti, 9 May	
1802 *The Welsh Methodists Vindicated*	1802 The death of Thomas Foulks	
1802 Addresses the Religious Tract Society on need for Welsh Bibles		
1803 Settles Robert Saunderson as printer in Bala		
		1804 British and Foreign Bible Society formed
1805 First part of *Geiriadur Ysgrythyrol* published		

Life of Thomas Charles	Related Matters	Other Dates
1805 *Casgliad o Emynau*, in-cluding Ann Griffiths's hymns	1805 Death of Ann Griffiths	
1806 First consignment of BFBS Welsh NT reach-es Bala, 25 September		
1807 *Yr Hyfforddwr*		1807 Death of John Newton
1807 *Y Sillydd*, a Welsh Primer		
1807 First consignment of BFBS Welsh Bible reaches Bala, 24 Sep-tember		
1809 Recommenced publi-cation of *Y Trysorfa*		
	1810 SPCK edition of Welsh Bible published	1810–20 The Regency Period
1811 First Welsh branch of BFBS formed, at Llan-gollen, 7 January		
1811 Draws up the services for, and officiates in the first CM ordinations		
1811 Fourth and last part of *Y Geiriadur Ysgrythyrol*		
1813 Rules for the Sunday Schools		
1814 Death of Thomas Charles, 5 October		
1814 Death of Sally Jones, 24 October		
1816 *Cofiant y Parch. Thomas Charles*, Thomas Jones, Denbigh		
	1817 Death of John Evans, Bala	
	1820 Death of Thomas Jones, Denbigh	1820 Accession of George IV

Life of Thomas Charles	Related Matters	Other Dates
		1821 Death of Thomas Scott
	1823 *Calvinistic Methodist Confession of Faith* first published	
1831 *Life and Labours of Thomas Charles*, Edward Morgan, Syston		
		1833 Death of William Wilberforce
	1834 Death of David Charles	
1836 *Essays, Letters and Interesting Papers of the Late Thomas Charles*, Edward Morgan, Syston	1836 Death of Simon Lloyd, Bala	
		1837 Accession of Victoria
	1841 Death of John Elias	
	1845 Death of Thomas Jones, Creaton	
	1855 Death of John Davies, Tahiti	
	1864 Death of Mary Jones	
	1867 Opening of the Calvinistic Methodist College at Bala	
	1869 Death of Edward Morgan, Syston	
1908 *Life of Thomas Charles*, D. E. Jenkins		

Map of Wales
showing place-names associated with Thomas Charles's life.

1

THE METHODIST REVIVAL IN WALES

THE significance of the life of Thomas Charles may be understood only if it is considered in the context of the Welsh Methodist Revival of the eighteenth and nineteenth centuries. The Revival began twenty years before he was born, he was converted under the preaching of its foremost preacher, he himself participated in a number of the awakenings that contributed to the development of the Revival, and similar awakenings continued for some twenty years or more after his death. John Hughes (1796–1860) of Liverpool, the first historian of Welsh Calvinistic Methodism and a leading preacher, pastor, and elder statesman of his denomination, said of him:

> [Charles] joined them at a time when Methodism [in Wales] was at a low ebb. Forty years and more had passed since the beginning of the Revival. In the south, many ordained men of the Church had joined the first fathers, but *not one in Gwynedd*.[1] Scores of unordained preachers had arisen in north and south, and some hundreds of small congregations were already scattered throughout the principality, yet, for all this, Methodism had little influence until the days of Mr Charles. This was particularly the case in north Wales. Very few places of worship had been built there: where there are sixty today [1851], there were then only six [1783]. ... The people of the north looked to the south for ordained clergy and for the ablest preachers. ...

[1] Gwynedd is the north Wales region corresponding to the old counties of Caernarfon and Merioneth. The statement was equally true for the other three counties of the north: Anglesey, Denbighshire, and Flintshire.

> There was an urgent need for a man of some stature to take the lead amongst the brethren in the north. ... And when it might have been dangerous for them to choose anyone from amongst themselves in that they were all of about the same general level of knowledge and influence, God saw fit, so as to keep them from contentions and divisions, to raise up Charles for them. ... He sat amongst them, the humblest of them all and the least assuming and ostentatious, but the greatest in influence. He presided over them, not by man's appointment, but by God's, not from any formal decision but from a natural promotion, not by force but by evident qualification.[2]

To appreciate the many important points in this statement it is necessary, before beginning to consider the facts of Thomas Charles's life, to review the early years and development of the Methodist Revival: in south and mid Wales; in north Wales; and, particularly, in the town of Bala, Merioneth (the centre of Charles's ministry from 1783 onwards).

The Methodist awakening in south and mid Wales (1735–62)

The land of Wales is bordered by the sea to the north, west and south, and by England to the east. It is of irregular shape, about forty miles wide at its narrowest and a hundred miles at its widest. Its length is about one hundred and forty miles. Its total area of just over eight thousand square miles comprises about eight percent of the area of the United Kingdom. In the eighteenth century (and up until 1974) it was divided into thirteen counties — the 'old counties.' Six of these were in south Wales: the counties of Monmouth, Glamorgan, Carmarthen, Pembroke, Cardigan, and Brecon; five were in the north: the counties of Anglesey, Caernarfon, Denbigh, Flint, and Merioneth; and two, Montgomery and Radnor were in mid-Wales. The population of the country was around 300,000 — about five percent of that of England and Wales.

---

[2] John Hughes, *Methodistiaeth Cymru* (Wrexham: Hughes and Sons, 1851), Vol. 1, 330.

Early in the eighteenth century four men were born in south Wales within a period of four or five years: Daniel Rowland (1713), Howel Harris (1714), Howel Davies (1716) and William Williams (1717). Just over twenty years later, within a period of four years, the four men were converted: Rowland in the winter of 1734/35; Harris in 1735; Davies in 1737; Williams in 1738. The blessing of God upon the subsequent ministries of these four men was the predominant factor in the beginning and development of the Methodist Awakening in Wales. The characteristics of the movement at this early stage were:

• the relative youthfulness of the men involved, all being in their early twenties;

• the fervour and intensity of their itinerant preaching;

• the means they devised to nurture and teach the converts, making use of farms, out-houses, and other dwellings to gather the believers in small groups which they called *seiadau* (societies), where they prayed, exhorted, studied the Bible, and shared their spiritual experiences;

• the emergence of a group of laymen to assist in the work of preaching and teaching. The first 'Calvinistic Methodist Fathers,' as the four men are known, were all,[3] apart from Harris, clergymen of the Church of England. As the leaders of the movement came to realize that many of its converts were gifted preachers, they appointed these over specific societies and encouraged them in their itinerant work. But in that these were laymen they hesitated to call them ministers and instead used the term 'exhorters.' In this way they hoped, if at all possible, to avoid any accusations of acting illegally by encouraging the ministry of men who were not ordained.

Connections were soon made with those involved in the parallel Methodist awakening in England. Both John Wesley and George Whitefield visited Wales many times and formed friendships with the leaders, particularly with Howel Harris. Harris was a gifted

---

[3] A fifth south-Walian, Peter Williams (born 1723, converted 1743) was to join them in the work in 1747.

organizer and set up a hierarchy of meetings in order to regulate the activities of the movement. The Monthly Meetings, or Associations, were meetings for the exhorters of a particular locality (eventually, of individual counties) and the Quarterly Associations, where all clergymen and exhorters were expected to be present, were arranged at different venues. The first Association was held in Cil-y-cwm, Carmarthenshire on 8 January 1742. A 'General Association of the Calvinistic Methodists of England and Wales' was also set up, to meet every six months. The first of these was convened in January 1743 at Caerphilly, Glamorganshire, when George Whitefield (who was on a preaching tour of Wales at the time) was appointed moderator.

While acknowledging the preaching and organizational abilities of these young men and the great courage and faith that they displayed, it is clear, from their own accounts and those of other witnesses, that the remarkable effects of their ministries sprang from the powerful influences of the Holy Spirit that accompanied them on so many occasions. Thus, for example, in the early period of the work (sometime around the year 1736) Rowland was in his own pulpit in the church at Llangeitho, Cardiganshire, and was at that part of the service where the Litany was read. When he reached the words, 'By thine agony and bloody sweat, by thy cross and passion, by thy precious death and burial, by thy glorious resurrection and ascension, and by the coming of the Holy Ghost, Good Lord, deliver us,' a 'strange influence fell on his spirit; his tone was most melting; his voice shook with feeling; the whole congregation was struck by the same influence; they too saw him whom they had pierced, and they mourned for him as one mourns for his only son; but soon the mourning turned into unspeakable glory.' The result was a general spiritual awakening that influenced a considerable area around Llangeitho. In 1743 Rowland wrote to George Whitefield:

> There is a general, fresh, and uncommon stirring in most places. Many come anew under convictions, especially old, wordly professors, and backsliders return. And there is such

a power as I never felt before given me in preaching and administering the Lord's Supper. The Lord comes down amongst us in such a manner as words can give no idea of … Such is the light, view, and power that God gives very many in the Ordinance, that they cannot possibly help crying out, praising and adoring Jesus, being quite swallowed up in God. And thus I was obliged to leave my congregation, being in many hundreds, in a flame … This is our condition generally every Sabbath.[4]

Whitefield was himself to be present at a Communion Sunday at Llangeitho soon afterwards and reported, 'The power of God at the sacrament, under the ministry of Mr Rowland was enough to make a person's heart burn within him. At seven in the morning I have seen, perhaps, ten thousand from different parts, in the midst of the sermon, crying "Glory", "Praise", ready to leap for joy.'[5]

In 1746 it was noted that about three thousand received communion at the hands of Daniel Rowland and his assistants at the monthly celebration of the sacrament at Llangeitho. At the same period, about two thousand communicants were served each month by Howel Davies in Pembrokeshire.[6]

Howel Harris was experiencing similar visitations of the Holy Spirit's power. He noted in his *Diary*, in November 1738, a comment he made at the time to Rowland, 'Sure the time here now is like New England.'[7] Harris had been reading Jonathan Edwards' account of the beginning of the Awakening in America, *A Narrative of Surprising Conversions*, published in England in 1737. Even at this early date, the Welsh Methodists realized that they were part of a much wider work of God.

[4] Eifion Evans, *Daniel Rowland and the Great Evangelical Awakening in Wales* (Edinburgh: Banner of Truth Trust, 1985), 74,

[5] *Ibid.*, 74.

[6] Henry Hughes, *Diwygiadau Crefyddol Cymru* (Caernarfon, 1906), 101.

[7] Eifion Evans, *Daniel Rowland*, 69.

North Wales

In the five counties of north Wales the activity of the Methodists did not meet with similar success. There were no ordained clergymen associated with the movement in the north, indeed most of the clergy were fiercely opposed to them and they warned their congregations against hearing the few men who ventured from the south. No church pulpits were offered them from which to preach and no sympathy extended when they were attacked by local mobs while preaching in the open air. Harris twice visited areas in the north in 1740, on the first occasion very narrowly escaping serious injury. On a further visit, to Bala, in 1741 he was so violently attacked and trampled upon that he believed he was on the point of dying Stephen's death. Rowland's visits to the north from 1740 onwards also met with little success. On occasions, in 1743 particularly, he encountered considerable opposition. The same treatment was received by Peter Williams. Stones were thrown at him in Newtown, Montgomeryshire, in 1747, but he was better received in Llŷn, Caernarfonshire, and on the island of Anglesey, where he was allowed to preach in many places. However, in 1748, while passing through Denbighshire, he was apprehended and fined £20 by the local landowner and magistrate, Sir Watkin Williams Wynn, who from that time until his death in 1749 maintained a fierce opposition to any Methodist who ventured into his jurisdiction.

On the back of his 1747 *Diary*, Harris noted the societies that there were then in existence. There were a total of a hundred and twenty eight in south and mid Wales and only two in north Wales (at Bala and in the Llŷn peninsula).[8] To this number must be added the twenty to thirty further societies established in south Wales by this time by Daniel Rowland in Cardiganshire and Howel Davies in Pembrokeshire.[9] An increasing number of lay preachers, a detailed planning in the quarterly meetings of their itineraries (particularly for the north of the country), and the continuing local and regional

[8] HMGC1, 182.

[9] Eryn M. White, *Praidd bach y Bugail Mawr* (Llandysul: Gomer Press, 1995), 3-5.

awakenings brought about a remarkable growth in the next few years. It is estimated that by 1750 nearly three hundred and fifty societies had been formed in the eight counties of south and mid Wales, and a further eighty-two in north Wales.[10] If the average number of members in the societies was about twenty (it was considerably higher in some of the south Wales groups but only single figures in isolated places and in the north) these numbers suggest that there were around ten thousand committed Methodists by this date, thirteen years after the beginning of the Revival.

The beginnings of Methodism in Bala, Merioneth

A description of the common Welsh pastimes of the period before the Revival was given by John Evans, one of the first elders of the Bala society:

> The common people were more willing to attend the church services on a Sunday morning than the gentry, but on the afternoons they also would run after their games. There would hardly be a Sunday afternoon without there being a games competition somewhere in the region. In these, the young men would demonstrate their strength and many of the people of the neighbourhood would come to watch them. On Saturday nights, in the summer especially, the young people, men and women, would hold what they termed their *Nosweithiau canu* (Singing evenings) and amuse themselves with dancing and with the harp until sunrise on the Sunday.
>
> Here in Bala, in the afternoons, there would be singing and dancing in the taverns, tennis playing in the *Hall*, and football. In every corner of the town some game or other would be played throughout daylight on the Sunday. In the summer, *Interludes* would be held on the stage in the *Hall* in the afternoons. In such a manner the gentry and commons would amuse themselves, profaning the Lord's Day.[11]

[10] Derec Ll. Morgan, *Y Diwygiad Mawr* (Llandysul: Gomer Press, 1981), 16.
[11] 'Conversation between Scrutator and Senex' (*Trysorfa Ysbrydol*, April 1799), 30-31.

As mentioned above, Howel Harris first visited Bala and preached in its streets in February 1740, returning again in November 1740 and January 1741. It was during this last visit, and from the hands of Bala people, urged on by the Rev. Robert Jones, the rector of Llanycil Church, the parish church of the town, that he endured the worst physical attacks that he ever experienced in his life. 'But the Lord intervened for him in a way that was almost miraculous, and he escaped from their grasp.'[12]

After this near-lynching, Merioneth was avoided by most of the itinerant preachers. However, a Methodist society of eight members began to meet in the town in 1745. Its leaders were two brothers, John Moses, the blacksmith, and Evan Moses who later became an exhorter. Harris visited the little flock in 1747 and then again in 1748 and 1749. A further eight years passed after the last of Harris's visits before the town's Methodists, still numbering under a hundred, ventured to build a chapel in 1757. By 1760 the Bala society was confident enough to invite, and be accepted to host, the north Wales Calvinistic Methodist Association in the town. About two hundred people attended. Although the society at Bala was one of the first two to be established in north Wales, Merioneth was about the last Welsh county to accept the Methodists. To a large extent, this was because of the attachment of the population to the Established Church. 'What surprised Merioneth churchgoers most in the Methodist preachers was their *extempore* preaching rather than a read sermon, and spontaneous prayer rather than a recital from *The Book of Common Prayer*.'[13]

The Disruption

Unfortunately, throughout the late 1740s onwards, tensions arose within the movement (and particularly between Harris and

---

[12] John Morgan Jones and William Morgan, trans. by John Aaron, *The Calvinistic Methodist Fathers of Wales*, Vol. 1 (Edinburgh: Banner of Truth Trust, 2008), 172-73.

[13] E. D. Evans, 'Methodist Persecution in Merioneth in the late Eighteenth Century,' JHS, 28 (2004), 26.

Rowland) mainly as a result of Harris's increasingly authoritarian behaviour and doctrinal waywardness. These tensions eventually brought about a separation in 1750. Harris removed himself from all itinerant work and retired to his 'Family,' a religious community that he set up at his home in Trefeca, Breconshire. 'Rowland's people' sought to maintain the remaining societies and to continue supplying preachers for north Wales but the loss of Harris's extensive travelling and his organizing genius could not be offset. More importantly, the quickening and convicting ministry of the Spirit was, to a large extent, withdrawn from the movement. A comparative dearth prevailed over the work for twelve years. 'A long night and a barren winter were the results' wrote Robert Jones, Rhos-lan.[14] Very many of the societies disappeared (especially in south-east Wales where the societies had been most strongly associated with Harris), their members returning to the world or leaving to join local Dissenting congregations. As Harris was the main link with the work in England, and with Whitefield in particular, this separation resulted in the Calvinistic Methodist movements of the two countries developing independently, to a large degree, from 1750 onwards. Not until the fresh awakening known as the 'Llangeitho Revival' of 1762 were the Welsh Methodists to experience again the extraordinary powers that they had known in the early period of the Revival.

[14] '*Hir nos, a gaeaf diffrwyth a fu yr effeithiau.*' See *Gwaith Robert Jones, Rhos Lan*, ed. by Owen M. Edwards (Wrexham: Hughes a'i Fab, 1898), 89.

Top: Present-day ruins of old Pant-dwfn, Thomas Charles's home.
Bottom: St Teilo's Church, Llanddowror.

2

BIRTH, CHILDHOOD AND CONVERSION
(1755–75)

Family background and birth

THOMAS Charles was born on 14 October 1755, probably at Long-moor Farm, about a mile and a half east of St Clears, in the parish of Llanfihangel Abercywyn, Carmarthenshire. He was the fifth child of Rees Charles and his second wife, Jael. The couple had married on 19 December 1743 and at the time of his birth were living at Longmoor, a 68-acre tenement farm. They moved within a few weeks to the considerably larger farm of Pant-dwfn, about a mile south of St Clears.[1] This was a farm of 367 acres with a yearly rent of £120. The exact date of the move is not known, hence the slight uncertainty regarding Charles's place of birth.[2] There were at least thirteen children born to Rees Charles: two, most probably, by his

[1] The buildings of Longmoor Farm no longer exist. Their position is shown on sheet 41, Carmarthen, Ordnance Survey (*Old Series*), 1866 (reprinted David and Charles, 1969). They were demolished around 1850 and their stones used elsewhere. In 1908 DEJ (I, 11) noted that they stood in a field belonging to Asgood Farm, but the field is now part of the holding of Penyrheol. The present owner pointed out a clump of trees where, according to family tradition, the farmhouse once stood. The present day Pant-dwfn is a modern building. A few stone walls remain of the old Pant-dwfn. (See the photograph at the head of this chapter.) Asgood and Penyrheol are to be found on Ordnance Survey Landranger Map 159 and Pant-dwfn on Map 158.
[2] See DEJ, I, 12-16, where Jenkins shows, from a detailed study of letters relating to rents and leases, that Charles was almost certainly born at Longmoor.

first wife, Jane, and eleven by Jael Charles.[3] In later life Thomas
Charles had most to do with his older sister Elizabeth, born before
the family settled at Longmoor, and his younger brother David,
born at Pant-dwfn. Though Pant-dwfn was considered a mansion
in the eyes of the neighbourhood, the family was not rich but lived
comfortably.[4]

Within the family the greater influence on Thomas Charles
was that of his mother, Jael. She was born in 1726 and was much
younger than her husband. She came from a wealthy farming
family not far from Carmarthen. Her father, David Bowen,
was well respected in the locality,[5] and when Thomas was eight
years old, his grandfather became mayor of Carmarthen. When
discussing the later careers of the brothers, Thomas and David,
one modern scholar notes that: 'The two brothers could quite
appropriately be called "Methodist aristocrats," even though that
seems such a contradiction in terms when considering the peasant
nature of eighteenth-century Methodism. It is significant that both
brothers were always referred to as "Mr Charles" in their respective
spheres.'[6] Edward Morgan, Charles's first biographer,[7] emphasized
his modesty but a more recent assessment of Charles states that 'it
is not inappropriate to notice how natural it was for him to lead. It
was a matter of surprise to Howel Harris and John Elias that providence had made leaders out of them. Charles took it for granted.'[8]

That the family did not prosper to the extent of others of Jael's
relatives was probably due to the inadequacies of the father, Rees

[3] William (born 1735) and Sage (1742) from his first marriage; Jane (1745),
Elizabeth (1746 or 47), David (1749, died in infancy), Jael (1752), THOMAS
(1755), Rees (1757, died in infancy), Ann (1760), David (1762), John (1766),
Rees (1768), and Charlotte (1770) from his second marriage.

[4] DEJ, I, 22-23.

[5] *Ibid.*, I, 15.

[6] E. Wyn James, 'David Charles (1762–1834), Caerfyrddin: Diwinydd,
Pregethwr, Emynydd,' JHS, 36 (2012), 18.

[7] Edward Morgan (1783–1869) of Syston, Leicestershire; Charles's first
biographer in English.

[8] RTJ (1979), 11.

Charles. He was respected sufficiently in the community to have served on three occasions as church warden in the parish, but he was not much of a farmer. In later years he encountered considerable financial difficulties, which proved a burden on Thomas Charles. At one point he was caught brewing illegally and had to pay a heavy fine. Although in comfortable circumstances it is probable that he could afford to send only one son (Jael's eldest boy, Thomas) to Oxford.

Childhood and first religious influences (1755–69)

The area of land south-west of Carmarthen towards the Pembrokeshire border is noted for its contribution to evangelical teaching over many generations. In the sixteenth century the puritan Robert Holland (1556/7–1622?) was a parson in the region, first at Llanddowror, two miles south-west of St Clears, and then at various parishes in Pembrokeshire. He published translations of books by William Perkins together with works of his own. Stephen Hughes (1622–88), vicar of Meidrim, three miles north of St Clears, was an early Nonconformist who travelled through south-west Wales, keeping school, preaching, establishing churches and, in particular, producing cheap evangelical literature for the common people. He helped to translate the first Welsh edition of *Pilgrim's Progress* as well as publishing *Canwyll y Cymry* [*A Candle for the Welsh*], the influential evangelical verses of Vicar Rhys Prichard, in 1681. His greatest achievement was the production in 1677/78 of a cheap edition of the Bible in Welsh.

'Serious impressions'

Of these heroes of the past, the individual who influenced Charles most, although only indirectly, was Griffith Jones (1684–1761). He had come to the district when he was appointed vicar of Laugharne in 1711 and was eventually settled as vicar of Llanddowror in 1716, remaining there until his death. His achievement in setting up circulating schools to teach the common people to read their Bibles is discussed in a later chapter.[9] He has also been termed the 'Father of the Welsh Methodist Revival': Daniel Rowland was awakened under his preaching; Howel Harris, for many years, visited him when in need of advice; all of the Methodist Fathers received much help and encouragement from him. Very many of the early Methodist exhorters were schoolmasters in his schools for a period. All this was in spite of the fact that as a committed Church of England clergyman he strongly disapproved of many of the Methodists' methods, and could never bring himself to engage fully with the movement. As the itinerating and lay preaching of the Methodists increased, the frequency of his own preaching tours, a notable feature of his early ministry, decreased, and he confined his preaching to the Llanddowror area.

Six years or so after the death of Griffith Jones, Thomas Charles was sent (at about ten or twelve years of age) to the school at Llanddowror, and was there for three or four years. It was during this time that he first became concerned over the state of his soul. He later wrote, in a brief autobiographical section at the beginning of his *Diary*:

> During that time I first felt serious impressions. The first cause of any thoughts about my soul I do not recollect. My convictions of sin were for a year or more but very slight and at intervals; but I had almost continually, though sometimes weaker and sometimes stronger, powerful impressions made on my mind inclining me to attend the preaching of the gospel, to read the Bible, and the best books I could get.[10]

He writes of walking some distances 'to hear gospel sermons,' and of reading John Bunyan's 'Treatise on the Two Covenants.'[11] In particular, 'that part wherein he shows the dreadful state of those

---

[9] See pages 131-33. E. Wyn James, 'Pererinion ar y Ffordd: Thomas Charles ac Ann Griffiths,' JHS, 29-30 (2005-06), 74.

[10] *Memoir*, 3-4. The *Memoir* includes many selections from the diary that Charles wrote in the period 1778 to 1785.

[11] John Bunyan, *The Doctrine of the Law and Grace Unfolded* (c. 1660). A Welsh translation was published in 1767.

who are under the covenant of works affected me very much and made me several times to cry bitterly.'[12] He also noted in the *Diary* that at the time he had no one with whom he could talk on spiritual matters. This is surprising in that there were already strong family connections with the Methodists. John Bowen, his uncle, who was twenty-five years older than Thomas, had been converted under the preaching of George Whitefield. The first Methodists of the town of Carmarthen met for worship in a small cottage of his, near his farm in Llangunnor. He eventually became one of the elders of the Methodist society in Carmarthen.[13] It is strange that he did not speak to his young nephew. It may be that the separation between them — of twenty-five years in age and of fifteen miles in distance — was too much for them to be closely acquainted. It may be also that the two families were not close: there was clearly no evangelical influence in Thomas's home at this time, and his parents may have kept at a distance from the Methodist ways of Llangunnor.

Spiritual fellowship and help were to come from another direction:

> At last Providence brought me acquainted with an aged, holy, and pious man, by name, Rees Hugh, who lived a few miles off; on whom I constantly called once or twice a week, and his conversation was much blessed to me. Sometimes he was filled with great joy and comfort in talking to me; and when that was the case, I never was unaffected. I loved him as long as he lived, as my own soul, and always looked upon him as my father in Christ. The remembrance of him will be pleasing to me as long as I live. He was an old disciple of Mr Griffith Jones of Llanddowror.[14]

Yet, as he also says in his *Diary*, he still had only limited knowledge of 'the gospel scheme' and was seeking answers to his questions and using all means to obtain them. He began to take communion in the parish church and even attempted to maintain

---

[12] *Memoir*, 4.
[13] DEJ, II, 153.
[14] *Memoir*, 4.

family worship at Pant-dwfn:

> I hope also that my feeble attempts were not ineffectual
> in the end. Considering my age and my little knowledge,
> the authority I maintained in a family so large, generally
> about eighteen, was surprising. What was deficient in other
> things was supplied by my earnestness and zeal. My temper
> and disposition being naturally mild, I was always generally
> beloved by all my relations; and this helped me greatly in
> passing through many difficulties.[15]

The Llangeitho Revival of 1762–64

During this period in which the young Thomas Charles was first
becoming aware of spiritual realities, he could not have avoided
hearing also of the new power and energy that had suddenly
returned to the Methodist movement in the country. The main
instruments in this awakening were the preaching of Daniel
Rowland and the recent publication of a new hymnbook written
by William Williams. Robert Jones, Rhos-lan, described the events:

> About the year 1762, in the face of great unworthiness
> and baseness, God remembered His covenant, by visiting
> graciously a great number of sinners in several parts of Wales
> ... There was a real difference between this revival and that
> which began at first through [the agency of] Mr Harris: the
> mode of proceeding in that was sharp and very thunderous:
> but in this, as in the house of Cornelius long ago, great
> crowds magnified God without being able to cease, but
> sometimes leaping in jubilation as did David before the Ark
> ... When these powerful outpourings descended on several
> hundreds, if not thousands, throughout south Wales and
> Gwynedd, there arose much excitement and controversy
> concerning the matter; many were struck with amazement
> and said, 'What can this mean?' ... It is noteworthy
> that it was on the day that Mr W. Williams brought the
> hymn-book entitled *Y Môr o Wydr* ['The Sea of Glass'] to

[15] *Memoir*, 5.

Llangeitho that the revival broke out, after the long winter which had enveloped the churches because of the schism which has already been mentioned.[16]

The title 'The Llangeitho Revival' is something of a misnomer in that, as mentioned by Robert Jones, it spread during the next two years to several parts of the country, including, for the first time, large areas of north Wales. The Llŷn Peninsula, Anglesey and the Bala region were the places first affected, but in the next decade more and more societies were formed in the north-east of the country. On three different occasions in the 1770s Daniel Rowland was asked to preach at the opening of newly-built chapel buildings: in Denbighshire in 1771, Flintshire in 1775 and, during his last journey to the north, Caernarfonshire in 1777.

Not the least of the blessings of this period was the reconciliation brought about between Howel Harris and his fellow-labourers of old in the gospel. In late 1762 Harris heard of the spread of the revival and acknowledged that the Lord was owning his servants — Rowland in particular. He longed for a part in the work with them again but feared that he was not worthy. He had been brought to realize that his own authoritarian behaviour had been one factor that had brought down the chastisement of the separation upon them: 'When I heard of the life among them, feared lest I should bring death. When I heard of their success, I was humbled and kept from envy or judging, blessing God for raising them and not me, yet fearing lest I should fall by my affections and hindering God's End of the Separation.'[17] Meetings were arranged between himself and Rowland and Williams. He was welcomed warmly and invited to return and to preach among the societies again. 'Sure this is the year of Jubilee,' he wrote in his diary, 'the time is come, the shadow of prejudices fly away, old love and simplicity return, and what did let and hinder seems to remove, and self seems to come down.'[18]

[16] Quoted in Emyr Roberts and R. Geraint Gruffydd, *Revival and Its Fruits* (Bryntirion: Evangelical Library of Wales, 1981), 22.
[17] HMGC1, 400.
[18] *Ibid.*, 401.

Thomas Charles at Carmarthen Academy

> When I was about fourteen years of age [1769] my father
> sent me to the Academy at Carmarthen, where I went with
> much fear and dread; and my old dear friend [Rees Hugh]
> was very fearful and anxious for me in my new situation. He
> prayed earnestly with me and for me before I went; and I
> have often thought I have received many blessings in answer
> to his prayers to God for me.[19]

The academy can trace its origins to the minister of an Independent cause in the town, William Evans (d. 1718), who opened
a dissenting academy in about 1704. No other college or academy
in Wales can compare with it for its wanderings, both geographical
and theological. Its main financial support came from the Presbyterian Fund Board in London, and when a tutor died the academy
would be transferred to the home of his appointed successor. Thus,
in the period from 1704 to 1795, it wandered from Carmarthen to
Llwyn-llwyd (near Hay-on-Wye, Breconshire), to Haverfordwest,
Pembrokeshire, back to Carmarthen (Thomas Charles's period),
then to Swansea, Glamorgan, until settling finally in Carmarthen
again in 1795. William Evans was thoroughly Calvinistic and a
translator of the *Westminster Confession of Faith* into Welsh, but
subsequent tutors included Calvinists, Arminians, Arians, and
Unitarians. Students destined for Baptist, Independent, Presbyterian, Unitarian, Calvinistic Methodist, and even Church of England
ministries received their theological preparation here.

A student at the academy in the latter half of the eighteenth
century noted that there were at least twenty Nonconformist
students there and a further twenty studying for ministry in the
Established Church. These Church of England students however
did not tend to remain more than a few years at the academy.
Thomas Charles, with his six years of study there, was therefore
a notable exception. Thomas Morgan, another Carmarthen
Academy student during these years, recorded that the curriculum

[19] *Memoir*, 6.

included the study of the Greek of the New Testament, a selection of the Psalms in Hebrew, Pictet's *Systematic Theology*, Chronology, Astronomy, Conic Sections, Trigonometry, Natural Philosophy, Pufendorf's *Law of Nature*, Goodwin's *Moses and Aaron*, and Lampe's *Ecclesiastical History*. Other authors studied were Hutcheson, Clarke, and Wollaston in Ethics and Natural Religion; Keil, Muschenbrock, and Fergusson in Natural Philosophy; Isaac Watts, John Locke, and Duncan in Logic. Most of these authors are indicative of the rationalistic and deistic nature of the theological training of the academy at this time. In contrast, Benedict Pictet (1655–1724) was a Calvinist and his work was a translation of his *Theologia Christiana* (1696), written when he was professor of Theology at the University of Geneva. It is significant that in 1760 the Arian minister of Llwynrhydowen, Cardiganshire, David Lloyd, rejoiced to hear that Pictet's works were to be removed from the Carmarthen curriculum. It would seem therefore that Thomas Charles was allowed only one or perhaps two years' study of the one decidedly Calvinistic author read at the academy.[20]

But as far as the teaching of languages is concerned Thomas Charles was to profit from the best training that was available in Wales at that time. The foundations of that linguistic knowledge which he was to use so effectively in later years were laid down here by his tutor, Dr Jenkin Jenkins (d. 1780). Jenkins, the principal of the academy during Charles's time there, was an Arian in belief, and perhaps the most wayward in doctrine of all its eighteenth-century principals. As well as being principal of the academy, Jenkins was minister of Water Street Independent Chapel, and David Morgan, Llanfyllin, an Independent minister and historian, says that during this period he nearly killed the cause by his lack of seriousness and the anti-evangelical nature of his ministry. It was public knowledge also that the students during his time at Carmarthen were noted for their irreligious behaviour[21] and at the end of the course the

[20] Dewi Eirug Davies, *Hoff Ddysgedig Nyth* (Swansea: Tŷ John Penry, 1976), 121-22, 127-30.

[21] Thomas Rees and John Thomas, *Hanes Eglwysi Annibynnol Cymru*, Cyf. I (Liverpool, 1871), 274.

majority were called to Arian congregations in England, while some entered secular professions.

Nevertheless, Jenkin Jenkins inspired in Thomas Charles an abiding interest in Latin, Greek, and Hebrew in particular, and in the study of languages generally. Thirty-five years later, in the preface to his *Geiriadur Ysgrythyrol* (*Scriptural Dictionary*), Charles wrote: 'I have no greater pleasure in the world, nor any means more profitable, than reading the Holy Scriptures in the languages in which the Holy Spirit delivered them; namely the Old Testament in Hebrew, and the New Testament in Greek.' His *Dictionary* cites nearly three dozen classical authors such as Pliny, Strabo, Herodotus, and Josephus. In addition, although not fully fluent in French and Italian, he was familiar enough with them and had a considerable interest in the various theories on the development of the Welsh language and in the etymology of its words.[22]

During these years at Carmarthen, Thomas Charles lodged with his older sister, Elizabeth, and her husband, Joseph Thomas respectable merchants of the town. Two significant events in the history of Methodism in Wales occurred during this period. In July 1773 Howel Harris died at Trefeca, and in May 1774 John Elias was born at Aber-erch on the Llŷn Peninsula. But there had been an earlier third event, in January 1773, which was to have far greater significance for Welsh Calvinistic Methodism than either of these.

Conversion

It is difficult now to know with any certainty Thomas Charles's religious condition during his first three years in Carmarthen, the period up to the winter of 1772/3. He mentions in his *Diary* that he soon joined the Methodist society of the town and appreciated the spiritual conversation of its godly members. 'But all had been well-nigh ruined by a set of careless, high-spirited jolly professors[23] with whom I contracted too much intimacy soon after I came

[22] R. T. Jones, *Grym y Gair a Fflam y Ffydd*, ed. D. Densil Morgan, (Bangor, 1998), 243-44.

[23] That is, professors of faith.

there.'[24] Whether these were friends from the academy or from the town is not known. Nor is it known what effect nearly three years of the baleful teaching of Carmarthen Academy had had on him. However, he writes in his *Diary* that he was kept afloat by James Hervey's *Dialogues*, 'which were made very useful to me in giving me a clearer knowledge of the doctrines of the gospel, concerning which I had hitherto been very much in the dark.' He was helped also by 'many other useful evangelical books,' but more particularly by 'religious conversation.'[25] What is certain is that, whatever his beliefs, they were intellectual rather than spiritual; 'head-knowledge' alone rather than the 'heart-knowledge' that the Methodists sought. Then, in his fourth year at the academy occurred the great event of his conversion. On 20 January 1773, aged seventeen years and three months, he went to New Chapel to hear Daniel Rowland preach.[26] The latter's text was, 'For we have not an high priest which cannot be touched with the feeling of our infirmities; but was in all points tempted like as we are, yet without sin' (Hebrews 4:15, KJV). The following is his own account:

> A day much to be remembered by me as long as I live. Ever since the happy day I have lived in a new heaven and a new earth. The change a blind man who receives his sight experiences does not exceed the change I at that time experienced in my mind …
>
> Then I was first convinced of the sin of unbelief or entertaining narrow, contracted and hard thoughts of the Almighty. I had such a view of Christ as our High Priest, of

---

[24] *Memoir*, 6.

[25] *Ibid.*

[26] No agreement has been reached as to whether Charles was referring to 'the New Chapel' (the building built for Daniel Rowland in Llangeitho, Cardiganshire, after he was thrown out of the Church of England) or to the building at Capel Newydd (New Chapel), Pembrokeshire. The first view used to be the majority view (see DEJ, I, 35-37; RTJ (1979), 13.) The authorised history of the denomination argues for the second view (see HMGC2, 65.) The most recent symposium on Thomas Charles opts not to decide between the different viewpoints (DDM (2014), see 3, 160, 193).

his love, compassion, power, and all-sufficiency, as filled my soul with astonishment — with joy unspeakable and full of glory. My mind was overwhelmed and overpowered with amazement. The truths exhibited to my view appeared too wonderfully gracious to be believed. I could not believe for very joy. The glorious scenes then opened to my eyes will abundantly satisfy my soul millions of years hence in the contemplation of them.

I had some idea of gospel truths before floating in my head, but they never powerfully and with divine energy penetrated my heart till now. The effect of this sermon remained upon my mind above half a year, during which time I was generally in a comfortable and heavenly frame. Often in walking in the fields I looked up to heaven with joy and called that my home, at the same time ardently longing for the appearance of the glorious Saviour to take me forever to himself.[27]

Throughout his life, Thomas Charles remembered it as a unique day in his experience and celebrated its anniversaries. Five years later he wrote: 'Today is a special day, to be greatly remembered. So glorious was the revelation of divine truths on this very day. By mercy they are to this hour as glorious and valuable as ever; they are always new, always awakening. O, may I live and feed upon them more and more!'[28] Again, in 1781, he wrote: 'O the happy return of this most beneficial day! A day to be happily remembered for on it the light of the knowledge of the glorious gospel first shone brightly in my soul in the face of Jesus Christ. On the return of this sacred day let every other thought give place to thanksgiving and praise …'[29]

Commenting on Charles's description of his conversion R. Tudur Jones states:

This revelatory paragraph is the key to the whole of Thomas Charles's career, and the key also to the source of the strength

[27] *Memoir*, 7-8.
[28] DEJ, I, 69.
[29] *Ibid.*, I, 244.

of the evangelical movement to which he eventually attached himself. Two things happened to him at Llangeitho. At a stroke, the scattered, disconnected knowledge of Christianity which he possessed hitherto had formed into a clear pattern. He could see 'the plan of the Gospel.' It would not be inappropriate to call this experience his intellectual conversion. And for the rest of his life he gave priority to the intellectual content of Christianity — to the Bible, to doctrine, to theology, and, as a consequence, to education. This is the first thing involved in that which occurred at the New Chapel in Llangeitho. The second thing was that the truths had 'penetrated' his heart. And he says that they had done so 'with divine energy.' This is what the Protestant Reformers meant by 'the inner witness of the Holy Spirit.' This was not only an intellectual matter. A new unity had entered his whole personality — understanding, will and feelings.[30]

This was not the only time that Charles heard Daniel Rowland preach. Some years later, writing to Sally Jones of Bala, he notes, 'I am glad that you returned safe from Llangeitho ... The remembrance of the sermons I heard there six or eight years ago does me more good than anything I have since heard. When at school at Carmarthen my excursions there in the holidays, twice a year, were more profitable to me than all the sermons I heard in the intervals between. I have therefore every possible reason to think highly of that great and good man of God.'[31]

Charles remained at the academy for a further two years after his conversion, summarising the time as follows: 'During the whole of my stay at Carmarthen, the Lord was in general very precious to me; I enjoyed very abundantly the most powerful means of grace, and also much of the divine presence in them. At the same time I was not without great temptations and snares which more than once or twice had well-nigh ruined me: but in

[30] RTJ (1979), 14.
[31] *Memoir*, 179.

Top: Memorial to Daniel Rowland, Llangeitho.
Bottom: Llangeitho Chapel and Rowland's Memorial.

all, God's invisible hand preserved me — the everlasting arms were underneath.'[32] He notes the help he received at this time from reading Luther's exposition of Galatians 1:4, '[The Lord Jesus Christ] who gave himself for our sins.' It 'was very much and particularly blessed to me, as it has been many times since.'[33] In that comment, Luther wrote:

> Say with confidence, 'Christ, the Son of God, was given not for the righteous, but for sinners. If I had no sin I should not need Christ ... The truth is, I am all sin. My sins are not imaginary transgressions, but ... unbelief, doubt, despair, contempt, hatred, ignorance of God, ingratitude towards him, misuse of his name, neglect of his Word, etc. ...
>
> Let us equip ourselves against the accusations of Satan with this and similar passages of Holy Scriptures. If he says, 'You shall be damned,' you tell him, 'No, for I fly to Christ who gave Himself for my sins. In accusing me of being a damnable sinner, you are cutting your own throat, Satan. You are reminding me of God's fatherly goodness toward me, that He so loved the world that He gave His only-begotten Son that whosoever believes in him should not perish, but have everlasting life. In calling me a sinner, Satan, you really comfort me above measure.' With such heavenly cunning we are to meet the devil's craft and put from us the memory of sin ...
>
> Make ample use of this pronoun 'our.' Be assured that Christ has cancelled the sins, not of certain persons only, but your sins. Do not permit yourself to be robbed of this lovely conception of Christ. Christ is no Moses, no law-giver, no tyrant, but the Mediator for sins, the Giver of grace and life.

We meet with this use of personal conviction of sin in order to confirm dependence and trust in the Saviour and thus to strengthen assurance of salvation many times in Charles's letters. When, in future years, he needed to help and comfort members of his

[32] *Memoir*, 8.
[33] *Ibid.*

widespread flock who were sinking under a sense of sin, his certainty as to the basis of his own assurance enabled him to express simply and clearly the comfort of the gospel.[34]

[34] See, for example, the letters below on pages 61, 66, and 350.

3

OXFORD AND SOMERSET
(1775–80)

Oxford

In the year 1775, Providence very unexpectedly and very
wonderfully opened my way to go to Oxford, what neither
my parents or myself nor any of my relations had any the
least idea of till just at this time, but now all obstacles were
removed and it was determined I should go. The manner in
which the Lord opened my way to go thither gave me great
satisfaction and strong assurance that I should be kept by
God's grace from being burnt in the fiery furnace, though
very often my spirits were much oppressed with fear and
doubtful apprehensions of my future safety; but he who
can keep us in one place, can with the same ease keep us
in another. There are no difficulties with God. Difficulties
wholly exist in our unbelieving hearts.

In May I set out on my journey thither. On the road
the Lord gave me very comfortable views of himself as my
Father in Christ; yea, that Christ's Father was my Father and
his God my God.[1]

CHARLES's period at Jesus College, Oxford was from 26 May
1775 to 1 July 1778. His uncle, his mother's brother, Thomas Bowen,
had been a student there twenty-three years before him and was
serving as vicar of Turkdean, Gloucestershire, only thirty miles
away. It is probable that he helped him at this time with advice and
material support, and Charles spent some of his student vacations

[1] *Memoir*, 8-9.

at Turkdean. An Oxford education at the end of the eighteenth century did not perhaps mean as much as it did later, after the educational and administrative reforms of the early nineteenth century, but it proved of immense significance to Charles's cultural and social development. A fellow Welshman and contemporary of his at Jesus College wrote in his diary: 'In every college of both Universities there are, doubtless, great opportunities for instruction; but I have been long persuaded that it is of more consequence to a young man what coffee-house he frequents than what college he enters: very much depends upon the choice of his companions …'[2]

This was certainly Charles's experience at university. In his own words, 'I soon got acquainted with several serious pious young gentlemen there, which could not but prove very great comfort and profit.'[3] He looked out for godly, evangelical believers and having found them, he cultivated their friendship and fellowship. In the nature of education in the English Universities at that time, all of these of necessity were members of the Church of England, and the majority of them destined for the ministry of that church.

Thomas Charles's cheerful, optimistic and kindly personality meant that he made and maintained friendships very easily, but of his many Oxford friendships four were to prove of enduring significance.

Oxford friends

John Mayor (1755–1826) was born in Dolgellau, north-west Wales, but he was only half Welsh. His father, whose family were from Upminster, was a businessman from London and had married a Welsh girl from Dolgellau. Mayor was a student at Worcester College, Oxford. His friendship with Charles was perhaps the strongest bond of the four relationships, certainly during their

---

[2] Written in 1814 by William Jones of Abergavenny and Jamaica; quoted by DEJ, I, 76-77.
[3] *Memoir*, 10.

John Mayor

Watts Wilkinson

John Newton

Simon Jones

Thomas Scott

college days. He eventually settled as vicar of Shawbury near Shrewsbury, in Shropshire.[4]

Edward Griffin (1755–1833) was the son of a gentleman from Worcester and had matriculated at Trinity College, Oxford two years before Charles arrived. Although they knew each other only for eighteen months or so in the university, their friendship lasted throughout the years.[5] He was appointed rector of Little Harwood in Buckinghamshire.

Watts Wilkinson (1755–1840) was born in Horsley, Northumberland and entered Worcester College in October 1776, following his friend John Mayor. He served churches within the City of London for a period of sixty-one years. A letter which he wrote to Charles during his first curacy suggests something of the pleasure and benefit that these four friends obtained from, and treasured in Charles's Christian optimism and faith: 'How often have I trudged from Worcester to Jesus College with low spirits and a heavy heart, but, cheered with my dear friend's pious and enlivening conversation, have returned cheerful and rejoicing.'[6]

Simon Lloyd (1756–1836) was the son of another Simon Lloyd, of Plas-yn-dre, the largest town-house in Bala, north Wales, at the time. His father had joined the Methodists and visited Howel Harris's 'Family' at Trefeca. There he fell in love with Sarah Bowen of Llandinam, Montgomeryshire, a member of the 'Family,' and its first 'matron.' Because of her great usefulness to him, and perhaps because of the money she had brought with her, Harris objected to their marriage. Eventually, however, through the intercession of one of the Bala society's elders, John Evans, he relented and the couple were married, within four months of meeting.[7] Simon,

---

[4] He suffered for many years from angina. In his obituary it is said that 'he had adorned the clerical profession by the extent of his biblical learning, the soundness of his doctrine, and the holiness of his life.' DEJ, III, 642.

[5] The last surviving letter between them dates from 1812.

[6] DEJ, I, 98.

[7] Sarah's sister, Hannah Bowen, succeeded her as matron of Trefeca, then, from 1771, became matron at the Countess of Huntingdon's College at Trefeca.

their son, at first attended a school at Bath but, coincidentally, was at the free-school in Carmarthen, the Queen Elizabeth Grammar School, for some of the time that Charles was at Carmarthen Academy. Whether they ever became acquainted in Carmarthen is not known. Simon arrived at Jesus College in April 1775, a month before Charles. As will be seen, the life of Simon Lloyd, and of his family at Bala, is closely bound up with that of Thomas Charles.

The letters, to and fro, between these five friends provide one of the main sources of information for Charles's life for the period from 1775 to about 1800. By them they kept each other informed of their activities, recommended the books they found most helpful and, over a period of nearly forty years, though separated far from one another, maintained their interest in each other's ministries and their faithfulness in prayer for one another. They were all of the same age and very loyal in their allegiance to the Established Church. This last point has particular significance in the light of Charles's subsequent career and relationship with the Church of England.

The Evangelicals within the Church of England

One historian of Welsh Calvinistic Methodism has commented: 'There were many streams represented by the converts of the eighteenth century revival – the Moravians, the followers of Wesley and those of Whitefield, as well as the Countess of Huntingdon's Connexion. Thomas Charles did not associate himself with any of these, but instead made his home amongst the Evangelical Anglicans.'[8]

One important element that characterised these evangelical clergymen was their allegiance to the ecclesiastical order of the Established Church: its doctrine, its homilies and liturgy, and the Book of Common Prayer. To them the parochial system was essential to the constitution of the church and episcopal authority had to be accepted. As a result, they considered itinerant preaching to be irregular and would never condone preaching by unordained

[8] J. E. Wynne Davies, 'Thomas Charles (1755–1814),' JHS, 38 (2014), 60.

laymen. In their opinion, to build meeting-houses or chapels would be tantamount to separation.[9]

The first consequence of this alignment' was that Charles (and his four friends) did not suffer any of the contempt and persecution that usually arose against other 'serious, pious' men who breached church orders in any way, by indiscriminate preaching, for example, or by association with Nonconformists. The memory was still fresh in Oxford of the case of six students from St Edmund Hall who in March 1768 had been sent down because of their 'too much religion.' A further case occurred during Charles's third year. In his very first letter to Edward Griffin, after the latter had departed to a curacy in Leicester, he wrote:

> It grieves me to inform you that poor Roe, of Brazen-nose College, has had his degree refused to him by the Society on account of his Methodistical principles; which at once deprived him of the honours of the University and of the fellowship which he was sure of as soon as he had taken his degree. Perhaps he acted indiscreetly in some things: but that can never justify the rigorous severity of their persecuting spirit.[10]

Robert Roe had been guilty of attending services in Wesleyan chapels, and Charles reveals his Church of England loyalties when he adds: 'By what he told me he seems to have performed what *he* thought to be his duty in an upright, sincere, conscientious manner; though I should not think it *my* duty to act as he did.'[11]

A further element in this connection with evangelical friends was that, apart from Simon Lloyd of course, these new friends were *English* evangelical clergymen. There was at the time no equivalent body of men that could be referred to as Welsh evangelical clergy. A handful of men (David Jones, Llan-gan, and Nathaniel Rowland, Daniel's son, for example) were scattered about south Wales, but in England their numbers were sufficient to constitute

[9] Wynne Davies, 'Thomas Charles (1755–1814),' JHS, 38 (2014), 61.
[10] DEJ, I, 59-60.
[11] *Ibid.*, 60.

a party within the National Church. Charles's name now began to become known to the leaders of this group, both to its senior members, such as William Romaine, John Berridge and John Newton, and, eventually, to the rising generation, such as Thomas Haweis, Henry Foster, Richard Cecil, Charles Simeon, John Venn and William Wilberforce. In later years it was these men, together with other Englishmen with whom, through them, he came into contact, both Church of England and Nonconformist, who would provide the initial support for Charles's activities, at a time when the numbers of Welsh Methodists in north Wales were insufficient to finance them.

A financial crisis

In March 1777, when approaching the end of his second year in the university, Charles suddenly received bad news, the consequences of which threatened to put an end to any possibility of university graduation and a career in the church. His supplies from Wales dried up and he already owed his college £20. He shared his bewilderment with John Mayor, and as a result Charles relates, 'A few days after, a gentleman sent for me to dine with him. I went, and before we parted, to my great surprise, he produced the £20 I wanted, and at the same time told me that I should not want during my stay at Oxford. I was much rejoiced and very thankful. The gentleman was as good as his word. This introduced me into a new connection, and considerably enlarged my sphere of acquaintance.'[12] It was through one of these new Church of England friends that he and Mayor received what must have been an exciting offer. They were invited to spend the summer of 1777 at Olney, Buckinghamshire, as the guest of the Rev. and Mrs John Newton.

John Newton and Olney

Charles could not have dreamt that his new-found connections would have resulted so quickly in a friendship with perhaps the most eminent of them. An entry in his *Diary* reads: 'In the year

[12] *Memoir*, 10-11.

1777 I spent the summer vacation with Mr Newton at Olney. The visit proved very comfortable [i.e. strengthening] and very profitable indeed.'[13] He and John Mayor arrived at Olney on 12 July and stayed there for three months, returning to Oxford for the new academic year on 16 October. John Newton was fifty-two years old at the time

Thomas Charles described his experiences at Olney in a letter (8 August) to Watts Wilkinson:

> Having a Newton to be instructed by, both by edifying discourses in the pulpit, and by conversation in the closet, what place or situation can I be in, more pleasing and delightful? I had formed in my mind great ideas of him, but really he has exceeded my most sanguine expectations ...
>
> Had I the strongest constitution and the best advantages of human literature, yes of all learning, both sacred and profane, yet I am perfectly convinced that all this would be much too little to make me a gospel preacher. One may speak a great deal, and that very orthodox, but unless he has a little of the unction of the Holy Spirit, he might, for aught I know, *as well be silent*. This is what I want in my prayers, studies and meditations. And that God would grant you and me a great share of it, when we come to act in a public capacity ...[14]

Charles was in Olney at the time that the Rev. Thomas Scott (1747–1821) was having serious conversations with Newton about the faith. He was a curate at Ravenstone, just three miles from Olney and with his rationalistic and Socinian doctrines he scornfully opposed evangelical truth. On his conversion, he wrote up his experience in a work that became an autobiographical classic, *The Force of Truth* (1779).[15] How much of his conversations with Scott were mentioned by John Newton to Charles is not known. But

[13] *Memoir*, 11.

[14] *Ibid.*, 12-13.

[15] Thomas Scott, *The Force of Truth* (1779; repr. Edinburgh: Banner of Truth Trust, 1984), 75-76.

the latter would certainly have known of them very shortly, if not from Newton then from Scott himself. The two Thomases, Charles and Scott, became good friends from this time, and corresponded together for the remainder of Charles's life. Scott, who was eight years older than Charles, was to be one of his greatest supporters, morally and financially, in his various activities.[16]

On returning to Oxford, Charles continued to correspond with Newton, and in later years requested his advice at crucial points in his career. The following is part of a letter that Newton wrote to the two students after they had returned to Oxford:

> Time was when I thought a minister a sort of superior Being, and hardly could be persuaded they had the like infirmities with other men. Perhaps you may have thought so likewise. But by and by, when you shall be admitted behind the scenes, you will find that the office, though it calls us to difficult services, and exposes us to dangerous snares, yet will not of itself afford us one additional grain of grace or strength. If when we commence teachers, we do not continue learners, if we do not watch unto prayer, if we think because we have been ordained, and can read Latin and Greek, we have a right to go forth as if we were wise or good, experience will soon teach us, or observation will soon convince others, that we are but empty and broken cisterns – and can do nothing right.[17]

The final year at Oxford

Charles's main concern during the six months of his final session (1777–78) at Oxford was to find a curacy. Two possibilities arose early in the new year: one was for a curate under Thomas Haweis at Aldwinkle, Northamptonshire; the other a curacy under James Stillingfleet at Worcester.[18] Both of these fell through but he then

---

[16] Scott was also the author of the immensely popular *Scott's Bible Commentary* (1792).

[17] DEJ, I, 55-56.

[18] Thomas Haweis (1734–1820) was rector of Aldwinkle. James Stillingfleet

received an offer, through the mediation of Edward Griffin, of a position in Somerset. The vicar, whose name was Henry Newman, a recent convert to the Methodists and known to John Newton, was in possession of two livings in the county and was in need of a curate. Having accepted this offer, Charles could now turn his attention to two other events that lay before him. The first was his ordination as a deacon in the Established Church. The importance and seriousness of the step impressed him greatly, and he shared it in a letter to his friend, Edward Griffin:

> Sometimes, I hope I can say, that God's glory and the salvation of immortal precious souls are my greatest concern: though at other times I must, with grief and shame, confess myself guilty of harbouring and caressing a traitor to heaven and an enemy to my own peace and comfort. I mean pride or self-interest – an enemy, of all others, the most bold in his enterprises and the most covert in his plots, aiming at nothing less than dethroning God himself; and who frequently under pretence of extending God's dominion, erects an empire of his own. I find him so entwined about me, that I almost despair of ever disengaging myself. But praised and for ever adored be Jesu's name for that precious scripture, '*He must reign* till he hath put *all* enemies under his feet.' He is no king upon terms. I hope you will pray for me.[19]

Charles was ordained on Trinity Sunday, 14 June 1778, but as his appointment was not to commence until Michaelmas (29 September), he had time on his hands and arranged, through the kindness of Simon Lloyd, a five-week tour of north Wales, including a stay at his friend's home in Bala, followed by a six-week period for the two of them together at Charles's home, Pant-dwfn, Carmarthenshire. The friends travelled together from Oxford to Bala, a journey

---

(1729–1817) was prependary of Worcester and rector of Hartelbury; he was the grandson of the famous Latitudinarian bishop, Edward Stillingfleet (1635–95). Both men were friends and supporters of the Countess of Huntingdon's work.

[19] *Memoir*, 15.

of more than 150 miles. How different would the evangelical ethos of Bala's Methodists have seemed to Charles compared to the evangelicalism of Oxford in which he had been immersed for three years. How interesting it must have been for him now to make the acquaintance of those of whom he would have heard so much from Simon Lloyd: the fifty-five year-old exhorter John Evans, one of the earliest members of the Bala society; Simon Lloyd, Senior; Sarah Lloyd, particularly, with her accounts of Howel Harris and of life with the 'Family' at Trefeca. He would also have met twenty-one year-old Lydia Lloyd, Simon's sister.

During this stay Charles accompanied some of the Bala Methodists to hear the preaching at a monthly Methodist Meeting at Clynnog, Caernarfonshire. And as he and Simon travelled down to south Wales they spent two days at the August Methodist south Wales Association at Llangeitho, Cardiganshire, and heard two sermons from Daniel Rowland, 'with inexpressible pleasure,' according to Charles's *Diary*. This might be judged inconsistent behaviour in that Charles did 'not think it *my* duty to act as he did,' in the case of Robert Roe's attendance at Methodist meetings. It might be the case, however, that Charles did not consider attendance at open-air meetings in rural Wales as being in any way similar to attendance at Methodist chapels in Oxford, particularly when the preacher, certainly at Llangeitho and, for all we know, at Clynnog also, was not a lay exhorter but an ordained clergyman of the Church of England.

Charles's return to Pant-dwfn at this time was to be his final visit to the home of his youth. His father, as a result of financial difficulties, was about to relinquish his lease on the farm and move to another holding, Cil-y-coed, a much poorer farm about four miles to the north.

On 16 August, Charles preached his first sermon, and in the congregation was his old friend, Rees Hugh. He wrote: '... preached at Llanfihangel.[20] I was very comfortable and very earnest: my heart exceedingly rejoiced to see once more my old very dear Christian

[20] Llanfihangel, Abercywyn, Carmarthenshire.

friend Rees Hugh. I could almost have cried for joy. It was the last interview I had with him in the world. In a month afterwards he went to heaven.'[21]

A curate in Somerset

The Rev. Henry Newman held the two livings of Shepton Beauchamp and Sparkford, which were about twelve miles apart. The villages comprised 85 and 41 houses respectively. Attached to the former was a rectory, where Newman lived. In September 1778 Charles wrote to Watts Wilkinson (who was at the time enjoying his own period of tutelage at Olney) describing his new situation:

> ... I came here about a week ago ... I know you would ask me, how does preaching agree with you? My friend, it is hard work. I find I have to do with two enemies, each of which is much my superior; that is, with *old Adam*, and the *old Serpent*. The one is hardy, unfeeling and obstinate; and the other is cunning and crafty. When I attempt to work upon and affect the hard, stupid and dead heart of a perverse sinner, the devil never fails to devise a scheme to disappoint me. Yet, weak and ignorant as I am, I despair not of obtaining a complete and glorious victory at last, for the Lord of Hosts has promised to be with me. 'Lo, I am with you,' this is all my comfort and support; and indeed I want no more.[22]

Like many a godly man beginning to realize the enormity of the spiritual task of the work of the Christian ministry, particularly in the light of his sinful heart, Charles could only fall back on the promises of God. He wrote in his *Diary* for 8 November:

> My soul being much depressed with the sense of my inability for the work of the ministry, and fearful lest any soul should perish through my ignorance or negligence, and lest I should bring a reproach upon the glorious gospel, the

---

[21] *Memoir*, 22-23.
[22] *Ibid.*, 24.

Lord was pleased to apply the following words with great power to my soul, 'I will instruct thee, and teach thee in the way which thou shalt go; I will guide thee with mine eye.' Help me, O Lord, to rely on thy sure word of promise, and to look to thee in all things, who perfects strength in the weakness of thy people, and from whom alone is their sufficiency for every work.[23]

Newman more or less entrusted the Sparkford living to Charles and he conducted his first marriage there on 30 November 1778. He would ride over to Sparkford on a Saturday morning, conduct whatever parish duties were required during the day, take the morning service on the Sunday (the only service of the day) and then return to the rectory at Shepton. A note in his *Diary* for 29 December suggests that he was already beginning to know something of that which would be his frequent experience for the next six years: 'It rejoices me that my name is cast out as evil for the Lord's sake. I hope I am enabled to choose to suffer affliction with the people of God rather than the pleasure of sin for a season.'[24]

Charles paid a visit to Oxford in the February of 1779 in order to receive his degree from the university and a few weeks later wrote to Simon Lloyd, in a letter bearing a new address at its head:

Queen Camel, 15 March 1779

… Last week I exchanged Mr Newman's lodging for another within a small mile of the church I serve [i.e. Sparkford], which is far more convenient and I hope will prove more beneficial for the people. When this parish heard of my coming to live amongst them, some of them expressed a good deal of uneasiness. They had a Doctor and a Presbyterian (the man with whom I lodge) before, they said, and now again they were to have a Methodist Parson (the name by which I am called in the neighbourhood) amongst them! One more is wanted (added they) to make our misery complete, i.e. the Devil. Here, however, they are much

[23] *Ibid.*, 25.
[24] DEJ, I, 112.

mistaken; for I am sure from the respect showed, and the love expressed to him, he never could be so unpolite as to be absent from them long – nay, has had such a work carried on here, for many years, and so many hands constantly employed, that I am morally certain the work could not be so elegantly accomplished if he himself did not superintend it. And I hope to convince them, by and by, that *we* are not *very great and intimate friends*, by some disputes I expect with him …[25]

His *Diary* entries in following weeks reflect the difficulties he was beginning to encounter. It would seem that Newman had a degree of pragmatic interest in moving him to Queen's Camel. He not only reduced his salary from £45 to £40 but may well have found it convenient also to have the 'Methodist Parson' with his 'earnestness and pointed sermons' twelve miles away from his own parishioners. This would explain such entries in Charles's *Diary* as:

> 22 March: I find the Lord is graciously determined to bring me from everything to live only upon him. I depended upon a broken reed and it hath pierced me to the heart. At present I have no friend but the Almighty.
> 4 April: How long must I dwell in Mesech? My soul is sore vexed at their iniquity who are enemies to God. Surely the fear of God is not in this place! … may the Lord bless my poor labours in this ungodly neighbourhood.[26]

On learning of these events, Edward Griffin offered him a vacant curacy that came with a living in Buckinghamshire that he was about to accept. Charles's response, however, was swift:

> When a person is once settled in a place, and as he thinks, by an all-wise Providence, he should, in my opinion, be very cautious in exchanging that for another, though more agreeable to flesh and blood and much more lucrative. My situation is indeed at *present* by no means desirable. I have

[25] DEJ, I, 116-17.
[26] *Ibid.*, I, 118.

no Christian friend to speak to within fifteen miles. Mr Newman's unexpected behaviour has produced a coolness between us. All these circumstances, together with the fair prospects your kind proposals hold out to me, strongly incline me to accept your offer. But would this be taking up the cross? Is this a proof of that undaunted fortitude which a gospel-minister *especially* should be possessed of? Or is it not rather shaking off the cross impatiently which God in consummate wisdom has laid upon me? When Providence appears dark and mysterious, we are not to be dejected and murmur but wait patiently on the Lord, who knows best what weather is most suitable to our constitutions. I am persuaded that a few rough storms are much wanted to rouse me; though the Lord knows how weak I am to bear them. He has promised that strength shall be *proportioned* to the day, and this is my stay and comfort.

For these reasons I find myself, after some thought and prayer, at least some attempts to pray, disposed to decline the offer, lest influenced by selfish motives, I should dishonour God and quit the post he has assigned me. At present I am strongly persuaded God sent me here: for what end it does not yet appear very clear.[27]

A great comfort at this time was the friendship he now made with John Lucas, vicar of Milborne Port. They had been slightly acquainted at Oxford but Lucas had been settled at Milborne, about eight miles from Queen's Camel, since May 1778. Charles wrote to Lloyd:

> 10 January 1780
>
> ... Mr Lucas' solicitations have prevailed upon me to keep this curacy a little longer on Mr Newman's own terms, viz. £30 per annum. This is the *third time* that Mr Newman has altered my salary since I came to him. You may easily conceive that it is very disagreeable to have anything to do with such a person, nor should I have stayed here on any

---

[27] *Memoir*, 35-36.

account had it not been for Mr Lucas, *who is a Christian friend indeed to me*. Next Lady Day I am going to live with him and to be a kind of an assistant to him. Though he does not want any assistance, the main intention is to make it a subsistence to me (*towards which he contributes*) and more comfortable to us both …²⁸

Milborne Port was some eight miles from Sparkford and Lucas would lend Charles his horse to carry him to his duties there. ²⁹ There were some rays of light amongst the general darkness:

The people here show me all the outward civilities I could expect, but a very great contempt of the gospel and godly living. Yet after all I am in great hopes that the Lord *hath* blessed and *will* bless my ministry among them … Religion is a new and strange thing here, and operates variously according to the different tempers and interests of the persons who hear it. But most look upon it as something very bad, though they know not what it is; and they are exceedingly afraid of taking the infection.³⁰

²⁸ DEJ, I, 152-53.
²⁹ The parish of Milborne Port was not large enough for Lucas to require a curate. Charles assisted him in small duties during the week for which Lucas paid £10 – the amount by which his salary had been reduced.
³⁰ *Memoir*, 45-46.

4

BALA AND SALLY JONES:
COURTSHIP AND MARRIAGE
(1778–83)

Bala

BALA, Merioneth, lay at the heart of a growing rural economy that was not yet affected by the industrial revolution emerging in other parts of the country. At this time, Merioneth was a community of spinners, weavers, and farmers, and Bala was the commercial centre where the Saturday morning market provided a worthwhile trading opportunity. Between 1800 and 1821 its population rose from about 850 to 1,163. In 1775 the stage coach route passed through Bala for the first time, reflecting the improvement in the roads servicing the town.

The Rev. John Evans in his *Tour through North Wales in the Year 1798* wrote:

> The small town of Bala ... in the parish of Llanycil ... is regular in its form, consisting of one particular street, the rest of the streets crossing it at right angles; and deriving its name from its situation as a place where a river runs into a lake.[1] Much of its consequence arises from its large fairs and markets, which owing to its central situation are numerously attended from distant parts of the country. It has a very considerable manufactory of knit woollen goods, such as stockings, gloves, etc. Knitting being the common

[1] DEJ corrects this to, 'a place where a river runs out of a lake,' a reference to the river Dee which proceeds through Llangollen, around Wrexham and through Chester.

employment of the neighbourhood, for both sexes and all ages: even the men frequently take up the needles and assist the females in the labour, whence the chief support of the family is derived. You see none idle; going out or returning home; riding or walking they are occupied in this portable employment ... No conjecture can be made of the quantity manufactured at Bala, and its vicinity; it must be very considerable, when from two to five hundred pounds worth are sold every market day.[2]

Some of this trade passed through the stores run by David Jones in Bala High Street. David Jones of Llanelltud, Merioneth, had married Jane Jones of Trawsfynydd, Merioneth, sometime after 1737, and as part of the marriage settlement they received a house at Bala, which served as their home and as a general purpose store. Jane Jones became one of the first members of the Methodist society at Bala, established in 1745.

Sally, their only child, was born on 12 November 1753 and named after her aunt, Sarah, but she was always called Sally. David Jones died when Sally was about six or seven years old, and in May 1761, when Sally was eight years old, her mother remarried. Her stepfather, a widower, Thomas Foulks, or Foulkes (1731–1802) came from Llandrillo, Merioneth. He had worked as a carpenter in Gloucestershire as a young man, and had been converted there in 1756 under the preaching of John Wesley. He kept his connections with the Wesleyan Methodists throughout his life but as there were none of Wesley's people in the Bala area he joined the Calvinistic Methodist society in the town and became an exhorter, or lay preacher, among them. Sally held her stepfather in great respect and loved him deeply.[3] David Jones had established a busy and profitable grocery and drapery shop on Bala High Street and Thomas Foulks took over the management of it on marrying Jane. As she grew up, Sally also began to work in the shop, serving at the

[2] John Evans, *Letters Written during a Tour through North Wales in the Year 1798* (1804), 67-8; quoted by DEJ, I, 419.

[3] DDM (2014), 194-95.

counter, travelling to fairs at Corwen, Wrexham, and Chester (all
to the north-east of Bala) to buy stock, supervising the servants
and maids, and paying the bills. It soon became evident that she
possessed as much, if not more, commercial skills than her natural
father. As she took on more and more responsibility in the family
business, her stepfather was released to minister more regularly
in the Bala society and to undertake preaching itineraries further
afield.

Simon Lloyd would have found it an easy task to persuade
Thomas Charles to pay a visit and stay at his home in Bala in the
summer of 1778 because Charles had long wished for an opportunity to meet Sally Jones. William Williams, the hymn-writer from
Pantycelyn, had described her as '*flodeuyn Gwynedd dir*' ('the flower
of Gwynedd'). He even wrote a poem to Sally in February 1776,
when she was a young woman of twenty-two years of age. The
tradition is that Williams hoped she would marry his son John.

With all the cares related to the shop, Sally had plenty to exercise her strong common sense. She was a kind-hearted, intelligent,
and godly young woman and was generally well-known for these
qualities in the societies. Thus it was that Charles had heard of her
from his Methodist friends in Carmarthen, five years previously.
Rumour also had it that she was very pretty and had some money
behind her. By 1780, she was 26 years old, two years older than
Charles and very capable of looking after herself.[4]

A postscript in a letter from Charles to Simon Lloyd, some
months after the Bala visit, contained the unamplified sentence: 'I
think sometimes of Miss Jones. Am undetermined as yet.'[5] A year
later (22 November, 1779), matters were much further advanced
in his mind:

> I thank my friend for the favourable intelligence you have
> kindly communicated to me concerning dear Miss Jones. I

[4] E. Wyn James, 'Pererinion ar y Ffordd: Thomas Charles ac Ann Griffiths,'
JHS, 29-30 (2005-06), 76-77; RTJ (1979), 18-19; Gwen Emyr, *Sally Jones:
Rhodd Duw i Charles* (Gwasg Efengylaidd Cymru, 1996), 22-23.

[5] DEJ, I, 110.

Plas-yn-dre, the home of Simon and Lydia Lloyd, as it is today.

frequently think of her and should think much more were
not my thoughts necessarily employed of late about other
important and unexpected affairs; which when they are
settled I believe my *Dear Sally* will engross more of my time
and thoughts …Thus I have explained the important affairs
which occupy so much of my time and thoughts; but at
times, notwithstanding all, *Dear Sally* steals in insensibly,
and before I am aware gets possession of my heart; '*haec
omnia inter nos.*'[6]

The first exchange of letters

That this was hardly the full story is demonstrated by the fact that,
six weeks later, in the first week of January 1780, the said Miss
Jones was opening her post to be confronted by the following:

28 December, 1779

My very dear friend,

Such an unexpected address from a person who never
saw you but once, and that at such a long interval of time,
will I suppose at first not a little surprise you: however … I
assure you that long as the interval is since I had the pleasure
of seeing you, you have not been absent from my mind,
for a whole day, from that time to this. The first report of
your character (which I heard at Carmarthen by some of
our religious friends about six years ago) left such an impression on my mind as, I am sure, no length of time can ever
obliterate. I immediately conceived an ardent desire, and
a secret hope, that my Heavenly Father's wise and good
Providence would so order subsequent events that I should
in due time see that beloved person of whom I had formed
such a favourable opinion When Mr Lloyd gave me a kind
invitation to spend part of the summer with him at Bala 'tis
inexpressible what secret pleasure and joy the prospect of
seeing you afforded me. Nor was I disappointed. The sight
of so much good sense, beauty and unaffected modesty,
joined with that genuine piety which eminently adorns

---

[6] 'All this between ourselves.' DEJ, I, 134-35.

your person, administered fuel to the fire already enkindled, and which has continued burning with increasing ardour from that time to this ...

Ever since I came to England I have anxiously expected ...that some favourable circumstances would open a door for my return to *Wales* (a place for ever dear!) but hitherto I have been discouraged. Finding that any longer delay would serve only to distract my mind and by constant uneasiness in some degree, unfit me for the proper discharge of that very important office in which I am engaged, I determined upon the resolution which I now put in execution of writing to you, and solicit the favour of a correspondence with you till such time as kind Providence indulges us with an interview, which on my part is most ardently desired ...[7]

The letter continues for quite a few pages. Charles would have had an anxious wait for the best part of four weeks before receiving the following reply:

Bala, 17 January, 1780

Reverend Sir

Your letter doth indeed seem something strange to me. I can neither give it full credit nor throw it aside heedless. May He who knoweth your motive in writing give me simplicity to answer and let the consequence be what it will.

The liberty and privilege of my present state are very dear and valuable to me. I often wish I had no temptation to part with them; but I can't say I have ever determined, or known the will of God concerning it. I trust his Providence will in time make this clear. I have several reasons that I do not choose to engage in a correspondence of this nature. But if any letters be exchanged between us I would wish each of us should have free liberty to drop the correspondence at pleasure. Probably after receiving this you will not wish to write again. This will be no disappointment to me. I quit my claim of every profession in your letter excepting one,

---

[7] DEJ, I, 146-48.

which is the remembrance of me at the throne of mercy. This is a pleasing thought which I am willing to cherish, and though I do not expect to see you in this vale of troubles yet I shall meet you where I hope my gratitude will be in full perfection there to express it to the glory of Him that heareth the prayer of His people for one another and blesses them in the remotest parts of the earth.

I have by your permission shown your letter to my father. He and my mother join in cordial respect and love to you. I believe my poor father is an Israelite indeed in whom there is no guile. He, dearest of mortals, thinks everything sincere. I join with him in best wishes for your prosperity in the glorious and very weighty work you are engaged.

Who am your well-wisher,

Sally Jones.[8]

Clearly Charles had made no great an impression upon her when they had met the previous summer. She has answered him courteously and has accepted his proposal to correspond, but there is no mistaking her reluctance and suspicion. We might wonder why it was that she accepted at all. In this and in subsequent letters there may perhaps be seen hints that her stepfather's influence had been at work. Perhaps he had heard something of the respect in Methodist circles for this young man and for his prospects. When she writes, 'He, dearest of mortals, thinks everything sincere,' she shows her respect for her father's judgement, but there is perhaps a hint that, in this specific case, she may not agree with it.

Thomas Charles's second letter and its answer

Thomas completely understood her situation – for the last month, if not for the last eighteen months, he had probably been imagining what her reactions would be. All he could do in his reply was to repeat his affirmations of sincerity, and he was not so subservient as to refrain from warning her of the danger of cynicism.

[8] Gildas Tibbott, 'Sally Jones' first letters to Thomas Charles,' JHS, 31 (1946), 39-40.

… But of the sincerity of all these warm professions of love and esteem, you seem to be dubious, and to suspect some sinister motive at the bottom. This I am very sorry for, because, at present, deprived of all other means to convince you of the contrary, but pen and paper. I can only assure you, upon the word of a Christian, that whatever I have written to you, was nothing but the real truth, expressed in the most simple manner I could. I am aware of its being a true though humbling consideration that the deceitful depravity of the human heart renders it necessary for us to exercise the prudence of the serpent in our mutual dealings with each other; still, I think, there are bounds here set which, doubtless, may be transgressed by a too cautious scrupulosity …[9]

On this occasion Charles had again to wait for nearly a month before receiving a reply, and it cannot have provided him with much encouragement.

Bala, 14 February 1780

Reverend Sir

It being tonight post-night, I withdraw from business to answer your letter. Little did I think I should ever be called of you to this employment. After such unmerited profession of esteem you would think me ungrateful if I was to tell you with what reluctance I go about it. If it was not in compliance to your request I would think silence the best return I could make. Yet I would not have you think a personal correspondence more satisfactory nor more agreeable to me than the scribbling one. If I could be open and free in any I would be so over my innocent paper that never looks me in the face nor puts me to the blush. Never think of seeing poor Bala on that occasion, if you have a call of Providence to these parts on some other account. Let us drop this correspondence first, that we may have no talk about it. I can't look upon it, but as a thing to be dropped. However,

[9] DEJ, I, 148-50.

for the time we hold it a serious subject may be profitable. Our happiness does not consist in anything transitory. Perhaps while our thoughts are employed about settling in this vale of tears we may be called out of it. To me such a call would be alarming. I have slept in outward profession of religion, without ever coming to a certainty whether my future destiny be the extreme of woe and sorrow or of joy without end. O may the melodious sound of the gospel awake me. And may a dear Redeemer be precious. While I make wishes for my own happiness, I hope my heart will be enlarged to pray for the welfare of Zion and peace on all that love her. I trust he to whom I am writing is included in the happy number. So shall we at the distance of perhaps a hundred miles mingle intercession at the throne of mercy. This is the best friendship we can wish to commence – and the only one I desire to know,

Who am, Reverend Sir, your well-wisher, Sally Jones.[10]

Sally's confession in this letter that the call of death 'would be alarming' to her is surprising, as is her comment: 'I have slept in outward profession of religion, without ever coming to a certainty whether my future destiny be the extreme of woe and sorrow or of joy without end.' How was it possible that someone so lacking in assurance had a name throughout Welsh Methodist circles for being godly and pious? Furthermore, how could Charles ever think of continuing a relationship with someone so doubtful of her own faith? The biblical commandment, 'be not unequally yoked with unbelievers,' was scrupulously adhered to by the Methodists. But to have been present in one of the society meetings, or to read some of the many reports of them, would very soon reveal that Sally was not unique in her experience. Such confessions were common. There was no benefit in the discussion of those societies unless the members were thoroughly honest with one another. They had little sense of competitiveness or spiritual rivalry; they fought against any pretence or maintaining of a public image. In those

---

[10] Tibbott, JHS, 31 (1946), 40-41.

days of revival, of the overwhelming sense of God's presence, the reality of eternal things was unavoidable. With God being aware of every thought, word, and deed, any pretence of experience to one another was wickedly foolish. Furthermore, Sally might indeed have been lacking in personal assurance but she was very definitely not lacking in faith. Even when she writes most pitifully of her longing to be assured of her salvation, the strength of her faith shines out. Thus, in a letter, later in their correspondence, dated 22 June 1780, she writes:

> I need not repeat the Scripture to you; but my heart can dictate nothing like them. May the Holy Spirit of God engraft them there: for in them is the seed of everlasting life. In them is to be found the pearl of great price. O that I could call it mine for from the want of this confidence proceeds all my complaints. Some cursed root of unbelief lies deep in my heart. If angels know this mystery of iniquity they must needs wonder.
>
> But the Angel of the new covenant knew what He should find in man before He took upon Him to redeem the fallen race and hath wrought out a complete redemption. I want nothing but assurance of my interest in this dear Redeemer. For this I hope to wait all the days of my life until my change comes.[11]

Of the reality of her faith there is no doubt. It was the strength of this faith, as shown by her works of love and loyalty, that had given her a name among her fellow believers. Thomas Charles never doubted it and it is very evident that he always addresses her in his letters as a firm Christian. He understands her troubles also and always supplies her with relevant scriptural comforts and counsels. It may well be that it was for this reason that Sally was happy to continue the correspondence, though flatly refusing at first to view it as a stepping-stone to marriage. Charles's third letter to her provides an illustration of the pastoral element that was always present in his correspondence:

11 DEJ, I, 194.

… I feelingly sympathize with you when you inform me that the 'thoughts of death are alarming to you.' It was the case with me for many sorrowful years. But through the abundant goodness of my heavenly Father, it is not generally the case with me at present. That Scripture, 1 Cor. 15:25-26, was very remarkably blessed to me for the removing of all the very alarming and anxious thoughts about death, which till then deprived me of lasting comfort. Death is considered there not so much our enemy as Christ's, and he must reign till he hath put all enemies under his feet, and though death will be the last enemy, yet death must be destroyed. I saw I had nothing to do but enjoy the victory, Christ is engaged to conquer. The victory is obtained by the arm of omnipotence, and we shall ere long bear the palm in our hands as a token of it. Till that happy time arrives may it be our constant care and study to live in the fear and to the glory of him who has thus loved us, and vanquished our strong enemies for us. O! it is pleasing, it is comfortable! to view Christ in the field of battle, bearing the weak believer on his shoulder, through whole legions of hellish foes, to the blessed mansions in his Father's house …

I sincerely thank you for the remembrance of me at the throne of grace. You never can do me a greater kindness, though you have it in your power to oblige more than any person on earth. God has promised to hear our prayers, 'ask and you shall have' is his unlimited promise …[12]

In part of her reply, Sally reiterates her position with respect to their correspondence:

… If that charity which hopeth all things, admits me the place of a Christian friend in your heart, it is more than I have merit to claim, and all the esteem I can desire or wish. I do not know what happiness there may be in conjugal union, whose friendship is grounded on that Christian love you have described, I think it bid fair for happiness in the

---

[12] *Ibid.*, I, 156-58.

nearest connection; but it would be a bold adventure to prove it. I must look at this at some great distance, or as a thing never to come to pass, or the thought will become intolerable. The wheel of Providence is in a good hand, and I can be easy about it. If we had to turn it for ourselves, we were undone, for we are often blind to our own happiness, and seek it where it is least to be found. Some seek it in riches, others in honour; but these are perishing things, and always on the wing ...[13]

The correspondence continues

On reading the letters that continued to pass between Bala and Somerset over the next months, many interesting points arise. If we assume that each of these early letters took up to a week or so to arrive, then the average time in which Thomas answered Sally was within seven days. She, on the other hand, in keeping with her cooler approach to the correspondence, took on average thirteen days before replying. He would address her with increasing familiarity; the 'my dear friend' of the first letter becoming 'my dear, dearest friend' within a few months. With Sally, it is invariably, 'Reverend Sir.' It is worth noting that they corresponded together in English. Any spoken conversation between them would naturally have been in Welsh, their mother tongue, but all the education that they had received (other than when Sally was first taught to read her Bible) would have been through the medium of English. The few comments in Welsh that they do exchange show a reasonable syntax but atrocious spelling. This would have been typical of the educated Welshman of the day. It is only later, after his extensive studies in the Welsh Bible, that Charles's grammar and style when writing Welsh became so idiomatic and accurate.

Sally would often pass on news that she would have heard from her Methodist friends, particularly any news obtained of the progress of the many spiritual awakenings in the land:

---

[13] DEJ, I, 162-63.

Bala, 12 May 1780

… I suppose you have heard of the great revival of religion that is in South Wales. This last crop probably that the first Reformers shall here upon the earth reap of their labours. One I hear, whom we highly esteem, is ready to fly out of the cumbersome clay, the person is William Thomas of Peel,[14] he is very sick if he is still alive. May the Lord of the harvest call others that will be able workmen into the vineyard. I hear that some clergymen in South Wales are called and made flaming ministers of the sanctuary and that there has been upwards of three hundred received into the society at Llangeitho since Christmas. Oh may they be such as shall be saved. The work seems to be at a stand in Bala at present, but it is sometimes darkest before the break of day, and the devil is afraid of the foolishness of preaching which spoils his kingdom. Notice was given by the Magistrates and Clergy here to our exhorters, that if we meet in any house that is not recorded, and the person licensed to preach, that they will prosecute us.

Strange that their eyes have been shut so long, and now opened. But poor swollen worms, they know not what power they oppose; O that grace would subdue them …[15]

I remain your affectionate friend and Scrawler, Sally Jones.[16]

Along with his joy and satisfaction on reading of the progress of Christ's kingdom in Wales, Charles would also not have missed that first use of 'affectionate friend,' a considerable advance from 'your well-wisher.'

His next letter to Sally was written from Oxford and in his *Diary* he noted his impressions:

[14] William Thomas (1723–1811) of Pyle, Port Talbot, Glamorganshire, an early Methodist exhorter, who in fact recovered from this illness to live a further 31 years.

[15] DEJ comments: 'Several revivals broke out at Llangeitho and their dates are not clear by any means.'

[16] *Ibid.*, I, 178-79.

This morning was ordained priest, when I most solemnly and with my whole heart devoted myself with all I have to the service of God. Time, talents and all, I hope, I have been enabled to lay down at his feet. Nor would I upon the most serious consideration, and in my most deliberate moments, wish to retract one word I have spoken. I hope I can say that the constant and rooted desire of my soul is after God and his service.

O Almighty God, who has given the will, grant also power to perform the same. Accomplish the work which thou hast begun in me. Endow me with a double portion of thy Spirit and clothe me with power from on high. Increase my love to souls. Impress my mind deeply and constantly with a sense of the solemn account I must one day render unto thee of my stewardship. Enable me to exercise the gifts given me. Lift up my hands whenever they hang down and strengthen my feeble knees. Help me to be in thy hands as clay in the hands of the Potter, willing to be ruled, fashioned and employed by thy godly wisdom in the manner and for the service thou thinkest proper. I am nothing in myself; mine eyes are directed unto thee in whom the fatherless findeth mercy. O never leave me. Thou art a faithful God who never failest those who depend upon thee.[17]

After six months of correspondence Sally has begun to write a little more naturally, sharing something of her warmth of character. The following extract again reveals her lack of assurance, yet ends with a little leg-pulling:

> 25 May 1780
>
> … I am ashamed to own that the things of time and sense have such root in my heart … My feet are often in the mire of some earthly affection and weary of the assaults of outward temptation. I am often ready to yield the day. It is a wonder indeed that I am not given up to hardness of heart and a reprobate mind which of all others is the judgement I must dread, for sin makes me harder than before …

[17] DEJ, I, 185-6.

I love to pour my complaints to you because I believe
you think of me at the throne of grace. I can make but a
poor return for you there. I sometimes attempt to commit
you to Him that intercedes for you.

My father bids me tell you that he would rather have a
letter from you than write himself. Considering his habitual
seriousness he is rather light about it. He says that he has
nothing to preach to you, '*Mai ofer yw dweud pader i berson.*'[18] He talks of you often, if not too often, to me.

I am, your friend

Sally Jones[19]

And now Charles made a bad mistake. Perhaps in response to
her warmth, he begins a letter with, 'My Dearest Love,' and then
added, 'I expect Mr Lloyd to pay me a visit this summer, when I
intend making the proposal to him of accompanying him to [Bala]
… if it be possible, when he goes there next.' He then goes on to
say, 'I have already given some of my friends to understand that I
am under an engagement to a young lady, though never mentioned
your name, and I hope you will always give me leave to consider
myself in that light. I am positive I shall never consider myself in
any other, and shall I consider you so too? Will you say, Yes?'[20]

This was all too much for Sally: talk of an engagement; a direct
proposal; the prospect of a face-to-face meeting, and, reading
between the lines of her reply, the input of Miss Lydia Lloyd who,
as Sally's reply shows was now party to the affair. Gone is the 'affectionate friend,' her next letter reverts to formality and, towards the
end of the letter, her response to any mention of engagement is
devastating.

My dear Miss Lloyd … presents her Christian love to you,
wishing you may prosper in every good work and your pen
a better employment than professing an esteem which she
as well as myself thinks impossible to be real for the object it

[18] 'There's no point teaching prayers to a parson.'
[19] *Ibid.*, I, 190.
[20] *Ibid.*, I, 191-93.

is directed. Do not deceive your friends with such a genteel term, 'Engagement with a Lady.' If you must talk to them of this unaccountable correspondence, tell them that you have something like a dream with a country girl among the barren hills of Wales, and promise them no further account of the matter, for like it hath begun it will end abruptly, *hep ychwaneg o hanes am dano*.[21]

If Mr Lloyd's company and the seeing your old friends in Bala will answer the end of your journey, I wish you that satisfaction. Only drop the mask and make no other pretence. I would rather converse with you at a distance in this calm retirement than have a personal discourse with you. I do not know why we have begun nor what leads us on to converse, but I have cause to put up daily that petition, Lead us not into temptation. This is my request for you as well as for myself. May Jesus be our guide through every passage in life.[22]

Charles's immediate response to this apparent rejection is found in his *Diary* for 29 June:

How difficult is it to use God's creatures and not abuse them? The use of them is lawful but the abuse of them is sinful. Everything is abused when it is not kept in its proper place of due subordination in our minds, and when they have not a tendency in the enjoyment of them to bring us nearer to God. Everything in the place which God has appointed for it is proper, innocent and comfortable. I am at present in danger of inordinate affection.[23]

It is clear that Sally appreciated their correspondence and profited from it, but when Thomas became too passionate in expressing the strength of his love for her she would then become uncomfortable, and suspicious thoughts as to his motives would arise in her mind. By August, matters are back on an even keel; indeed, Sally is

[21] 'With nothing more to be said.'
[22] DEJ, I, 194-96.
[23] *Ibid.*, I, 198-99.

writing at her most relaxed. This is when her character is seen at its best. Here she again reveals her struggles against lack of assurance, her caring, social concern for those around her, especially those of the Methodist society, her need to keep her 'secret,' and her willingness to tease her correspondent:

> Having now thought of a letter in which you have dismissed the subject of our correspondence, may I not be permitted to copy after your example, without looking for a direct answer to your last to me? It now better suits my frame to talk of Llangeitho. Many of our people are gone there and dear Miss Lloyd has been able to go with them. I think it may be applied to that place what was said of Jerusalem of old, 'Thither the tribes go up, even the tribes of the Lord, to testify unto Israel to give thanks unto the name of the Lord.' 'For my brethren and companions' sake, I will wish thee prosperity.' Whatever is real in me I think this is, though I have reason to turn and say, 'Prove me and try me lest there be an unrighteous way in me,' when I think I have found the footsteps of the flock and tread in them. It is immediately asked me, 'How comest thou hither?' I fear that I have not the wedding garment, the righteousness of the saints, and that in the day when the Lord makes up his jewels I must be excluded from the assembly of the firstborn and have my part with the hypocrites and unbelievers.
>
> > Lord if thou canst not work the cure
> > Then I am contented to endure.
>
> There is balm in Gilead and a Physician there; 'For guilt not innocence His life He poured.' This shall be my only plea in spite of obstinate unbelief ...
>
> If you are in the same mind about coming to Bala, it may be proper for you to know that no one of the family at Plas-yn-dre knows of our correspondence besides Miss Lloyd. She has kept it from the others. If you would ask Mr Lloyd to cloak your conversation with me with some excuse

(*heb ormod o gelwydd*[24]) of business for somebody with my father, or acquaintance with some of Mr Wesley's people, or I know not what, something as you think of, I would rather. For if it is known but to a few it will soon be in a blaze about the country.

We have never refused a bed to any that have asked. Our house is small; but we have holes in the roof where we put pilgrims to lie.

Sally Jones[25]

An agreement, of sorts, arrived at

Thomas Charles made another visit to Bala in September 1780, leaving Somerset on Monday, 4 September, and arriving at Bala about eight at night on the Friday. This was only the second occasion for Thomas and Sally to meet face to face, the first meeting since they had begun to correspond and two years after they first saw each other. There are indications in subsequent letters that some sort of agreement was arrived at between them at this time, but the letters still show the same features: Thomas's irrepressible ardour and love and Sally's coolness and realism; Thomas's constant discomfort at their being apart; Sally's awareness that circumstances might still prevent a marriage; Sally's continued lack of assurance and Thomas's spiritual counsels to her, and, in every letter, their constant prayers for one another. Some of these features are seen in the following letter. It contains also a comment by Charles on the process of falling in love which provides good advice for a Christian couple of any culture or period.

18 November 1780

My Dear, Dearest Heart

To be persuaded that I possess a place in your affection and esteem affords me more real satisfaction than anything of a temporal nature possibly could, or, I am certain never can. Not because I vainly suppose that I deserve, in any

[24] 'Without too much lying.'
[25] Tibbott, JHS, 31 (1946), 42-44.

degree, a place there, but because I sincerely love you, my dearest love, and wish for a place therein.

And I am still more satisfied, that this regard proceeds not so much from blind passion as from clear conviction. Passions are unsteady things; they are no sooner excited but they subside again, and cannot be depended upon. But what proceeds from conviction is likely to be lasting. Passions are blind and dangerous *leaders*, but when they faithfully *follow* conviction they preserve their proper place, and are not amiss …

While I am expressing the present state of my heart towards you, I would not willingly, at the same time, forget to say something that may have, by the blessing of God, a tendency to establish your faith in, and increase your love towards him, to whom we are under such infinite obligations as will forever challenge and distance all returns. What returns can *we* ever make for Christ, the gift (what a gift!) of the Father? The very thought confounds and oppresses the mind … 'Christ died for the ungodly' – I love to repeat the words, because all my hopes and comforts in time and eternity are grounded upon them. I am not afraid to depend upon this foundation – I am sure it will never fail. This is the children's bread, and why should you think 'you have no right to meddle with it'? Are you not ungodly? You cannot deny it. Well then, 'Christ died for the ungodly'; is not this enough? O let us no longer doubt but believe in him, love him, delight in him, and set forth his praise not only with our lips but in our lives!

It comforts my soul that you remember me at the throne of grace. Continue to pray for me. I cannot forget you whilst able to remember myself. 'May the God of all consolation fill you with all joy in believing.' Farewell, my sweet love,

I am your own

Thomas Charles[26]

[26] DEJ, I, 225-27.

Thomas Charles as a young man.

Seeking a curacy in Wales

Now that the possibility of a marriage had been admitted there remained the task of facing the practical realities that might arise. The strength of Thomas Charles's love enabled him to ignore all difficulties in the way. His attitude is revealed as he expands upon a throw-away remark in one of Sally's letters:

> 11 December, 1780
>
> ... I wish you had written the following sentence, 'It will be equal for me to *direct to* you at one place as another,' thus: 'It would be equal for me to *live with* you at one place as

another,' for you may depend upon it, that soon after I am removed from here (be it when it will) I shall come and ask you to come and live with me. Your silence on that head induces me to suppose every place equally agreeable to you if you leave Bala – so it is with me if I leave Milborne Port. Therefore I think our minds to be in a proper frame to be guided by Providence. But your disapprobation of any place would be a sufficient proof to me that it is not the will of Providence that I should go there.[27]

Sally, however, with her more dispassionate viewpoint, was already aware of the possible insuperable problems that might lie ahead. In January 1781 she expresses her fears very clearly:

… But we should look what suitableness there is in external circumstances for the regard we have (and permit it to be real) for each other may only be a trial whether we account anything dear for the sake of Christ and the Gospel: my lot being cast among the dear despised Methodists and my small talent for the world of business and your calling and usefulness being in the Established Church and a connection with any other denomination likely to be destructive to it. Should not we weigh these things and stop our proceedings?

Wherever you think you can be most useful to precious and immortal souls, there I would wish to hear you are fixed to settle. I have not believed yet that it is appointed for us to live together nor am I anxious to determine one way or other. I ardently wish for your happiness and pray that the Lord may direct your course and keep you as a star in his right hand …[28]

For Charles, the guiding of providence, realised by a call to an appropriate living, would decide where, having married, they would live. For Sally, on the other hand, that guidance would decide if they ever were to marry. And always in the back of her

[27] DEJ, I, 232.
[28] *Ibid.*, I, 242-43.

mind was the worry: How could Thomas, a Church of England priest, marry Sally, a member of the despised Methodists, the daughter of a Methodist itinerant preacher? It would ruin his career in the church or, more importantly, it would ruin any opportunity of spiritual influence in the church.

The non-resident rector of Coychurch in the Vale of Glamorgan, the parish where the clergyman David Jones of Llan-gan (a leader of the Methodists in south Wales) lived, was Edward Davies. He lived in London, was a friend of John Newton, and 'a pious and evangelical clergyman of the Establishment.' The permanent curate acting for him at Coychurch was about to retire and, on hearing this, John Newton persuaded Davies to offer the post to Thomas Charles. Charles immediately wrote to Bala on 18 January 1781, passing on this information, not realising the devastating effect it would have (Llan-gan is over 150 miles from Bala). 'I am inclined to accept of it, if there should be a house in the parish for me to live in, and also (without which I shall do nothing) you should approve of it. It is certainly a very good curacy, equal to any one of £60 per annum in England. I shall give him no positive answer till I hear from you …'[29]

Within a week he received his reply, but its nature was such that it must surely have 'perplexed' immensely:

> … I shall not omit writing this post, though I fear it will be to perplex you instead of to help you to determine the present circumstance. I thought that you had determined to settle at Llanganna and that your call seemed clear to go there. This being the case, I had no doubt, but the Lord would enable me to be perfectly satisfied with that dispensation of Providence, which must have been a final separation between us, for I knew my father and mother would never consent for me to go that distance from them, therefore had no doubt of my own duty, as well as inclination to live in this country. It may be still that the Lord calls you there, and that he has work for you to do in those parts. I would not be a hindrance to you for the world …

[29] DEJ, I, 243.

You see that the best information I can give you is full of confusion, and nothing in it to be depended upon. Looking upon all difficulties, is it not the easiest and safest way to put an end to our acquaintance, than to be perplexed with it? I seriously think that there is some impropriety in it. I wish you would make so free to speak of that, as of your regard for one who has no right of it for any worthiness that you can find, nor any suitableness to accompany you through the rugged path of life ...[30]

Sally was acutely aware that had it not been for their relationship, Charles could have been settled for some years by this time and ministering usefully as a curate in Glamorgan or in any of the English curacies that he had been offered. The fear that she might be a hindrance to God's work inhibited the expression of her love to him. D. E. Jenkins is surely correct when he suggests that this letter would not have been written without considerable heartache.[31] Charles responded to the letter by taking the four-day journey to Bala again. As they then talked over their situation, Sally, presumably, drew strength from his words and presence, and Charles realised something which he had, perhaps, not fully grasped before. It was certainly during this period, and perhaps during this visit in March 1781, that he made up his mind on one point at least. He wrote to Watts Wilkinson:

It is true that dear Mr Newton kindly recommended me to a curacy in South Wales, and I entertained some thoughts of accepting it; but when I came to consult with dear Miss Jones, I found it would not do. She is an only child of tender and affectionate parents. When it came to the point, I found that it would be worse than death for her to be removed, whilst they live, to any considerable distance. Indeed when I saw how their minds were affected at the thought of it, I immediately laid aside every such idea; for I would not for the world be the means of bringing their grey hairs with sorrow to the grave. Everything, therefore, must remain as

[30] *Ibid.*, I, 247-49.
[31] *Ibid.*, I, 250.

it is, till I meet with a situation within a convenient distance
of the place where they live in North Wales.[32]

Such a situation, however, was not to be found so easily. In the
period between January 1781 and September 1782, Charles was disappointed in not obtaining opportunities for curacies in five places:
Cerrigydrudion, Llandyrnog, Oswestry, Mallwyd, and Llanuwchllyn. All of these places would have been close enough to Bala for
some acceptable domestic arrangements to have been arrived at.
The vicar of Oswestry refused his application because he had heard
that, 'I was tinctured with what they call Methodistical principles.'
Matters were further complicated in that by now Charles's friend,
Simon Lloyd, was also seeking a curacy near his home town. Sally,
aware of all the steps being taken by both men, found herself at
times in difficult situations. Simon Lloyd's endeavours for a curacy
proved more successful than his friend's. He was appointed to the
churches of Llandegla and Bryneglwys (Denbighshire), beginning
his work on 12 January 1783.

These continued disappointments took their toll on Sally's
spiritual confidence. Charles would often have to remind her that
the strengths of her fears that she might prove to be unconverted
was a true indication of a renewed heart. Thus, in April 1781,

> You condemn yourself without mercy for unbelief. But is
> it really unbelief that is the cause of your distress? For there
> is a spiritual jealousy in a renewed heart about the love of
> Christ, which has the love of Christ as its foundation, and
> which is often mistaken for unbelief, to the no small per-
> plexity and distress of the soul.[33]

And again in October 1782,

> This brings into my mind the substance of a conversation I
> had with you one night when last at Bala. I believe the fears
> you then expressed respecting your spiritual state were the
> effects of love to Christ. You did not fully enjoy Christ, nor

[32] DEJ, I, 246.
[33] *Ibid.*, I, 254.

had an absolute certainty of enjoying him, but you loved him and desired to enjoy him, and therefore you feared you should be disappointed. Have you not more fears of losing Christ than of anything else in the whole universe? And does not that prove that you love him supremely? Far, far above all other things put together. Let your fears then add strength to your faith and encouragement to your hope. You can never have any surer proof of anyone's love to you than from his fears of losing you – and love and fear are always proportioned to each other without absolute enjoyment. Christ also looks kindly upon our fears, sees sincere love at the bottom of all, and is not backward to confirm our hearts in his love.[34]

An awakening at Bala, 1781

A letter from Sally in mid-June 1781 contained full accounts of two remarkable occurrences. In the first half of the letter, dated 19 June, she described the results of a Methodist Association meeting in the town:

> We had many preachers from south Wales but Mr Rowland could not come. There were more people assembled this time than ever was before. The Spirit of rejoicing was poured abundantly upon a great many. I believe there were many hundreds singing and praising in the streets; their voice at some distance from them was like a sound ascending to the clouds. Some that went among them, to hear the words, were taken captive and joined with them, and others that went to oppose them like mighty giants whom none could resist, were obliged to retreat in disgrace. Every stripling flung his stone at them, and their threatening was no more regarded than the chaff which the wind scattereth.
>
> I was but a spectator upon the scene, only I felt some inward desire that the name of the Lord should be glorified, for there is much disorder in it. Yet, in all probability the

[34] *Ibid.*, I, 373.

Lord works powerfully upon some and takes them as it were into the third heavens. Some young people that were never religiously affected before met the first night after the Association in a room where someone prayed, and there they spent that night, in prayer and praises. The next night they met in the chapel, and it was between 4 and 5 in the morning before they parted.

If they take root downward as they spring upward, much fruit may be expected. But I have more cause to suspect myself on account of my deadness than anybody else. Yet, this I think: that good and bad are now caught in the net, and that a time of separation will come when there shall be difference between those that serve the Lord in spirit and in truth and them that serve him not. I believe there is danger of serving self in every outward show, at least to me there is.[35]

It is in letters like these that we see and appreciate something of the spiritual maturity and personal humility in Sally that had so attracted Thomas Charles. Her comments suggest that she might have arrived at her opinions from studying and profiting from some of Jonathan Edwards's discussions on revival. These were certainly known in Wales (by Howel Harris and Daniel Rowland, for example) by the early 1740s but it is perhaps unlikely that a shopkeeper's daughter in rural Merioneth would have met with them even forty years later. It is more probable that she was helped to such a balanced view of the complex nature of a period of spiritual awakening by the writings of her much-respected friend, William Williams, Pantycelyn.

Whatever emotions this account might have stirred in Charles's heart, they were probably as nothing compared to his reaction on reading the second half of Sally's letter, bearing the later date, 21 June. She had been in grave danger of losing her life! As she was returning to Bala from Llanuwchllyn Fair in a storm of thunder, lightning, and torrential rain, the River Twrch burst its banks, sweeping away five bridges and thirteen houses in the immediate

---

[35] DEJ, I, 274-75.

neighbourhood of Llanuwchllyn. Surrounded by flood waters, Sally had to climb hedges and wade through ditches to find safe ground.[36]

After expressing his alarm on reading the second part of Sally's letter, Thomas also comments on the news of the Bala Revival:

> Thunders, storms and floods only declare the majesty, the glory, and the rich treasures of the Heavenly Father, let everything then encourage us, for everything proclaims our happy lot in having God for a portion ...
>
> A thought so replete with comfort and joy is enough to make anyone jump and sing, and sing and jump again; and if it be this which influences the jumpers in Wales, I wish them from the bottom of my heart success – may they pierce the clouds with their melody and amaze the angels of the third heaven with their songs of praises, to the utter confusion of Satan, and all his agents – but as you very judiciously observe 'There is a great danger of serving self in every outward show,' and when the lives of such as distinguish themselves in that manner do not correspond with their profession, the devil has a great handle to reproach religion and bring the cause and interest of Jesus into contempt. For my own part, I am so fearful of saying anything upon the subject that I think it best to be silent, but I am clearly of opinion that such things should not be encouraged, nor any distinguishing marks of approbation showed to those who so distinguish themselves, by those who are in authority in the church, but rather every time examined as to the motives which every time influenced them.[37]

It was at this time that Charles received his first invitation to preach at one of the chapels of the Countess of Huntingdon's Connexion. The Countess requested his help for six Sundays in her Bath Chapel.[38] He was unable to help at that time because of

[36] *Ibid.*, I, 275-76.
[37] *Ibid.*, I, 280-81.
[38] *Ibid.*, I, 285.

the demands of the various churches that he served while at Milborne Port. He now had varying responsibilities in five churches. At St John's Church in Milborne Port he would sometimes relieve John Lucas, preaching on Friday evenings and occasional Sundays. His main responsibility remained at Sparkford, but he also served South Barrow, Lovington, Chilton Candelo, and North Barrow (all in Somerset). In a letter to Simon Lloyd he states, 'I have had reason to believe the Lord has in some degree blessed my poor labours in this dark corner. Some are under concern about their souls and my congregations in general increase.'[39]

The decision to remove to Bala

With this concentration on the correspondence between Thomas and Sally an unbalanced perspective may have been provided of Charles's labours during his years in Somerset. Throughout the period he preached on Sundays and week-nights in the various parishes where he laboured. He made frequent pastoral visits to his flock but was keenly aware of how little spiritual work was being accomplished among them. In all this he was learning more about himself. He wrote in his *Diary*: 'I find it much easier to be active for Christ than to be passive to his will, by yielding myself up to his disposal and resting satisfied with the issue. For by the honour derived from activity the pride of the *old* man within is gratified; and self finds something to feed on.'[40]

A letter to Sally, dated 23 January 1783, shows how frustrated he felt at the relative failure of so much of his labour amongst his people:

> I should certainly embrace this occasion of disengaging myself from a situation in which I can be of little use – every repeated attempt I make being frustrated – were I not fearful of running before the Lord in it. In everything we need to watch ourselves, and in few things more than in an over-hasty spirit.[41]

[39] DEJ, I, 282-83.
[40] *Memoir*, 44.
[41] DEJ, I, 391.

An example of Thomas Charles's handwriting.

By February his mind was made up. If his labours were to be predominantly at the disposal of a friendly vicar, sending him to whichever parish needed a supply at any time, this could just as well be accomplished in Merioneth as in Somerset. He laid out his plans in a letter to Sally on 28 February, 1783:

> … The scheme I hinted at in my last, is this: to ask leave to serve one of Mr Jones of Mallwyd's churches for nothing till I am able to get a curacy of my own in that country.

For I understand that he has two; one besides Llangunog. I do not suppose he would deny the request for he offered me the whole curacy for one quarter or longer if it would anyhow suit me.

If you and your parents would come in to it, I see no impropriety in it, for I am able now to procure a gospel minister to supply my place here and one who would be likely to suit and to stay here, which I do not intend in any case, at present.

I should not be idle – God forbid I should – but it may be, more active by far than I can be now; and also should be on the spot to apply for any place that offered. Besides, another advantage occurs to me which I could not so fully enjoy were I absolutely engaged to take care of a parish, that is, I should be more at liberty and less confined if occasional calls should offer to enlarge my sphere of action. I must always be thinking of something; my mind cannot be easy till I am able to bring things to bear; and after my last two disappointments, this is the only thing I can think of ...[42]

Charles was now quite determined to be married and living at Bala by the end of the summer. Necessary arrangements at Milborne Port were already in hand – his successor had been appointed – and he had decided on the 23 June as the day on which he would leave Somerset. Things were not quite so decided at the Bala end, but John Jones of Mallwyd, Meirionethshire, had written a positive response to Charles's request to be allowed to serve, unpaid, in one of his churches.

In response, Sally was as diffident as ever. Even in this, her last but one letter (29 May 1783) to her betrothed before his journey to her and their subsequent marriage, her unwillingness to commit herself entirely is evident. Just as evident is the fact that her lack of confidence was bound up with her lack of Christian assurance:

Everything shows the importance of the affair we have in hand, and we have need to be directed from above. I am not

[42] DEJ, I, 396.

An example of Sally Charles's handwriting.

unhappy in my mind for anything hitherto, and however it turns I hope we shall be enabled to know and to do the will of the Lord. For my part I am not positive nor confident how it will be; but I am easy about it whether everything is to come to nought between us or not. In that case we shall both I trust have strength according to the day. At present I think it my duty (whatever change may yet happen) to view things in the same light as you do in coming on, and I endeavour to weigh the matter seriously from what motives my regard for you proceeds and whether they are likely to hold my head above the waters, should outward comforts fail.

I have many fears concerning myself and doubtings whether I have ever received of the Lord the least grain of saving grace, and sometimes think that trials must come to prove what is in me.[43]

From the very beginning of their correspondence Charles's love, optimism, and confidence had had to be sufficient for both of them, and so it proved right up to their wedding day. Thereafter, things were to change remarkably quickly. On the morning of 23 June, after writing a last letter to Sally from Somerset, Charles wrote in his *Diary*:

June 23. I left Milborne Port this morn. Fully persuaded, be the consequence what it will, it was the will of the Lord I should do so.[44]

He knew better than to go immediately to Bala: Chester Fair was held on 5 July, and Bala Fair on 11 July. He therefore used the fortnight to visit, firstly, his friend Edward Griffin at Little Horwood, Buckinghamshire, and then a second old friend, John Mayor, at Shawbury, Shropshire. On Sunday, 13 July, he preached for John Jones at Llangynog Church, Merioneth, and arrived at Bala later that week.

The marriage of Thomas Charles and Sally Jones

While the marriage arrangements were proceeding in the Foulks household, Thomas took the opportunity to hear again the preaching of Daniel Rowland, his father in the faith. In a letter to Sally in 1781 he had expressed his longing: 'I should be very glad, if the will of the Lord were so, to see once more the old venerable

---

43 DEJ, I, 406.
44 *Ibid.*, I, 415.

Prophet before he takes his flight.'[45] The Llangeitho Association of that year met on the Tuesday and Wednesday, 5-6 August, 1783 but he travelled down earlier to Cardiganshire in order to attend other services on the days leading up to the Association. He described his experience in a letter to Edward Griffin:

> There were, at the Association, about twenty clergymen and between sixty and eighty lay preachers, though not all that are in the Connexion. You may suppose how glad I was to hear once more the old grey-headed Elijah proclaiming the deep things of God with that pathos, perspicuity and energy peculiar to himself. I heard him twice, and three clergymen besides, and also several lay-preachers, endowed with excellent gifts. Preaching began on Saturday and lasted till Wednesday morning ten o'clock. I shall add no more but that it was good to have been there.[46]

Clearly, his previous belief that no lay person should preach was by now considerably weakened, if indeed he had ever held it with any conviction. The minutes for the Tuesday private meeting of this Association note that eight clergymen and twenty 'exhorters' were present.[47] The ministers included Daniel Rowland; Nathaniel, his son; William Williams, the hymn-writer of Pantycelyn, Carmarthenshire; David Jones, Llan-gan.

Charles returned to Bala and he and Sally Jones were married on 20 August 1783 at St Beuno's Church, Llanycil (the parish church for Bala). Simon Lloyd and his sister, Lydia Lloyd, were the witnesses. He was two months short of his twenty-seventh birthday and she, three months short of her thirtieth. Thomas wrote in his *Diary*:

> This morning I was married – and I hope I can with truth say, 'in the Lord.' I have seen much of the Lord's goodness both in the person he has bestowed upon me and in his

[45] *Ibid.*, I, 268.
[46] *Ibid.*, I, 426.
[47] 'A Journal of the Welsh Association from 1778 to 1797,' JHS, II (1926), 58.

manner of giving her – the person most suitable in every view of all others I ever saw; and the manner in which she has been given me was best of all calculated to bring me to a right spirit in asking her and in receiving her of my heavenly Father. Every obstacle in the way was abundantly useful, and the delay, though to me was exceedingly tedious, was exceedingly beneficial and absolutely necessary. The Lord will not suffer his people to have the little of earthly things he is pleased to bestow upon them, in the same manner that worldly people enjoy them. Trials and crosses and disappointments shall be sent to drive them to the throne of grace, to bring them to deny themselves, to be resigned to his sovereign will, and to believe before they possess, in everything they shall live by faith.[48]

The contrast between Sally's cold, cautious letters of their courtship and the examples we immediately find in these, the very first months of marriage, is very evident. Only now when all bridges had been burnt does she disclose more of her natural warmth of character and her particular love for Thomas. Thus, in a letter dated 23 October 1783 she writes:

Most dearly beloved
    Your kind letter came just in time. Mr Pugh came here last night and said you was not come to Shawbury. What great cause have I to be thankful that the Lord has preserved you on your journey? When I see a cause in myself that the Lord should visit me with a rod, I fear for you and think the cross will come somehow or another that way. However I am persuaded of this that your life is precious in the sight of the Lord, and to his tender care and loving kindness I endeavour to commit you daily.
    I am, dearest of mortals, wholly yours
                                    S. Charles[49]

[48] DEJ, I, 424.
[49] *Ibid.*, I, 434.

And in another, dated 13 November 1783:

> My dear, dear husband
>
> The contents of the letter could not but give me great pleasure, at the same time I am almost tempted to complain on your letters. I formerly acknowledged the power of them, at that time it gave me full satisfaction to hear from you, but I am not in that state now. The idea of being reduced to live on letters again is not pleasing. Indeed, I long to see you, and I have a right to live with you *till death us do part*. But I would not be found to complain on the Providence that separates us. The Lord help me to be resigned and thankful, it is enough that he does not leave you comfortless in the work of the ministry, and he has a greater right than I have to dispose of you according to his blessed will and pleasure. I am happy that he is your father-friend and guardian …
>
> I do not love to write short letters. I would rather trouble you with three-quarters of the sheet of nonsense, than conclude too soon. I wish Somebody was like-minded. I have a good mind to send ____'s letter back to be filled, however I'll wait to know what Friday's post brings me.
>
> … I hope to see you in good time Monday night if the weather permits, but if the weather is bad you'll oblige me more by not setting off, and if you do come be sure to set off early. The journey will be more pleasant when you are sure of having time before you to accomplish the journey. If you see Robert Shôn give my kind love to him and tell Mr Parry that I am sorry that I am so shy in my letters that I say so little to him. If you should know where Mr Jones, Officer, lives, you would do well to see Mrs Evans of Bodwenny's little children with some little fairing for they maybe will enquire for them.
>
> I am called; here are two shopkeepers. Tonight you may know I am busy. Mr Chidlaw was buried today. Mrs Chidlaw is very bad and I fear likely to go the same way. Jenny is also confined to her bed. Mr Chidlaw of Chester

is come down. Dear, dear, I have a thousand things to say;
I may as well conclude as soon as I can,
   Who am, *C. annwyl inne*[50]
   Your own

                                        S. Charles

… it rains very hard here tonight. Maybe the flood will be
out that the Post can't go. However I hope he will be able to
go before you set off to come home, and I beg of you not to
come through bad weather to make your cold worse.[51]

Thomas Charles had waited ten years between the time he first
heard of Sally and the realization of his hopes in 1783. Yet these
were years in which Charles learnt a great deal of the lessons of
patience and of submission to God's timetable. Far from damp-
ening ardour, Thomas's strength of love prevailed. It outlasted ten
years of uncertainties – uncertainty even in that aspect of his life
to which he was most committed: his ministerial duty as a servant
called by God. It is surely the case that his love for Sally was an
element of God's providential care of his church in Wales for,
without it, it is almost certain that Charles would have followed
the natural path, one which he had clearly contemplated at times,
of ministry in England. In doing so he would have joined the ranks
of so many evangelical Welsh clergymen of the period: men such
as Thomas Jones (1752–1845) of Creaton, Northamptonshire, and
Edward Morgan (1783–1869) of Syston, Leicestershire. Finding
no welcome, or places to minister, in Wales, they were obliged
to follow their calling in England. Had Charles's life proceeded
similarly his energy and leadership would have been lost to the
ranks of Welsh Methodism.

Twenty years (January, 1803) after his marriage, Charles was to
write to a lady who was uncertain as to whether or not she should
accept a proposal of marriage.

[50] 'My own dear Charles.'
[51] DEJ, I, 444-45.

I never wish to interfere or say much about such concerns; as I know from experience that such improper meddling does in general more harm than good, only I say this much: 'in patience possess your soul.' And go on steadily and discretely as the way opens or shuts before you ... Sometimes I have observed obstacles coming in the way of an event taking place entirely with the design of procrastinating it as to time. For there is a certain time for every event in the Lord's counsel and design. It is to be accomplished in the exact time fixed upon by him, which is the only proper time it can take place in. I have seen and observed much of that respecting myself. I have often found that 'in quietness and confidence was my strength.' Mind these words much, and wait upon the Lord in the belief of them.[52]

[52] DEJ, II, 437.

St Beuno's Church, Llanycil.

St Tydecho's Church, Llanymawddwy.

5

THE FIRST YEAR AT BALA
(1783–84)

> I am now waiting to see what the Lord has to do with me;
> making use of every means in my power to procure some
> employment in the Established Church; not for the sake
> of any emoluments I might have, but from a principle of
> conscience. I can live independent of the Church; but I am
> a Churchman on principle, and therefore shall not on any
> account leave it, unless I am forced to do so. But you can
> well conceive how disagreeable and uncomfortable it is to
> be doing nothing. I never felt before, in the same degree,
> the force of that expression, 'Woe is unto me, if I preach not
> the gospel.' I feel a necessity is laid upon me; and that my
> life would be a perfect misery, without engaging in the work
> with all my powers.
>
> *Thomas Charles to Watts Wilkinson, 2 September 1783.*[1]

The truths preached by Charles

THE description of Charles as 'the Methodist Parson' given to him
by some of his Somerset parishioners could not have arisen from
any formal links that they were aware of between Charles and
the Methodist movements in England or Wales – no such links
existed. It must therefore have been based on his preaching and
ministry among them. No record of any sermon preached in these
years (1779–85) seems to have survived but the truths which he
taught may be inferred from the main themes of his meditations at
this time, taken from his letters and the pages of his *Diary*, written
during this period.

[1] DEJ, I, 427.

The abiding thought in all Charles's ministry and service to God was his knowledge of *the love of God*:

> Nothing but the free, undeserved and eternal love of God, without any motive exciting it but what is in himself, can give us one gleam of hope, or one ray of comfort, in the midst of the horrid gloom into which sin has brought us … God's goodness to angels and holy beings is *infinite*. But what shall we call that goodness and that love which is freely extended to sinners, to rebels, to traitors, to the ungodly! Is not this, were it possible, more than infinite? A belief in God's love to us in all its freeness, fullness and immensity, works by love to him, with invincible strength and unwearied diligence in his service. The effect is always in proportion to its cause. So the more clear our comprehension of God's love to us, and the firmer our belief in it, the more ardent will be our love to him, and the more active will be our diligence in his service.[2]

This love, like God himself, is sovereign in all its actions and purposes:

> My mind this morning dwelt with edification and comfort on the firmness and stability of the covenant of grace, and also on its suitableness, in every view, to the various wants of fallen sinners. It is 'well ordered in all things and sure.' … May the Lord deliver me from the sin of making a god of myself, which we always do when we follow our own wills, instead of God's. Meditations on God's absolute sovereignty, I have often found a great means of mortifying self-will.[3]

But before any man, woman or child can begin truly to appreciate the nature of God they have to learn something of their own natures, and this *conviction is the work of the Holy Spirit*:

> When the Spirit thus worketh, what discoveries does He make! What infinite guilt does He show to be in every spot

[2] *Memoir*, 421.
[3] *Ibid.*, 28-29.

and stain of sin! With what horror and amazement does
the awakened sinner view his own pride, seeing it as com-
prehending all the atheism and enmity against God, which
actuate the inhabitants of hell! Envy, malice and revenge,
the natural off-spring of pride, he now sees to be the very
tempers and dispositions of the Devil himself ... When the
Spirit shows sin to be sin, every frame of mind unsuitable
to the divine majesty and purity is exceedingly felt and
lamented: shame, sorrow and indignation, the deepest
self-abasement and abhorrence, weigh down the soul, and
humble it to the dust. Yes, there is a sort of infinity in the
abasement of the soul, when the Spirit shows sin to be sin;
he would still be more humble, and sink, were it possible,
still deeper; he grieves, because he cannot grieve more; he
abhors himself, because he cannot be still more detestable
in his sight. He sees an infinity of evil in his sin, which he
cannot fully comprehend, any more than he can the holiness of the law, or the greatness of God, against whom it is
committed. He would therefore that his sorrow, humility
and self-abasement should bear some proportion to it.[4]

To satisfy God's law and reconcile the sinner to God would
require *an atonement* infinitely greater than anything that a guilty
man could provide. This is what the gospel of a crucified Saviour
offers:

By Christ's perfect obedience to the law, all possible and
more than all conceivable honour has been put on it: and
by his death on the cross, he hath made such an atonement
for sin, and such a satisfaction to God's justice, as ten thousand times ten thousand hells could not equal. Were we
oppressed with the united guilt of all the accursed rebels
of earth and hell, the inconceivable merits of this infinite
sacrifice would alone be sufficient to remove it all. Clothed

---

[4] Edward Morgan (ed.), *Essays, Letters and Interesting Papers of Thomas
Charles* (1836); repub. as *Thomas Charles' Spiritual Counsels* (Edinburgh:
Banner of Truth Trust, 1993 [2021]), 49-50 [37-38].

with the divine righteousness of such a dignified Person, in the sight of all our guilt, in the prospect of future judgement, we can joyfully say, 'Who is he that condemneth? It is Christ that died.'[5]

Christian conversion occurs when a sinner puts all his trust for salvation in Jesus Christ, believing that Christ's life and death are the only means by which he will find eternal life. It involves both *repentance for sin and faith for forgiveness*:

> Our sinfulness and misery are great; but there are no bounds to the riches of the grace of an infinite God: and forgiveness is dealt out according to those riches to guilty sinners who believe in Jesus. O how suitable is the Gospel to our wretched state! It is a joyful sound indeed! Forgiveness! Yes, and repentance too! We could not enjoy the comfort of pardon without a penitent frame of mind. It is impossible for an impenitent sinner to taste and relish divine consolations. A penitent frame of mind is the working of holiness in a peculiar way in the heart of a sinner. Holiness is the same, wherever it is; but it differs in its effects in different subjects. An angel hates sin; and so does God and Christ. Holiness in them manifests itself in the hatred of every thing contrary to it. But holiness in the heart of a guilty sinner can never exist, not only without hatred, but without a penitential frame of mind, conscious of criminality and inexcusable guilt. And the deeper our sense of God's immense goodness, love and grace in Christ, the more penitent and self-abhorrent we shall be … May the Giver of repentance and forgiveness cause them to abound towards us both, and the whole church of Christ.[6]

In these truths are found the elements of a *justification by faith*:

> Justifying faith then I conceive to be: firstly, a full persuasion of the all-sufficiency of Christ's righteousness and

[5] *Memoir*, 405. In later years he would address the same theme in more measured words (see pp. 343-4).

[6] *Spiritual Counsels*, 303-4 [226].

atonement, wrought by the Spirit of God in the heart of a
sinner, founded on the express declaration of God's word.
And secondly, through the same Spirit, a consenting or
acquiescence of the heart therein, submitting to the righteousness of God, and letting go every other hold. To this I
think nothing can be added without impairing the nature
of faith; which is to go out of ourselves, quitting our own
righteousness to obtain acceptance with God out of his
mere mercy. For which reason I conceive the apostle saith,
'It is of faith, that it might be by grace.' It could not be by
grace any other way than by *faith*. And if you add any thing
to the account given of justifying faith, it doth not appear to
be by grace. If you add *assurance* to it, this, inasmuch as it is
something in *ourselves*, makes us look there for acceptance:
whereas faith, as described, looks *out* of ourselves, entirely
to Christ for acceptance; and so justification continually
appears to be by grace … Consequently, as at first, so always
we must carry with us a sense of our own utter unright-
eousness, a full persuasion of Christ's sufficiency, and an
acquiescence in him, for the favour of God.[7]

But though our sin is forgiven, it lives on within us for as long
as we are in the flesh. *Within the Christian therefore a continual
warfare is being waged*, the new life of the Spirit engaging with the
enmity against God which remains stubbornly within us:

It is this enmity to that which is good which is the Christian's continual plague. Every where and in everything, it
lusteth and warreth against all good. In prayer, hearing,
reading and meditating, this enmity is the grief of his heart.
In believing, loving, hoping and obeying, it sets itself, full
of enmity, against that which is good, and the practice of it,
universally … This enmity is, as it were, the active principle
in every sin, setting it to work with vigilance, activity and
perseverance. And this is it which the believer principally
sets himself against; he hates this enmity, is deeply humbled,

[7] *Memoir*, 64-65.

THOMAS CHARLES OF BALA

grieved and distressed on its account; and he cannot but groan, being burdened, whilst he carries about with him this body of death ...

He who hath seen this enemy as he is, knows how desperate and how dangerous he is, spends much time in searching him out, that he may not be murdered in the dark, is well assured that he cannot be too much avoided, and all means for mortifying him too diligently used. The sense of this enmity fills him with godly sorrow, and keeps him in the dust all his days. He cannot live at large, as many do, in boldness and security, well knowing what a deadly watchful enemy he always carries about with him. He cannot indulge, as others do, in carnal joys and pleasures, and in what are called innocent amusements, nor pursue his earthly concerns with too much greediness, knowing that by all these things the old enmity will be fed and nourished, and will gain more strength to wage against the soul. If our eyes are not steadily fixed upon this point, if we are not diligently searching into our own hearts to know the enmity and deceit of sin ... we are in great danger of being found hypocrites in the end, however well pleased we may appear to be with the doctrines of grace.[8]

The Holy Spirit dwells within each believer, and how much we grieve him when we are half-hearted in this warfare:

We know but little of the condescension, love and grace of the Spirit, because we are so ignorant of the various workings of inward corruptions by which his great work is opposed and continually obstructed. But when every secret thing is laid open to full view, and we see with divine light how we have resisted his gracious dealings with us, his love will no less overwhelm us with astonishment than the love of the Father and the Son. He has our comfort and happiness, our complete holiness and glory so much at heart, that anything which is an obstruction to the progress of his work is said

---

[8] *Spiritual Counsels*, 173, 175-76 [130-31, 132].

to *grieve* him. We are not grieved but for what befalls one whom we regard and love … So it is with the Spirit of God. He is concerned for those to whom he is engaged by his love as their comforter, and is grieved with their sins when he is not so with the sins of others …

How unworthy a conduct, to grieve him who comes for the very purpose of giving us consolations and joy! He has condescended in infinite love to become our Comforter. He bestows his comfort willingly, freely and powerfully. Nor is there the least hope, peace or joy but what he works and bestows. No relief in trouble, no refreshment in perplexities, but what he gives. And shall we by our negligence, sin and folly, grieve him! Grieve him, without whom we cannot live, cannot think a good thought, cannot breathe a good desire! Grieve him whose presence is heaven in the soul, and whose absence is a hell of corruption, darkness and misery. Is it possible that we can make such base returns for such love and be such enemies to ourselves! O, what a creature man is! In what dust and ashes ought the best of us to lie down![9]

God's purpose towards us, the goal of Christ's death on our behalf, and the aim of the Spirit in his sanctifying work within us, is *to bring us to holiness*, to be like Jesus Christ:

Grace never expects peace and comfort but in the way of holiness, and never thinks the cost too much if it can by any means be obtained. Comfort unconnected with holiness, and not influential to promote it in the heart, is a comfort which grace never desires, and which never can proceed from the Spirit of God the Comforter …

Do you not love holiness? Yea, in your worst frame, and when most dull, even when you hesitate whether sin or grace has the dominion over you? You still love holiness and abhor yourself because you are not more holy; and there is no heaven that you desire separate from it; why then

---

[9] *Memoir*, 427-29.

encourage doubts respecting your state?

There is no beauty or loveliness like holiness. It is real, undefiled, unfading and eternal. It is to be like God; it is to be like Christ; it is the work of the Holy Spirit. I cannot bear to think of true Christians not being holy; for in that case they must be very hateful in the sight of God. We ought never to deem anything handsome which God does not consider so. A fine dress, a handsome house, a large estate – *He* does not value. But a meek and quiet spirit is in his sight of great price, though in rags or on the dunghill. No one shall see him without holiness, 'Blessed are the pure in heart, for they shall see God.'

May God grant that we shall be so much in love with holiness that we may not be able to live without it. To be 'partakers of his holiness' is an expression of the apostle which has often delighted me. It is well worth-while to bear chastisements to obtain it.[10]

These truths: the sovereignty of God and his love in Jesus Christ towards sinners; faith and repentance by the work of the Holy Spirit; justification by faith in the substitutionary death of Christ upon the cross; forgiveness of sins; the need to mortify sins, to walk by faith and live humbly before God, to seek holiness and the image of Christ, these were the basis of Charles's faith and would have been the basis of his sermons. To him, such evangelical truths represented the faith of the Protestant reformers of the Church of England and were to be found in the Thirty-nine Articles of that Church. They were the principal truths taught so carefully and in such detail by the Puritans (so many of whom had been faithful members of the Church of England), and also, in his own hearing, by that eminent servant of that Church, the Rev. Daniel Rowland of Llangeitho.

But since the Reformation and the days of the Puritans, the Established Church had, by and large, become affected by nearly a hundred years of the spiritually-deadening influence of the

---

[10] *Memoir*, 415-17.

Enlightenment and its teaching of Deism and of a rational theology that deeply undermined the nation's trust and faith in the
word of God. The Church of England was considered by some
to be no more than 'a useful branch of the Civil Service,' and
many of its parishioners, especially of the peasantry, had lapsed
into drunkenness, cruel and violent sports, and a religion charac-
terized either by deep superstition or complete indifference. It is
no surprise, therefore, that on hearing the above truths, pressed
upon their consciences by vehement, soul-searching, heart-felt,
evangelical preaching, many of Charles's parishioners in Sparkford
and Milborne Port would have concluded that their curate was
a Methodist: a member of that 'enthusiastical' sect of firebrands
who (in their judgement) were travelling through many parts of
the country with their wild ranting sermons, stirring up trouble in
the churches and rebellion against their priests. Charles's ministry,
therefore, had not been well-received in Somerset, apart from by
a few individuals. It remained to be seen what reception he would
be given in Merioneth.

Rejected in three parishes

The first months of married life brought no great change to the
week-day activities of Thomas and Sally Charles. Sally continued
with the management of the family shop. She was accustomed to
rise early, about five o'clock in the morning, to begin the day's
work in the shop. This was a habit she had learnt from her parents.
Her stepfather would rise between four and five in the summer
and between five and six in the winter, particularly on a Sunday
morning if he had a long journey ahead of him. On the frequent
occasions when he returned late on a Sunday night after preaching
two or three sermons and a long ride on horseback, he would still
be up in the morning at his business, as early as any in the town.[11]

Up to this time Sally had simply worked in the shop for her
parents, but in the months leading up to the wedding Thomas

[11] Gwen Emyr, *Sally Jones: Rhodd Duw i Charles* (Bridgend: Evangelical
Press of Wales, 1996), 33.

Foulks frequently asked her to take over the business completely in order to release him to give all his time to the ministry. She had been reluctant to take up his offer, for two reasons. The first was the uncertainty over her future: as the wife of an Established Church minister, would it be appropriate for her to continue as a tradeswoman? The second was her fear as to whether she had sufficient capital to take full responsibility for the business.[12] She had shared her concerns with Thomas and it was his suggestion in his answering letter that she eventually followed:

> As to settling your affairs, I doubt not but in the end the Lord will direct. You may possibly be troubled and perplexed but look for a comfortable issue from the Lord. Were I to advise you as a friend, I would not advise you to take the whole of the business upon you immediately. Consider what a world of cares, troubles and perplexities it will bring upon you. You will be hurried out of your life – at least so it appears to me; though you must know better. Suppose you defer it till sometime after we are married. Should we not then be better able to judge whether such a thing could be practicable?[13]

Charles's situation was unchanged in that he still experienced great difficulty in finding work. He had preached for John Jones in Llangynog Church on his way to Bala at the end of July. His second Sunday there was to be his last. Writing to John Mayor, he says: 'The church I was engaged to serve, in this country, I was dismissed from, after preaching there two Sundays. I now assist Mr Lloyd.' Simon Lloyd was unwell and had asked Charles to take his place in the pulpits of his two churches, Llandegla and Bryneglwys. Events, however, were to repeat themselves exactly, for his very next sentence to Mayor reads, 'One of his churches was the second Sunday shut against me by the parishioners; and I expect

---

[12] For Sally's financial circumstances and the marriage settlement, see DEJ, I, 421-22 and 'The Marriage Settlement of Thomas Charles and Sarah Jones, 1783,' JHS, 29 (1944), 35-36.

[13] DEJ, I, 414.

every Sunday to be my last in the other.'[14] This proved to be the case, as he described in a later letter to Edward Griffin:

> ... last Sunday, the whole parish, with two or three of the principal inhabitants at their head, came to me and accosted me in a rougher strain than I ever have been used to before. They insisted on my preaching no more in their church; for they added, 'You have cursed us enough already.' I took great care that nothing but the plain simple truth should give offence: nor is there anything else laid to my charge ... What the Lord means to do with me, I know not, but I hope I shall know soon.[15]

For the first time since being ordained, Charles was having to experience pulpit-free Sundays and weeks without the need of preparing mid-week evening sermons. He found the situation painful as shown by the quotation at the head of this chapter. He was, however, experiencing new responsibilities. As usual in the first week of October 1783, Sally was away at Chester Fair. A letter which Charles sent her deals with thoughts prompted by his daily study and shared with her, but the last paragraph details some of the new elements that had entered his life:

> ... I have found this afternoon more comfort and joy in the Holy Ghost than I have for some time past, in reflecting on the love of each of the divine Persons engaging them respectively to accomplish the work of Redemption. The Father loved us freely and gave his Son. The Son loved us freely and gave himself for us. The Holy Ghost loved and still loves freely and comes to sanctify, comfort and dwell in our hearts. This last dwelt upon and affected my mind most particularly as no unworthiness prevented the Son of God from coming to redeem us; so also, no depravity prevented or prevents the Holy Ghost from coming to sanctify, comfort and to dwell forever with his. He has loved them freely from eternity in their filth and abomination, therefore

[14] DEJ, I, 425.
[15] *Ibid.*, I, 426.

he comes to them, abides with them forever. Christ came freely to do all for them, and the Holy Ghost comes as freely to do all in them, and all his workings in them are infinitely free from beginning to end. May the Lord help us to believe this. I experience the difficulty of it this moment …

My dear mother desires me to tell you the following things are wanted, lest you should have forgotten to insert them in the memorandum – Broad French Tape; Large Band Box for hats or bonnets; Lemons. We have sent 3¾ lb of Beeswax, the side saddle, and a small cask for the brandy or rum, with Richard. My mother has done everything she could to procure some butter to send also, but she could not get it without paying an extraordinary price for it. But she will try again next week … My mother says I shall make an excellent shopkeeper. I think I see a pleasing smile on your countenance …[16]

From October 1783 to January 1784 he supplied the pulpit for his friend John Mayor, the vicar of Shawbury, Shropshire, more than fifty miles to the east of Bala. Also in that October, Thomas heard that Simon Lloyd had suffered the same fate as himself at the hands of the Llandegla parishioners. They had told him that because of his 'attending Methodist meetings' they would not have him as their minister. He seems to have kept his connection with the sister congregation at Bryneglwys for another three years.

In his *Diary* for 1 January 1784, Charles looked back on the previous twelve months:

Another year is past. When I reflect upon it I find more comfort in considering what Christ has done *in* me, than in what I have done *for* him. I can perceive that his hand has been upon me – giving me to see a little more of the total sinfulness of my nature, the exceeding sinfulness of sin: its deceit and guile. I have not been also without some glorious views of Christ in his person and offices. More so than I ever experienced before, but alas how little still do I

[16] DEJ, I, 429-30.

know of these profound mysteries – the mystery of iniquity and the mystery of godliness! I ought to lie low in the dust, but blessed be the Lord that he continues to give me a little divine light – I hope in an increased degree! But Oh how little have I done *for* him! Here I ought to be ashamed and confounded indeed! … may he direct and strengthen me! We must not only be supplied with strength to *work*, but also be taught continually and directed *how* to work and *where* to work.[17]

Towards the middle of January 1784, Charles heard that Edward Owen, the rector of Llanymawddwy, required a curate. He applied and was appointed to the post. Thus, on Sunday, 25 January 1784, after a break of seven months, he again preached to a congregation whose pastoral care had been placed in his hands.

Llanymawddwy, Merioneth, was a parish of some 800 inhabitants about fourteen miles south of Bala. Its population at that time was at the highest it would ever be: by the end of the nineteenth century it had been halved as a result of the depopulation of Welsh rural areas. The village lies on the upper reaches of the River Dyfi which rises on the slopes of Aran Fawddwy (2,971 ft) nearby. The road from Bala was a wild mountain road[18] crossing Bwlch-y-Groes, one of the highest passes in Wales, and linking Llanuwchllyn and Mallwyd. The impressive view from the pass encompasses the Dyfi Valley, Cadair Idris, and Aran Fawddwy nearby. The descent from the pass was 'an exceedingly steep and narrow zigzag path' like a staircase, rendered 'dangerous by loose shivering slate stones that slide beneath the feet.'[19] Charles would travel to Llanymawddwy on a Saturday and remain there until mid-day Wednesday, preaching on the Sunday and the Wednesday morning.

[17] *Ibid.*, I, 457-58.
[18] Now an unclassified road, with a 1 in 4 gradient in places. Bwlch-y-Groes was used between and after the wars to test prototype cars and their performance during hill-climbing. The southern ascent was renowned throughout the 1970s and 1980s as the most challenging climb used in the Milk Race, a round-Britain cycle race.
[19] George Borrow, *Wild Wales* (1862).

After only two months at Llanymawddwy, however, Charles's enemies caught up with him. He wrote to John Mayor:

29 March 1784

… as my time is short, having only four Sundays more, I would not on any account miss one opportunity of delivering my message to the very many who willingly attend to hear, even on week days. I had an absolute promise of the curacy; but promises are nothing when there is an heretic[20] in the case, 'no faith to be kept with heretics.' After my appointment three clergymen from Dolgelley and its neighbourhood, gave themselves no rest till they got me dismissed. However I verily believe the Lord sent me there, and I hope not in vain. He can bless one sermon as well as ten thousand. I was apprehensive my continuance would not be long; therefore I endeavoured to make the best of the short time I might be there.[21]

The ringleader amongst his enemies was the Rev. Rice Anwyl, rector of Llanycil, Bala. It is thought that it was Charles's efforts in catechising the children and young people of Llanymawddwy at the close of the Sunday services that caused offence. Anwyl, who could not stand Charles because he had married a member of the Methodist society in Bala, was a great friend of Edward Owen, the rector of Llanymawddwy who had appointed Charles. It is probable that Morgan dismissed Charles in order to please his friend. The Llanymawddwy parishioners got up a petition to secure their curate, but the man they chose to deliver the petition on their behalf was persuaded to destroy it instead. In this way, by a third dismissal from a curacy, Charles's career as a parish priest in the Church of England came to an end.

Time for a decision

By this time Charles had endured six years of unremitting frustration and failure. Throughout those years he had known only

[20] That is, himself, of course, as judged by his enemies.
[21] DEJ, I, 474.

uncertainty and disappointments with respect to the three things that mattered most to him: his seeking of Sally for a wife; his longing to be used for God's glory; an assurance of where it was that God intended him to labour. The first of these desires had now been met but the other two seemed as far away as ever. Two commentators, with almost two hundred years between them, have come to the same conclusion with respect to the purpose of these seeming fruitless years. Thus Iain H. Murray, writing in 2009, notes:

> ... there was in Charles the constraint of a prayerful faith. Uncertain of the future though he was, he had learned more necessary things in all the sore trials of the years following his ordination. His disappointments in Somerset and elsewhere, the long wait for Sally, and, worst of all, his conscious incapacity and the small influence for good which seemed to attend his work, had all worked for good. It is significant that the first chapters in *Spiritual Counsels* are on 'Spiritual Pride' and 'Humility.' He was brought low.[22]

And Charles's first biographer, Edward Morgan, wrote in 1828:

> When God intends a person for some great work, he prepares him for it. He makes him know and feel what he is in himself, sinful, depraved, weak, devoid of every spiritual good, and full of every evil ... [Mr Charles] was destined by heaven for great and glorious services. He was now undergoing a course of hard discipline, to fit him for his work. The success he met with in after life, and the honour to which he attained, would have found in the pride of his heart too ready a combustible, and might have proved his ruin, had not that pride been previously mortified ... The foundation of his humility was deeply laid: and it was laid, no doubt, during the first years of his ministry, by the realizing views he had of his own sin and unworthiness.[23]

---

[22] Iain H. Murray, *Heroes* (Edinburgh: Banner of Truth Trust, 2009), 125-26.
[23] *Memoir*, 198-200.

Charles himself held the same view. He knew that, 'here the religion of Christ begins; and our progress in the divine life is always safely estimated by our progress in humility. Humility is the strength and ornament of all other graces; it is the food that nourisheth them; the soil in which they grow.'[24] Throughout April, May, and June 1784, Charles looked for further vacancies, solicited the advice and prayers of friends, particularly his friends amongst the English evangelical clergy, and tried to wait patiently for the unveiling of God's path for him. That which he found most painful was the sense of not being useful in God's work. Writing to Sally while visiting John Mayor in Shawbury, he complained:

> I cannot carry a guilty conscience any longer about me; which I must do if my days are consumed in vanity. Indeed I seem at present to be a mere encumbrance on the Earth. I am in everybody's way and no one knows what to do with me. I hope this will teach me humility, and make me sensible of what little consequence I am in the world.[25]

In this same letter he commented, 'all friends here seem to give me up to the chapels in Wales.' The reference is to the many meeting-houses and chapels built by the Methodist societies.

The development of the Methodist Revival (1764–84)

To appreciate Charles's position at this time, we need to understand the development of the Methodist Awakening in north Wales in the years since 1764.[26] No revival as powerful and extensive as that of 1762–64 occurred for some years afterwards in Wales, though from 1770 onwards the societies in the region around Llandrindod, Radnorshire, were considerably strengthened by a period of blessing that continued for some four years and resulted in some hundreds of convictions and conversions. But from 1778 onwards another country-wide movement brought many thousands into

[24] *Spiritual Counsels*, 3 [2].
[25] DEJ, I, 486.
[26] See above on pp. 16-17 for the account up to that year.

Christ's kingdom, particularly in the counties of the north. In 1779 the ministry of a lay exhorter, Richard Dafydd of Clynnog on the Llŷn Peninsula, was crowned with such unusual unction and blessing that the awakening spread throughout the county of Caernarfonshire. He was soon being referred to as 'Rowland of Clynnog,' in that his preaching was now more like that of the great Rowland of Llangeitho than of the little-known old exhorter of Clynnog. Similar awakenings arose in Aberffraw, Anglesey, in 1776, and in many places in south Wales in 1780 (to which Sally Jones referred in her letter of 12 May, 1780[27]).

In 1781 a further outpouring of the Holy Spirit upon the ministry of Daniel Rowland at Llangeitho occurred. Very little of the history of this awakening is known, but that its effects must have been remarkable may be safely inferred from the fact that, among the numerous periods of revival centred about Llangeitho, this is the one that was referred to as '*The Great Revival*.' And then, in that same year, 1781, Bala town experienced, for the first time, these powers from on high, described so carefully by Sally in her letters to Somerset.[28] As a result of this revival the Bala society chapel had to be enlarged in 1782.

In the years up to 1755, the date of Charles's birth, the Calvinistic Methodists in Wales had built twenty-four chapels, every one of them being in south Wales. But by this present period, the summer of 1784, and as a result of the many awakenings in most parts of the country, the number had risen to 114. Sixty-seven of these were in south Wales, and forty-seven in the north.[29] These chapels in the north were distributed throughout the counties: six in Anglesey; eighteen in Caernarfonshire; five in Merioneth; four in Radnorshire; ten in Denbighshire and four in Flintshire. There were now thousands of believers gathering for worship and fellowship in the Methodist societies in the north but there was a desperate need for ministry, guidance and leadership. Of the twenty clergymen

[27] See above, page 55.
[28] See above, pages 67-68.
[29] HMGC1, 451; HMGC2, 533-42.

and sixty to eighty lay preachers mentioned by Charles as being present in the 1783 Llangeitho Association,[30] all the clergymen and the vast majority of the exhorters were from the south. The forty-seven societies meeting weekly in their chapel buildings were, of course, only a fraction of the number of societies that had been formed in north Wales. The majority in 1784 were still gathering in private houses and barns. They depended on a three-fold ministry: that of lay preachers from the south who undertook long itinerant journeys of two, three or four weeks throughout the north; that of the few north Wales itinerants, men like Robert Jones and Thomas Foulks; but predominantly, that of their own local elders, such as John Evans in Bala, who followed their own callings in the week and served the local societies on Sundays and week-nights. On very rare occasions, an itinerant clergyman from the south might pass by and administer the sacraments at one of the new chapel buildings.

Joining the Methodists

This is the reason why English evangelical *clergymen* in Shrewsbury, aware of the situation, could advise, or at least could be resigned to the prospect, that Thomas Charles should be 'given up to the chapels.' Charles himself, however, was not so ready to make up his mind. In the previous autumn of 1783 he had expressed to Watts Wilkinson the strength of his belief that he should stay in the Church of England sufficiently strongly for the latter to reply:

> ... I rejoice, at your sentiments respecting conformity. You know I formerly used to suspect you was rather lax in that point. Am happy in the change; may it continue. Nothing, I trust, will move you. I am not more sure that Archbishop Laud was a rogue, than that you would live to repent if you were ever to dissent ... I have no doubt you may get some emolument in the Church, especially as you have no regard to emolument. Take care of setting bounds for yourself, or determining not to take a church but within such a

---

[30] See above, page 75.

particular district as may best suit your convenience. Your dear Master may have work for you to do far from Bala or Merioneth. I heartily pray him to direct you.[31]

Now Charles writes to Wilkinson again in June 1784 explaining his new situation:

> I am in a strait between two things – between leaving the church and continuing in it. Being turned out of three churches in this country without the prospect of another, what shall I do? In the last church I served I continued three months. There the gospel was much blessed, as to the appearance of things. The people there are calling upon me with tears to feed them with the bread of life.[32] What shall I do? Christ's words continually sound in my ears, 'Feed my lambs.' I think I feel my heart willing to engage in the work, be the consequences what they may. But then I ought to be certain in my own mind that God calls me to preach at large. This stimulates me to try all means to continue in the church, and to wait a little longer to see what the Lord will do. I thank the Lord I want nothing but to know his will, and to have strength to do the same.
>
> The gospel spreads here, and thousands flock to hear it; and I believe thousands in all parts have received it in its power. I tremble lest the Lord should find me unfaithful, when I see so much work to do. I often think I hear my dear Master saying to me, 'Why standest thou here all the day idle?' This thought is still sharpened when I consider that the night is coming on apace, when no man can work. Your own feelings will tell you that my mind must be eased one way or other. O! to be clothed with power from on high, and to be faithful unto death …[33]

It was now practically certain that Charles would not obtain a position in Merioneth, or even in north Wales, but Wilkinson had

---

[31] DEJ, I, 443.
[32] That is, not in the Church but within a society.
[33] *Ibid.*, I, 490.

not previously considered that this should be any great obstacle to his remaining in the Church of England. Sensing what was in the wind, he wrote to John Newton informing him of Charles's wavering position. Soon a weighty letter arrived at Bala from Olney. Newton delivered his views with all his usual clarity and good sense:

> … I am sorry to hear that you have been dismissed from your curacies, but I can hardly think this circumstance alone will *in foro conscientiae* [34] require you to leave the Church of England; if indeed you could get no curacy at all in the Church, you might be more justified if you should leave it. But from what I can judge you seem to make your residence in Bala a *sine qua non.* So that I apprehend if you should give up your ministry in the Establishment, and go forth to preach at large, it would not be wholly from a principle of conscience that you ought to do so, for the sake of the Lord and of his work, but partly at least, if not chiefly, from a motive of convenience, because in some respects it suits your temporal concerns to live where you do, and you have in a manner determined as a previous step not to remove from thence.
>
> It appears to me that when we devote ourselves to the service of the Lord in the ministry, the surrender should include not only a purpose to preach the gospel in general, but likewise a willingness to be guided by his Providence into that particular situation in which it may be his good pleasure to place us. Now for aught I can tell the reason why the Lord has permitted you to be silenced in Wales may be that he has a work for you to do in Yorkshire or Northumberland, and that a resolution on your part to quit the Church except you can exercise your ministry in your present neighbourhood, may be so far contrary to his will …[35]

It is clear from the very determined tone of the arguments expressed in these letters by Wilkinson and Newton that Charles

[34] 'Before the tribunal of the conscience.'
[35] DEJ, I, 492-93.

was considered by the Evangelical Churchmen of his day as one of the most able and promising of their young men. They did not wish to lose him from their ranks. John Newton, at this time, was one month short of his sixtieth birthday. He had been twenty years in the ministry and was widely respected as a wise and godly counsellor. His prominent position in London and his connections with many of the eminent men of the day meant that he was considered a patriarch within the evangelical wing of the Church of England. To receive such a personal letter from such a man, with its heavily-weighted counsel in one direction, would stop most men in their tracks.

But what both these honest friends were ignorant of were the facts that Sally could not leave her parents and Charles could not endure a situation resulting in long separations from Sally. Both these truths were not mere matters of '*convenience, because in some respects [they suited their] temporal concerns*,' as Newton and Wilkinson believed, but existential facts of temperament and principle which long years of experience and hardship had brought to light. And, more objectively, what these two men, in their far away locations in London could not have had any real awareness of was the pull on an evangelist's heart at the sight of thousands of awakened souls attending the Methodist preaching services, with their deep hunger for God's word, and with so few shepherds in the whole of north Wales able to pastor them. It would have required a Whitefield or a Wesley to have appreciated the dilemma of Charles's circumstances at this time.

Within a few days of receiving Newton's answer, Charles had made up his mind. D. E. Jenkins identifies one undated letter as being the very day of the decision. He concludes that Charles wrote to Sally on 3 July 1784, while she was at Chester Fair:

> Saturday night in the shop
>
> Ever most dear wife,
>   Mother and I are sitting together in the shop, the hurry of the market being over. Mother is pondering over Father's letter, and this will inform you how I am engaged. We were

exceedingly glad to hear by Evan that you were well and hearty so near Chester. My fears tell me still that something might happen before you got to your journey's end. I endeavour to commit you to the Lord's custody. I cannot forget to pray for you. Asleep and awake you are near my heart. I hope the Lord is present with you abundantly supporting you.

… Robert Jones is come here; and *Charles bach annwyl inne*[36] begins to be uneasy. He was at the society last night. He was *glad* he went.

I hope the Lord will direct us: his counsel alone can bring us out of every wilderness.

Hasten to come home, my dearest heart. Every place here is gloomy, Sally not being here to enliven the scene. You would be received with more joy than ever by *Charles bach, etc.* Heaven is in your eyes, my dear; Charles loves to look on them.

My mother is much as usual. Sends kind, kind love. But not half so much as,

Your ever affectionate husband.

T. Charles.[37]

The letters from Wilkinson and Newton may have been in his pocket and their arguments in his mind, but on Friday night Thomas Charles had been in the Methodist society listening with gladness to the loving exhortations of Robert Jones, Rhos-lan. Whether this was his first visit to the society or whether he had been attending for weeks, it is impossible to say, but he certainly wished to impress upon Sally the joy he felt in his heart as he worshipped with them. Robert Jones (1745–1829) was the leader of the north Wales Calvinistic Methodists at this time. He had been a teacher in Griffith Jones's schools for twelve years but had been fully engaged since 1768 as an itinerant preacher. He was to become one of Charles's closest friends and a most trusted advisor.

[36] 'My dear little Charles,' Sally's pet name for him.
[37] DEJ, I, 495-96.

Robert Jones, Rhos-lan.

Tradition has it that during this visit he pressed Charles urgently to throw in his lot with '*pobl y seiat*.'[38] Charles is quoted as having said at some point during the summer of this year, 'I feel myself much inclined to take Wales, as I did my wife, "for better, for worse, till death do us part."'[39]

Rather than stand by in idleness, Charles had begun to keep a school for the poor children of Bala, holding it in his own house. As their numbers increased he had to look for larger premises and was happy enough to accept the offer of the Calvinistic Methodist chapel. With wife, parents-in-law, school, and friends weaving closer and closer bonds between himself and the Methodists, it is no surprise that he began to receive 'earnest invitations to exercise his ministry among them.' Certainly, at some time in July, or the first fortnight of August 1784, he enrolled as a member of the Bala Methodist society. Most probably it was the sixty-one-year-old

[38] 'the people of the society.'
[39] *Memoir*, 229.

elder, John Evans, who examined him before the gathered society and registered his name. He attended the Llangeitho Association of August 1784 and significantly (in contrast to the previous year) his name is included in the Association minutes as being numbered amongst the ranks of the Methodist clergy.

It is important however to realise what this decision to preach for the Calvinistic Methodists did *not* mean. It did not mean that Charles was turning his back on the Church of England. Far from it. It is true that ministering to the despised Methodists would immediately bar him from any future preferment in the church and also close the majority of church doors against him. He would most probably never preach again from a Church of England pulpit, at least not in Wales. He would now have agreed with the arguments that his friend Robert Roe had put up seven years earlier before the Brasenose College Senior Common Room when they refused him his degree because of his 'Methodistical principles': [40]

> *Principal*: Mr Roe … you attend illicit conventicles.
> *Answer*: I do not attend illicit conventicles, or any other Dissenting Meetings.
> *Principal*: What come to the same in *our* eyes is, that you have, and do, frequent, the meetings of the people called Methodists.
> *Answer*: I acknowledge I have.
> *Principal*: And do you not think this wrong …?
> *Answer*: I do not think it wrong, because they are no dissenters from the Church, and their Chapels are established by law.[41]

Of Thomas Charles's Oxford friends, the one who held to the highest Churchmanship was Watts Wilkinson. Years later (31 January 1804), he would write to his son:

> I dined last Friday in company with my old friend Mr Charles. He has no doubt been an instrument of *good*, of

[40] See above, page 32.
[41] DEJ, I, 62.

much good; but I *always did* – and told him so at the first –
and *still do* very much question the propriety of the step he
took when he joined that connexion.[42]

But having made his decision, Charles had no doubts. He still
considered himself a faithful priest and member of the church,
and he viewed his ministry as one conducted according to the
ordination vows of the Established Church. When he administered the sacraments among the Methodists he would do so using
the church services. When he baptised a baby he would understand that he was inducting that child into the community of the
Church of England. His disapproval of Nonconformity was as
strong as ever.

Most members of the Calvinistic Methodists of Wales at that
time considered themselves members of the church, parishioners
in their localities, dependent on the church for the conducting
of baptismal, communion, marriage, and funeral services, but
meeting to hear the preached word and to share their spiritual
experiences in their own society meetings. Even in these they
would be very careful not to appear to be in opposition to the
church. They would, for example, make absolutely certain that the
times of their meetings would never clash with those of the local
church. Only in one point was Charles, perhaps, at variance with
his previous standpoint. As mentioned before, he would not now
hold to any belief that lay preaching was illegitimate. How strongly
he held this conviction previously is not known, but once within
the Methodist fold it was quite obvious that the health of Welsh
Methodism depended almost entirely on the exhorters. Though
the clergymen provided some of the most powerful preachers –
Rowland; Jones, Llan-gan; Griffiths, Nevern, for example – it was
the countless unordained preachers and exhorters who sustained
and pastored the scattered believers. And Charles now gave himself
to provide for these, and the flocks they superintended, his loyal
and appreciative support.

---

[42] *Ibid.*, II, 455. Despite this view, Wilkinson still continued to support
Charles financially in his activities.

As the years passed, the religious life of an increasing number of the Methodists would separate more and more from their local parish church, and they would begin to adopt the attitudes and independence of Nonconformists. As a Connexion, however, this was never formally the case, and for nearly thirty years it certainly was not true of Charles as an individual, until the decisive separation of 1811.

Thomas Charles (as published in *The Gospel Magazine* of 1797).

6

ENTERING FULLY INTO THE WORK OF
THE REVIVAL
(1785–87)

Charles's first preaching journeys

It is believed that Thomas Charles began his itinerant preaching among the Calvinistic Methodists about the beginning of September 1784. By November he was travelling through Eifionydd and the Llŷn peninsula in Caernarfonshire, accompanied by a lay preacher, Humphrey Edward, from Bala. Such journeys were to be his main activity, apart from periods of ill-health, for the remainder of his life. In 1810 he was to say, 'I really would rather to have spent the last twenty-three years of my life as I have done, wandering up and down our cold and barren land than if I had been made an arch-bishop.'[1]

Charles's accounts of his six-year ministry (1778–1784) within the Established Church convey a period of much frustration and difficulty. A very different spirit may be discerned almost immediately as he commences his first itineraries among the Methodist societies. The change is due primarily not so much to any difference in external and ecclesiastical circumstances, though these must have been considerable as he, practically overnight, exchanged his parish-church pulpits for those of barns, private houses, and the open-air. Rather, he was now preaching to a completely different group of people. Whereas previously the vast majority of his hearers,

[1] D. Francis Roberts and Rhiannon Roberts, *Hanes Capel Tegid y Bala* (Bala, 1957), 22; quoted by E. Wyn James, 'Pererinion ar y Ffordd,' JHS, 29-30 (2005-06), 78.

both in Somerset and Merioneth, had been life-long attenders of their local churches, accustomed to the undemanding duties of their religion, suspicious of and unwelcoming towards any Methodist-tainted newcomers, he now faced the eager, expectant, and humbled converts resulting from the many spiritual awakenings of the developing revival. Charles has not left any written account of his experiences during these first years of itinerating. The diary which he had begun writing in November 1778 finishes abruptly in July 1785, which suggests that it was brought to an end by the pressure of his increasing preaching engagements. Other accounts however suggest that almost immediately the spirit of the revival was accompanying his ministry.

Thomas Jones (1756–1820) of Caerwys (later of Denbigh),[2] describes their very first meeting thus:

> It was about the end of September he made his first tour, as an itinerant preacher, through a part of Caernarfonshire. The Compiler of this his history remembers being with him, forming a first acquaintance with him, listening to him, and enjoying his profitable fellowship, in two or three places in that county: and from only that much experience, he formed such an opinion of him, as to his unostentatiousness, his application, and his entire Christian bearing, together with his vivacious spirit and excellent gifts, as a preacher, that he was willingly constrained to greatly reverence and love him from that time forth.[3]

During the Christmas week of December 1784[4] an Association was held at Bontuchel, about two miles from Rhuthun, Denbighshire. Charles preached on the text, 'But when the fullness of the

---

[2] Thomas Jones was raised at Caerwys, Flintshire; at various times he lived at Mold (1795), Rhuthun (1804), and Denbigh (1809); but he is generally referred to as 'Thomas Jones, Denbigh.'

[3] DEJ, I, 520-21; Thomas Jones, *Cofiant y Parch. Thomas Charles* (Bala, 1816), 164-65.

[4] Jones gives the date as December 1785, but D. E. Jenkins shows that he was mistaken (DEJ, I, 521-22).

time was come, God sent forth his Son, made of a woman, made under the law, to redeem them that were under the law, that we might receive the adoption of sons,' (Gal. 4:4). It proved to be one of the most notable sermons that Charles ever delivered at an Association. Thomas Jones was present and described it:

> In the days of Christmas of this year the Publisher, as one out of many, well remembers that he was listening to him preaching at an Association at Bont Uchel, near Ruthun, in Denbighshire (on Galatians 4:4-5) and that he spoke of an infinite person, and the active and passive obedience of the Redeemer, with such lucidity, authority and heavenly effect, as vividly surprised and gratified, lovingly melted and stirred the congregation, to a degree seldom witnessed.[5]

The memory of this service remained as part of the local Methodist tradition up until the end of the nineteenth century. The verses in Galatians were remembered, to the end of their lives, by those who were present as 'Mr Charles's text in the Bontuchel Association.' Jones heard him preach a third time in this, Charles's first year of itinerating, and described the occasion: 'About this time, or a little later, he preached at Lôn Fudr, in Llŷn; where his sermon was with power and acceptance so remarkable, that its fragrance filled that district, and spread also to the country around.'[6]

The relationship between Charles and Jones would develop into life-long friendship and fruitful co-operation. Although there was only a few months' difference in their age and they were comparable in intellectual abilities and spiritual fruitfulness, the younger man's respect for the older is seen in nearly every reference of his to Charles, throughout the rest of his life.

Leading the Methodist society at Bala

John Evans, the senior exhorter of the Bala society, had been a member there since 1745. He was born in Glan-yr-Afon near Wrexham, Denbighshire, in 1723, but the family soon moved to

[5] DEJ, I, 521; Jones, *Cofiant* (1816), 165.
[6] DEJ, I, 521; Jones, *Cofiant* (1816), 165.

John Evans, Bala.

nearby Adwy'r Clawdd. It was at Bala, however, that Evans had found his Saviour, his wife, and his life's work. In his secular work he was firstly a weaver, then a book-binder, and lastly, a candle-maker; and in his spiritual work, he was an indefatigable preacher who walked to venues up to thirty miles away to preach to the small scattered gatherings of the early north Wales Methodists, but was still present at his workplace early on the Monday morning. He was to become the leader of the Bala society and, along with Robert Jones of Rhos-lan, the most respected elder in the whole of the north Wales Association.[7]

It might be supposed that considerable tensions could have arisen between Charles and John Evans when the former committed himself in 1784 to the body of believers that formed the

---

[7] Gildas Tibbott, 'John Evans, Y Bala,' JHS, 46 (1961), 26-35, 53-60; Goronwy P. Owen, *Atgofion John Evans* (Caernarfon, 1997), 17-24; Jones and Morgan, *Calvinistic Methodist Fathers* (Edinburgh, 2008), Vol. 2, 30-47.

Bala society. Charles was a young man of twenty-eight and Evans was sixty years old, having led the society for more than thirty years by this time. He now had a new member on his hands – a clergyman (a B.A. and M.A) possessed of very evident spiritual and preaching gifts, a friend of John Newton, Thomas Scott, and other famous names, and who was married into one of the most influential families of the society. It says much of the godliness and humility of both men that they became the closest of friends and the most productive of fellow-labourers. There was little that Charles would undertake without first finding out Evans's views on the matter, and the older man held the younger in the greatest respect. They were united, for example, in their dislike of emotional, over-dramatic preaching, as the following description of Evans demonstrates:

> As might have been expected, John Evans was a solid preacher, declaring the truth in its simplicity. Many of the exhorters of the time appealed mainly to the emotions. Their purpose was to awaken the ungodly and while proclaiming the destruction awaiting an evil world they would shout and cry out, literally fulfilling the command, 'Cry aloud, spare not, lift up thy voice like a trumpet.' In many ways they met the needs of the day and were the means, under God, of convicting many. But this led some to conclude that shouting and roaring were indispensable elements of preaching. John Evans, on the other hand, sought to enlighten the mind and feed the people with knowledge; he appealed, certainly, to the emotions and feelings, but only through the understanding. He therefore spoke quietly, never in fact raising his voice. The more discerning of the people greatly enjoyed his ministry – the clarity of his style, the simple and scriptural form of his language, the solidity of his arguments and the very practical nature of all his preaching, were much appreciated by them. He preached with his natural speaking voice without any artificiality or assumed intonation. When asked why he did not shout or work up steam in the pulpit as most of his contemporaries, he replied, in the wry

manner that was his, that there was no need to sweat when telling the truth.[8]

The two men, Charles and Evans (with Thomas Foulks's assistance up to 1787) were to guide and pastor the Bala society between them for twenty-eight years. There are many anecdotes of their mutual respect for one another and their loving, affectionate relationship. One story describes Charles's hesitation over whether to set out one Saturday for a preaching engagement on the following day in a remote chapel in the mountains. He himself was recovering from illness and a heavy fall of sleet had made the roads treacherous. He sent to John Evans to ask him what he thought he should do. He received the answer: 'Ask Mr Charles, Is he master or servant? If master, he can do as he pleases, but if servant, he has but to obey the call.' This decided the matter and the engagement was kept, with no ill effects. In this and similar ways, the Oxford graduate and ordained clergyman showed his sincere respect for the old candle-maker. There is a letter to Evans from Charles, kept in the National Library of Wales, which begins, 'My Dear Old Faithful Friend.'

In her letters to Charles, the Countess of Huntingdon would ask to be remembered to 'honest John Evans,' and from the Countess's appointed successor, Lady Anne Erskine, one of the four trustees who administered the Countess's Connexion after her death, there is a similar greeting (31 May 1794): 'I hope the work goes on well at Bala and my old friend John Evans is in good health of soul and body. Remember me very kindly to him.'[9] John Evans was to die on 12 August 1817, at the age of 94, outliving the younger Thomas Charles by nearly three years.

Widening influences

In the years from 1785 to 1787 Charles's ministry and influence were to expand rapidly throughout the whole of north Wales. Apart from his itinerant preaching, the one single area of activity

[8] Jones and Morgan, *Calvinistic Methodist Fathers* (2008), Vol. 2, 36-37.
[9] DEJ, II, 133.

which was most significant in these years was his re-establishing of the Circulating schools of Griffith Jones, Llanddowror, and his championing of Sunday schools.[10] But in other, more general ways, he very swiftly became a force within the Methodist ranks in the north. By 1785 the Bala society had over 400 members, gathered from a large district around the town. Many hundreds more attended the preaching as hearers.[11] These now formed Charles's regular congregation when he was at home.[12] For the most part he was away on preaching tours. In February, his journeying took him south at least as far as Llangeitho; in April he undertook three weeks of travelling through Caernarfonshire and Anglesey. His experiences of preaching to such eager hearers greatly confirmed him in his decision to commit himself to the Methodists. He had written in his *Diary* at the beginning of the year 1785:

> I am this day beginning a new year: God only knows whether I shall see the end of it. May I be always found with my lamp burning, watchful and doing my Master's work – then all will be well whenever he comes! When I reflect upon the last year, I see great cause for thankfulness. I have reason to believe that the Lord has in some degree blessed my poor ministerial labours. I never found Satan so busy tempting me to unfaithfulness in my Master's service, since I have been in orders. It surprised me much, for the temptation continued in full strength for some time. It caused me to pray more fervently, to be humbled more deeply, and to see more of the fear of man and of the love of the world in me than I was aware of. Blessed be the Lord that I was enabled every time to overcome and not to act unfaithful. This affords me now great comfort. I believe Satan acted more violently than ever because the Lord blessed my ministry more than ever …[13]

[10] Described in chapter 8.
[11] That is, those of the congregation who were not members of the society.
[12] E. D. Evans, JHS, 28 (2004), 27.
[13] *Memoir*, 240-41.

In April, John Mayor wrote to him with the offer of a curacy. His response was immediate:

> ... as to the curacy, I believe I must not entertain the thought of accepting it and leaving my present line of labouring in the Lord's vineyard. The fields here all over the country are white for the harvest. Fresh ground is daily gained. Whole neighbourhoods, where the word has been heretofore opposed, call for the gospel. Thousands flock to hear and, in many parts of the country, we have good reason to believe, are effectually called. Whilst the prospects here continue so promising, I cannot in conscience quit the field here and remove to another place. My dear friend, pray for me. I am often from the ground of my heart crying out, 'Who is sufficient for these things?'[14]

He strikes the same note in a letter written in July to Edward Griffin. In it he also gives some further particulars of the Bala society and his own activities:

> At Bala there were but a half dozen hearers at the beginning, and the opposition continued without interruption for the space of 25 years. Now the congregation consists of about 2000 hearers, and there are between 400 and 500 communicants. In short, without enumerating particulars, for it would be endless, the Lord certainly has done a great work here: the preaching of the gospel has been attended, especially at seasons, with great visible power, and its effects in civilizing the country at large, and in bringing many to a saving knowledge of the truth, are evident to all...[15]
>
> ... As to my ministry here, I keep the two following objects in general view – viz, preaching the gospel in new places. Where our people here are much attached to the Church, a clergyman is much more acceptable. Secondly, attending those places on Sundays in the different counties, where it is convenient for the body of our societies to

[14] DEJ, I, 539.

[15] Richard Bennett, 'Llythyrau y Parch. Thomas Charles,' JHS, 5 (1920), 41.

attend, and administering the Sacrament there. Here at Bala I am every month. You see I have my hands full, as there is no clergyman but myself in the whole Six Counties. I am at times ready to sink under the burden, but having put my hand to the plough I dare not look back. My dear friend, do pray for me that I may finish my course with joy. Our Sacramental Seasons are often very precious and we have much of the divine presence.'[16]

Charles's rise among the Methodists is exemplified by his rising profile in successive associations at Llangeitho. In 1783 his presence was not formally recognised; in 1784 his name was found in the minutes; in August 1785 he was called upon to preach for the first time at this, the high feast of the Methodist year. A well-known passage in Thomas Jones's biography of him describes the outcome: 'About August of this year … the late reverend father Mr Daniel Rowland heard him preaching at Llangeitho. His glad response was: "*Charles is God's gift to the north*." This is indeed the case, and it may be added, to the south also.'[17]

In this new context of labour some of Charles's hitherto unused abilities began to emerge. Members of the societies began to resort to him for financial and legal advice in matters that concerned the societies. Thus, in the early 1780s, the members of the society at Waunfawr, near Caernarfon, were enduring considerable persecution as they worshipped together in a house in the village. This was drawn to his attention by John Evans, Bala. The result was that a strip of land was purchased for £40. By 1785, under Charles's supervision, Capel Bach chapel had been built in Waunfawr, and he, together with Robert Jones, Rhos-lan, John Evans, and two others, were named as trustees in the trust deed of 1876. In the same year, he is named, alongside John Evans and Thomas Foulks, on the trust deed of the chapel built for the Methodists at Dolgellau, Merioneth.

[16] *Ibid.*, 41-42.
[17] Thomas Jones, *Cofiant* (1816), 161.

Charles was also instrumental in helping to raise the first chapel for the Methodists in Liverpool, at Pall Mall, in 1787. It is said that he raised almost £400 towards the costs. In this way he began to shoulder what was to become a continual burden, namely, the financial responsibility for so many of the Methodist chapels in north Wales. In the early years much of the money came in response to appeals to evangelical Churchmen from across the border.[18] In later years the increasingly organized Calvinistic Methodist Connexion with its multiplying membership was able to finance its own developments.

The list of buildings built, in part or fully, by means of his fund-raising over the years include: Llandwrog (1789), Rhuthun, (1789), Denbigh (1792), Caernarfon (1793), Harlech (1794), Cefn Meiriadog (1796), Wrexham (1797), Bryn-crug (1800), Corwen (1802), Y Bont-ddu (1803), Llanelidan (1804), Abergynolwyn (1805), Arthog (1806), Capel y Graig (1806), Cynwyd (1807), Llany-cil, (1810), Cemais (1810), Llanegryn (1811), Capel y Bwlch (1811), along with many others. For most of these chapels, Charles would be a trustee and the man invited to preach at the opening services. His preaching skills and fund-raising abilities in themselves would have soon established him as a leader, but what was becoming more and more evident to the organizers of the movement was that in the person of Charles they had been given a leader of remarkable wisdom, spiritual insight, and statesmanlike qualities. His gifts were becoming more and more evident as he undertook increasing responsibilities with respect to the formation, development, and progress of the Methodist Connexion in the north.

Ministering to the Countess of Huntingdon's Connexion

Charles had been unable to respond to a request from the Countess of Huntingdon to supply the pulpits of her various chapels when he was at Somerset but in June 1789 she renewed her request:

[18] The correspondence between Charles and Thomas Scott at this period is typical of one of the main methods by which he gathered funds in these early days of his leadership in the north. See DEJ, I, 564-66.

Once more I make the most friendly and respectful offer for your services at Spa Fields for a few weeks – eight Sundays at longest ... Should the Lord dispose your heart to come from the sixteenth of August to the fourth of October I shall make no engagement with any other ... Dear Sir, your very sincere friend and willing servant,

S: Huntingdon.[19]

Charles's position now was very different in that he was not attached to any church and was therefore free to respond positively. Unfortunately, he fell ill at the beginning of August, and Nathaniel Rowland (Daniel Rowland's son) took his place from November 1789 to January 1790, but Charles was able to take over and minister for the first time at Spa Fields Chapel for eight weeks

Selina, Countess of Huntingdon.

[19] *Ibid.*, II, 43.

from 10 January 1790 onwards. A list of the other pulpit supplies for Spa Fields during 1790/91 shows the rank of ministers amongst whom Charles was now numbered. These were: David Jones, Llangan (March, April); David Griffiths, Nevern (May, June); David Jones again (September, October, November); Nathaniel Rowland (December, January, February). There was no differentiating with respect to remuneration: each man received two guineas a week and ten guineas for travelling expenses.

These periods of pulpit supply in London continued regularly for Charles throughout the remainder of his life. Every year in early July, from 1790 to 1800, then in the winter months from 1802 to 1805 and finally, 1809 to 1813, in late April/early May, he would make the journey from Bala to the capital and remain there for an eight-week period. The shop, and later the children, would keep Sally at home. In the last twenty-four years of his life he performed this ministry seventeen times, carrying on until only eighteen months before his death. These London visits were to prove immensely important to him and his work because of the opportunities they gave him to meet and befriend so many of the leading men in evangelical circles.[20] He already had close acquaintance with one group of influential Church of England clergymen from his Oxford days, but his London connections widened his sphere of correspondence and influence greatly, among both clergymen and Nonconformists. Invitations to serve as a director on various evangelical bodies would eventually arise from these connections, and he would then arrange his period of supply in order to be in the capital for the annual board meetings. The first such appointments were to the directorships of the London Missionary Society in 1797 and the Sunday Schools Society in 1798.[21]

[20] It meant, for example, that on each visit he could renew friendship with John Newton at St Mary, Woolnoth, from 1790 until the latter's death in 1807. Thus, in a letter of 15 August 1798 from Spa Fields, he wrote, 'I saw Scott yesterday, who is well. Cecil is poorly and sets off next week for Bath. Mr Newton is not in town; and I feel disappointed in leaving London without the usual annual interview with him. He is engaged in writing the life of Grimshaw.' (*Memoir*, 295-96.)

[21] See below, pages 176 and 143, respectively.

7

FAMILY LIFE
(1784–94)

> I bless the Lord that I have a *praying* wife. People are seeking
> this and t'other good qualities in their wives. I will say, 'Give
> me a praying wife.'
>> Thomas Charles to Sally Charles, 8 December 1783.[1]

A very happy marriage

THERE are very many occasions and circumstances in the life of
Thomas Charles that reveal his spiritual discernment and wisdom.
One of the clearest evidences of this is his choice of wife and his
long years of perseverance to ensure that he 'brought her to the
altar.' The repetitions of their expressions of love for each other are
to be seen in their letters whenever they were apart throughout the
years, and their temperaments and skills complemented each other
perfectly. Those same letters would still often refer to Sally's tendency to doubt her salvation but these were tempered by Thomas's
consistently sunny cheerfulness and his patience in counselling
her. He, on the other hand, was strongly sustained in his labours as
an itinerant preacher by her unwavering confidence in his abilities
and his call to the work. Her letters show that she felt his absences
from the home deeply but that this never undermined her encouragement to him to press on with his work nor her constant prayers
for God's blessing to be upon him.

Very early in the marriage she expressed her great satisfaction
at the way in which providence seemed to be hindering him from

---

[1] *Memoir*, 431.

further employment within the Church of England. Three months after their wedding she wrote to him:

> November 1783
>
> … I should be very unhappy on account of the long journeys if I did not think it answers a more glorious end than anything of a worldly nature, and I hope the Lord will honour you to be of use to his glory in the world. I was thinking today that it was in vain for one that had found mercy of the Lord and was determined to be faithful to his glory, to think of acting to that purpose under the wings of the Children of Darkness. It is evident that they 'hate the light and can't abide it.' I believe if there is any set of people among those that are called Christian that are given up more especially than others to blindness and opposition of the light that these black friends are they. I am glad my dear C. is separated from amongst them; may Jesus the Captain of his host commission you to go out in the face of devils, the door is wide open to preach the gospel out of their synagogues. The thought of the shortness of our lives affects my mind, and I know you will pardon me for expressing my thoughts in so rough a manner …[2]

With feelings like these there is little wonder that she had had doubts about being married to a minister of the Established Church. Sally's worries over the unsuitableness of their union had not been trivial. On the one hand, as has been mentioned, she was tied to Bala by her love for her parents, particularly by the need to care for her mother. Mr and Mrs Foulks depended upon her help for the continuance of their income from the shop. In addition, she was also a member of the Methodists. While this does not seem in any way to have been a matter of difficulty between the couple themselves, it certainly increased the prejudice of the clergy against Charles. It also resulted in his failure to secure a curacy, leaving him with no source of income. It is remarkable that Charles's decision to join the Bala Methodist society and commit himself entirely to

[2] DEJ, I, 446.

ministry amongst the Methodist community resolved, almost at a stroke, all these seeming incompatibilities.

Charles had never thought of marrying Sally for her money, and she herself, after testing him for so long, came to realise this. But it is a happy irony that it was Sally's money, or perhaps, more accurately, her business skills, conjoined with Charles's complete dedication to the ministry that was the perfect combination, under God's blessing, to bring about so much of the immense spiritual advancement throughout north Wales during the next thirty years. It has often been noted how much the early Methodism of the north owed to shop-keeping wives: for twenty-seven years, from 1783 to 1810, when she passed on the shop to her son, Sally maintained the family and maintained Charles in the ministry. Similarly, Elizabeth, the first wife of John Elias (1774–1841), supported him by running their shop for nearly thirty years. William Roberts (1784–64) of Amlwch, John Elias's cousin, was able to devolve all the responsibility for his shop to Sarah, his wife, which she undertook for over forty years. The same was the case also for John Jones (1796–1857) of Tal-y-sarn, whose wife, Fanny, owned a shop and managed it for over twenty-five years.

Sally's character

With Charles away from home so often, the running of the home and family depended to a considerable extent upon Sally. D. E. Jenkins provides the following description of her:

> Mrs Charles was altogether a remarkable little woman, though her talents shone chiefly in the affairs of this world. Somewhat small in stature, in figure inclined to sparseness, she was by no means frail; her movements were always lively, sometimes sharp. She could even flare up into a temper, and in her warmth she did not hesitate to give her offending apprentices the flavour of a rod or yardstick. Nevertheless she seldom, if ever, lost control of her judgement so as to throw her business arrangements into confusion. Her great capacity for work and her application made all around her,

if they had anything in them, exceedingly alert; and those who left her for other spheres generally carried with them marks of her influence in a certain fitness and ripeness of experience. Unlike many women of her business aptitude, she had also a great capacity for affection; all her servants, without exception, held her in much esteem and admiration. Mr Charles was no exception to his branch of the Charleses – he had but a poor gift for business affairs and the management of money; her gifts, therefore, enhanced as they were by deep religious longings, admirably supplied his deficiencies.[3]

Family joys and sorrows

In the first week of June 1785, Sally gave birth to their first child, Thomas Rice Charles. She wrote to Charles towards the end of the month, when he was away at the annual Anglesey Association:

> You will be glad to hear that our market is over and that I am as well as when you left me, only a little tired. I am now in our room hearing Gwen singing for little Tommy, who is sleeping sweetly …[4]

Within four months of the birth of her son, Sally lost her mother. Jane Foulks died in the last week of October, 1785, at sixty-eight years of age. She had been one of the early Bala converts of Howel Harris and was one of the very first members of the Methodist society in the town. She had remained faithful to her testimony throughout the worst years of persecution. In the last third of her life she had been witness to the most amazing turn-around, with the crowds now gathering weekly in Bala to hear the gospel where once they had gathered in order to mistreat its preachers. She had welcomed Thomas Charles warmly to her home on his marriage to Sally and attempted to pass on her shop-keeping skills to him.

[3] DEJ, III, 605-6.
[4] *Ibid.*, I, 540.

In June of the next year Sally wrote to Charles:

> My dearest C., take as much care of yourself as you possibly can. I would almost beg you would not speak so loud but I am afraid it is similar to the advice Peter gave to his dear Master, and deserves the like reproof. Well, I have one comfort still remaining, that if you are spent, you are spent in the best service, and I must endeavour to leave you in the best hands …
>
> Time calls for me to go to bed. I must take my leave of you tonight with much longing to see you once more at home. Tommy *bach* sleeps, here in the cradle by me, and Shanny in the other bed. We are all here as you left us only Peggy Wynn is gone home today …[5]

The references to Gwen, Shanny, and Peggy Wynn are to maids employed by the family, either in the home or behind the counter of the shop. Shanny (or 'Shani') was Jane Ellis, a member of the Bala society and the maid in the Jones, and then the Charles household, for many years. She was already in the home in the late 1770s when Charles first began his correspondence with Sally.[6] Whenever Williams, Pantycelyn, wrote to the family he would always ask to be remembered to her.

On 17 February 1787 their second child, Sarah, was born. Sally had been dangerously ill for some weeks before the birth. Charles passed the news on in a letter to John Mayor:

> What 'vague report' you have heard of dear Mrs Charles, I do not know; but the truth is this: she was taken extremely ill about three weeks before her time: but the Lord in mercy wonderfully interposed. I was obliged to live above a week (and a most trying week it was) tossed between hope and fear. She was extremely reduced and her strength was very nearly exhausted. The whole of her recovery is the Lord's

[5] DEJ, I, 546-47.
[6] In a letter of 1784, Sally writes, 'Shanny's compliments to Mr Newman and yourself – but you need not deliver it if you think it improper.' *Ibid.*, I, 517.

doing, and I believe in answer to prayer in extremity. It is well to have an *all-sufficient* Friend to go to. When I gave her up to him, I received her back from him by a favourable turn being given to her illness. We cannot but see the Lord's hand in it from first to last. It was he that 'killed and made alive.' She recovers but slowly, and is still very weak; but she is recovering: and what comfort that gives me, your own feeling must tell you; for I cannot.[7]

Sally's weakness at the time of Sarah's birth was reflected throughout the baby's short life. The letters of the next twelve months contain constant reference to her state of health. Thus Charles, for example, wrote to Sally while she and her stepfather were away at Chester Fair in October 1787:

… Sally *fach*[8] is much as you left her – rather better than worse. I hope you will be able to commit her to the Lord, and rest easy in your mind till you see her. If she alters at all you will be sure to hear of it …

Need I tell you that I love you? No; but still it is pleasing to me to repeat it, though you want no assurance of it. I bless the Providence that brought us together …[9]

Now, within the space of nine months, they were visited by a series of family sorrows and surprises. Rees Charles, Thomas's father, died in the first week of May 1787. The family had quitted the old home at Pant-dwfn in 1778, when Thomas Charles was just beginning as a curate in Somerset, and had moved to Cil-y-coed, a farm near Meidrim, Carmarthenshire. The new farm had not proved as profitable nor as easy to manage as Pant-dwfn; furthermore, mishandling of the deeds relating to the change of tenancy had resulted in legal difficulties. In addition, Rees Charles had been charged with breaking excise laws with respect to his work as 'a maltster and a maker of malt' and had been heavily fined. These

---

[7] DEJ, I, 568-69.

[8] That is, Sarah, the baby (*fach* is the feminine of *bach*, meaning *small*, but used here as a term of affection).

[9] *Ibid.*, I, 584.

A nineteenth-century print of the Charles's home,
with the shop on the ground floor.

circumstances had brought Charles's parents into a considerable
degree of adversity in the last years of his father's life, and Charles
and the family at Bala had shared in their sorrows.

In November of 1787 the family received some startling news.
Thomas Foulks informed them of his intention to marry again,
for the third time, and his bride was to be none other than Sally's
lifelong friend and contemporary, with whom she had shared all

her secrets, Lydia Lloyd. By this time, Sally had become the sole owner of the shop. Her stepfather would help her on occasions, especially during the arduous journeys to the fairs of north Wales to order stock. But all the responsibilities – commercial, financial, and legal – were upon her shoulders. The dynamics of the new situation arising from this marriage could have been very awkward – one's best friend and confidante becoming one's stepmother! There was the added complication that Thomas Foulks's savings were not adequate to maintain the couple, especially if there were to be children born to them. He would have to return to the one trade he knew: that of keeping a shop. With great tact and kindness Thomas Foulks ensured that nothing would come between him and his much-loved stepdaughter. Rather than embarrass her by opening another shop in Bala and thus compete with her for trade, he and his new wife eventually moved to live in Machynlleth, forty miles to the south, and opened their shop there.

The greatest sorrow of all occurred in the new year. Sally, or Sarah, the baby, had been continually unwell almost throughout the year. Whenever we read the many accounts that Charles wrote of his examining, catechizing, and hearing children recite verses, his delight and pleasure in their company is very evident. How much more must have been his delight in his little girl, Sally *fach*. On 22 January 1788, 'the only little girl with which Providence ever favoured him was taken from him.'[10] She was just four weeks short of her first birthday. The next day Charles wrote to John Mayor:

> I write this to you from a house of mourning. My little girl died yesterday, after a twelve-month existence in this our world, in almost continual affliction and sorrow. At last death prevailed and separated her soul from her afflicted body, to meet again when both the one and the other will be fuller of holiness and felicity than they were here of sin and sorrow. How free was the grace that saved her and took her to glory! It came to her unthought of, unsought for, and undesired. Her sin was taken away without any sorrow

[10] DEJ, I, 588.

for it, hatred toward it, or striving against it. Without any contest she got the victory for ever over all the enemies of our souls! Without travelling one step of the wilderness-road she got safe to Canaan. The grace implanted within her is got to its full growth without the nurture and discipline which others require and are exercised with. Here it was but as seed under-grown; but now it is full-grown and loaded with the richest fruits. Blessed be God for his full salvation! I think myself happy to be the parent of this little vessel of mercy to be filled with eternal glory. 'The Lord gave; the Lord hath taken away' – nothing but his own; 'blessed be the name of the Lord!'[11]

In 1788, Joseph Thomas, the husband of Charles's favourite sister, Elizabeth ('Betsie'), died. It was with this couple that Charles had lodged throughout the six years he had been at Carmarthen Academy. Then, in May 1789, Elizabeth herself died, leaving behind four orphaned children. One of them, a four-year old boy called David, was received by Thomas and Sally into their home as their own. He was a boyhood companion to their eldest, Thomas, being of the same age as him. The two boys are often referred to together in the family letters.

In August 1793, Thomas and Sally celebrated their tenth wedding anniversary though they were apart at the time. Charles was in London, supplying the pulpit at Lady Huntingdon's chapel at Spa Fields for a two-month period. He wrote:

> My Dearest Love
>
> It relieves my mind to write a few lines to you though I have nothing in particular to say. Our ten years together is now very near over – during that time the Lord has made you the means of great comfort to me. He gave me the only person I desired and hath blessed our connection. Though we have not been without our trials, yet we have not had them from each other. No person in the world is happier in this respect than myself; I would not change my situation

[11] *Ibid.*, I, 588.

for the Imperial crown. The gold of Peru is nothing when compared to what I possess in you. It comforts me to think the Lord can make you as comfortable as I could wish you to be, though it is out of my power. To him I look up daily in your behalf, and under the shadow of his wings I cannot but see you safe. His tender love can soothe your anxious mind amidst all your cares; and my absence when he is present is no more than the absence of a farthing candle when the sun shines. In patience possess your mind, and may his love prove a source of abundant consolation to you.

I have done very little about your business. What shall I buy? Shall I buy some silk shawls as last year? Shall I buy any Russian goods? You must not be too faint hearted, but give me some orders …

Dearest, kindest, and best of wives; I pray and bless the Lord every day for you. This is the only return I can make for such a blessing. I hope that this as well as every other blessing will lead me to the Giver of every good and perfect gift …"[12]

Sally was seven months pregnant at this time, and the Charles family was completed with the birth of a second son, David Jones Charles, in the second week of October 1793.

[12] DEJ, II, 123-24; *Memoir*, 431-32.

8

THE CIRCULATING SCHOOLS AND
THE SUNDAY SCHOOLS
(1785 ONWARDS)

I acknowledge my great indebtedness to my dearest children
of several places in North Wales, who learn with such eagerness, readiness, and such understanding, that the greatest
delight of my life is to visit them, and it is a delight to all
who hear them. The only repayment I can make to them is
to promise to be their servant in this pleasant work, while
the Lord gives me life and health.

Thomas Charles, from the conclusion to his work
Yr Hyfforddwr ('The Instructor')[1]

THE religious reformers of the period, Griffith Jones, Llanddowror,
and Thomas Charles among them, judged that the religious education of children was an immense responsibility that could not be
put aside. They fully believed that regeneration by the Holy Spirit
was the only means by which a child might be saved, but they
believed also that this fact did not in any way relieve parents and
clergymen from the responsibility of preparing that child's mind
by teaching it the contents of the Scriptures. The law of God, the
universality of sin, the vicarious sacrifice of Christ, along with the
other main doctrines of the gospel and the personal necessity of
repentance and faith: these needed to be the foundational truths
inscribed upon the slate of a child's mind. This had nothing to do
with the nature of a general education as conceived of today, nor of
the classical education that was provided at the time for the boys of
wealthy families. It was a religious necessity, and it was their duty,

[1] *Yr Hyfforddwr*, (1807), 104.

as much as lay within them, to provide an 'urgent religious teaching … the education and conversion (or education *for* conversion) of the illiterate and the indifferent, the ungodly and the ignorant, the rich and the poor. And always the young.'[2] In Charles's words,

> If we do not enrich their minds with the precious treasures of God, the world and the devil will fill them with the most cursed treasures mined from hell – it is sheer insanity to watch over the bodies and to neglect the souls of our children![3]

Early charitable education in Wales

At the beginning of the eighteenth century little provision for popular education existed in Wales. A few of the Tudor grammar schools (Carmarthen Grammar School, for example) still remained, providing a classical education for boys. The sixty or so schools that had been established in the Commonwealth period had provided a more elementary education but had been of very short duration. Only about a fifth of the population was able to read.[4]

In 1674 the Welsh Trust was formed by Thomas Gouge (1605?–1681)[5] of London. The main purpose of the Trust was the provision of day-schools for the children of the poor in Wales. The initial success of the movement saw the establishing of up to three hundred schools. On the death of Gouge, however, the work came to an end.

The next organization to set up charity schools in Wales was the Society for the Promotion of Christian Knowledge (SPCK), and

[2] Margaret N. Cutt, *Ministering Angels: A study of Nineteenth-Century Evangelical Writing for Children* (1979), 11, 28; quoted in Siwan Rosser, 'Thomas Jones, Dinbych, a'i Anrheg i Blentyn,' JHS, 32 (2008), 46, 50.

[3] Thomas Charles, *Catecism Byrr i Blant* (Trefeca, 1789), ii; quoted in Siwan Rosser, *ibid.*, 46.

[4] Eryn M. White, *The Welsh Bible* (Tempus Publishing, 2007), 53.

[5] Thomas was the son of William Gouge (1578–1653), one of the Assessors of the Westminster Assembly and the author of a massive commentary on the Epistle to the Hebrews.

the moving force behind the Welsh work was Sir John Philipps of Picton Castle, Pembrokeshire. The society established ninety-six schools in Wales between 1700 and 1727. Of the thirty-one schools established in Pembrokeshire, Sir John Philipps maintained twenty-two. In south Wales the medium of education was in English, but the SPCK committee realised that in monoglot areas of north Wales the teaching in English was a waste of time, and the use of Welsh was allowed. The archives of the SPCK suggest that the total number of Welsh children taught in their schools was about 1,670. Differences of opinion at the time of the establishment of the Hanoverian dynasty in 1714, however, hindered the work and by 1736 it was practically at an end.

Griffith Jones's circulating schools, 1734–79

In 1736, Griffith Jones, the evangelical rector of Llanddowror, Carmarthenshire, and the son-in law of Sir John Philipps, wrote,

> Experience has not taught me a better method of setting up a Welsh School than to have it published in several churches about the place it is intended to be at, that teaching and books will be given for three months to as many as may or will accept it, and it is not to expect such an offer again.

Griffith Jones's schools were immediately successful, far surpassing all previous efforts at mass education in Wales. In them, the children were taught to read the Welsh Bible and to learn the Church of England Catechism.

There were four main reasons for this success. The first was the superior organizational abilities of Griffith Jones himself. He undertook all the soliciting of funds, made all the decisions as to where schools were to be placed, acquired all the necessary premises (usually churches or church halls), and hired all the schoolmasters. He even trained his teachers, establishing what amounted to a training college at Llanddowror.

The second reason was that in both north and south Wales the language of education was Welsh. Griffith Jones's common-sense view with respect to teaching was exactly the same as his views on preaching: 'we cannot help thinking that English sermons to Welsh congregations are neither less absurd nor more edifying than Welsh preaching would be in the centre of England.'

The third and perhaps most important factor was the 'circulating' or itinerant nature of the schools. The schools were generally held during the winter months when farm labour took less of the people's time. They remained in one place for about three months, which was considered sufficient time to teach a child to read. Once this period was over the schoolmaster would pack his bags and move on to the next hamlet, village, or town assigned to him by Griffith Jones.

The fourth factor was that adults were included. Appreciating what their children were receiving in the day, parents and others would make the most of the schoolmaster's presence in their community and attend the school in the evening. In one note to the SPCK, Griffith Jones informed them that

> in many of the Welsh schools, the adult people, men and women, make up 2/3rds of the scholars and most of the masters instruct for 3 or 4 hours in the evening after school time about twice or thrice as many as they had in their schools by day, who could not attend at other times.[6]

By the time of his death in 1761 Jones had set up 3,324 schools and taught 153,835 scholars.[7] Madam Bridget Bevan (1698–1779) took over the running of the schools and they continued to prosper until her death in 1779. Up to that point, a total of 6,435 schools had been held and 310,926 pupils taught to read, at a time when the population of Wales was about 500,000. One of those taught was Thomas Charles himself who was a pupil at a school in Llanddowror up to his departure for Carmarthen Academy in 1769.

Griffith Jones left all the funds for the schools together with all his own money to Madam Bevan, and on her death, eighteen years

---

[6] Griffith Jones, *Welch Piety* (1740); quoted in David Jones, *Life and Times of Griffith Jones of Llanddowror* (London, 1902), 114-15.

[7] Gwyn Davies, *Griffith Jones, Llanddowror: Athro Cenedl* (Bridgend: Evangelical Press of Wales, 1984), 47.

later, she bequeathed £10,000 for the continuation of the schools. Unfortunately, however, her will was contested; the money was placed in Chancery and remained there for thirty years. In 1779, therefore, the circulating schools movement of Griffith Jones effectively came to an end.[8]

Thomas Charles re-establishes circulating schools, 1785

While working as a curate in Llanymawddwy in February and March 1784, Charles resurrected the old practice of catechising the children every Sunday after the vespers evening service. He found that the inability of the children to read frustrated him greatly in this work. On making inquiries he discovered that, apart from two or three children from wealthier families who were sent to school in the nearest town, no other children in the neighbourhood received any education whatsoever.

In his preface to a *Crynodeb o Egwyddorion Crefydd* (*A Short Catechism for Children*) that he published in 1789, Charles wrote:

> With unfailing diligence and great success did the godly and Reverend Mr Griffith Jones labour among the Welsh in this work. Just as his diligence condemns our neglect, so does his great success strongly urge us to grapple with the same task courageously.[9]

He could write in this way in that, from 1785 onwards, he had himself begun the work of re-establishing circulating schools after Griffith Jones's pattern. The first hint of this arises in a reference contained in a letter he sent to Sally in April 1786. He was at the time staying at Hardwick Hall, Ellesmere, Shropshire, meeting with Sir Richard Hill, the Member of Parliament for Shropshire, and brother of the evangelist, Rowland Hill:

> … I have some good hopes that our Welch charity schools will be considerably promoted by my journey and, if that should be the case, it will afford me great satisfaction indeed.

[8] Mary Clement, *S.P.C.K. and Wales: 1699–1740* (SPCK, 1954), 21-25.
[9] DEJ, II, 40.

> We know not what the Lord has to do with us and by us. O
> for grace to be passive in his hands and active in his cause![10]

The first detailed account of his work is found in a letter of his
to Thomas Scott.

> ... When I came a little acquainted with the country, I
> was surprised and grieved to find so many totally illiterate
> and not able to read a word in the Bible in their mother's
> tongue. I have attempted and succeeded far beyond my
> expectations in setting up charity schools, with a view *only*
> of teaching poor children and young people to read the
> Bible in a language they understood, and teach them the
> principles of the Christian religion by catechising them. We
> had seven schoolmasters last year in employ, and we think
> of increasing the number to twelve this ensuing summer.
> The schoolmaster's salary is £10 per annum. He stays but
> half or three-quarters of a year in the same place, then we
> move him to another neighbourhood. By these means we
> are able to teach the whole country with no great expense.
> I visit all the schools myself as often as I can. The money is
> raised by voluntary subscriptions among our societies.[11] The
> burden they have borne hitherto with the greatest cheerful-
> ness, and are abundantly satisfied to see the schools blessed
> to the rising generation.[12]

Seven years later his methods were not greatly changed and his
motive was as focused as ever: [13]

> ... We have now about twenty schoolmasters, employed in
> five different counties, to each of whom we pay ten pounds

[10] DEJ, I, 545-56.

[11] Offerings collected in the societies during a Communion Sunday would
usually be donated for the support of the schools.

[12] *Ibid.*, I, 566.

[13] This quotation is part of a letter written by Charles to John Campbell,
Edinburgh, dealing mainly with the 1791 Bala revival (see below, pp. 169-70).
The present comment follows on immediately after the quotation given on
that page.

per annum. They are entirely at our disposal, and we move them from place to place all over the country, and teach all that will attend them, rich or poor, gratis. Half a year we find sufficient to teach a child of moderate capacity to read the Bible well in the Welsh language. The only intention of these schools is to teach children to read their *own language*, and to instruct them in the first principles of religion, and to endeavour to impress their minds with a sense of the importance of divine truths ...

In some of the schools we have had general awakenings among the young; they have been a great means of *soberizing* the minds of young people, drawing their attention to the Bible; it gives them a taste for reading, and the next step will be to attend preaching, which is seldom without some effect on their minds. We take care that the teachers are men of piety and zeal for the conversion of sinners. We have but one only point in view in these institutions; that is, the *salvation* of souls.[14]

Comparing the circulating schools of Griffith Jones and Thomas Charles

When Thomas Charles began to establish his schools, he followed the pattern of the previous schools of Griffith Jones, with which he was very familiar. In his methods, his curricula and in the resources he used, he copied Jones. This is not surprising in that both men were moved by one single predominant purpose, that of saving souls.

Both Jones and Charles trained their teachers themselves: Jones in his training school at Llanddowror, and Charles at his home in Bala. As he mentions in his letters, he went from employing one master in 1785, to seven in 1786, twelve in 1787, and twenty by 1794. Both movements used Welsh as a medium of study. This was the mother tongue of the population and the medium therefore by which they would learn to read the Bible more quickly. Like Jones,

[14] *Ibid.*, II, 101-02.

Charles also wrote all the literature for the schools himself – the reading books, primers, and catechisms.

The differences between their two circulating systems are rather more significant than the similarities. Charles's plan was initially much less ambitious than that of Griffith Jones. The latter's schools were generally attached to the parish church and therefore potentially transferable to all parishes. Charles on the other hand set up his earliest schools in small scattered communities in mountainous and inaccessible districts. The longer, six-month, stay of the master in the vicinity meant that his schools became much more a part of the local community than were those of Jones. The narrower geographical range of the work at the beginning meant also that Charles could involve himself much more with each school. All the organization and arrangements were in his hands, and he would make a point of visiting each school, meeting the children and examining them in the progress they had made. Jones, with his wider field, depended necessarily on the co-operation of local parish clergy. In order to maintain that co-operation Jones would publish fixed rules and procedures which all schools had to follow. Charles's direct involvement meant that he could be more flexible in the arrangements for each school. He might decide that a school be kept for nine months or even longer in a particular neighbourhood if there was call for it. He might also extend the curriculum to include the teaching of writing if it seemed appropriate for the pupils of a particular school.

In their financial upkeep the two movements were also very different. Like the Welsh Trust and the SPCK, Jones's schools were dependent on the support of the Church of England. Without the sympathy of local clergy who would supply teachers and buildings, and of wealthy gentry who would supply money, the earlier circulating schools could not have multiplied as they did. Charles's early schools were financed entirely by himself and unlike Griffith Jones, he was entirely independent of the Established Church. This meant that he was in no way embarrassed by Methodist sympathies and Methodist support. On the contrary, he rejoiced in the close connection between his schools and local Methodist societies. He chose his schoolmasters primarily from the young men of the societies, and societies would send requests to him for a school in their area. In many cases the societies would then take over the financial responsibility for their school. The schools became Methodist breeding grounds and were one of the main factors in the spread and increase of Methodism in north Wales.

But Charles's evangelical Church of England friends were not lacking in their generous support also, and as his connections in London increased so did the number of donations from that direction. In later years a close friend, Joseph Tarn, the secretary of the British and Foreign Bible Society, would employ a man to collect the various London subscriptions. Contributions were received from members of the well-known Clapham Sect, including Henry Thornton and Charles Grant. William Wilberforce contributed, as did Lord Barham, who was to become the First Lord of the Admiralty.[15] Thomas Charles received money also from readers of *The Evangelical Magazine* and *The Gospel Magazine*, two periodicals that would on occasions publish reports of the progress of the Schools.[16]

There was never a time throughout the remainder of his life that Charles was not soliciting funds for the upkeep of the schools. On occasions there were exceptional gifts, such as the anonymous gift of £50 (the equivalent of about £6,000 today), or the remarkable bequest in the will of David Ellis, from Flintshire, who had made a

[15] Sir Charles Middleton (1726–1813), 1st Baron Barham, a leading evangelical and member of the Clapham Sect. He was a close friend of Thomas Clarkson, supporting him in his lifelong campaign for the abolition of slavery.

[16] *The Evangelical Magazine*, published in London, was begun by two Welsh brothers, Evan and David Williams, the sons of the Methodist exhorter, David Williams, Swyddffynnon, Cardiganshire. David Charles, Thomas's younger brother, was a trustee of the magazine. E. Wyn James, 'David Charles (1762–1834), Caerfyrddin: Diwinydd, Pregethwr, Emynydd,' JHS, 36 (2012), 30, 50.

fortune from lead ore and left £500 for the schools.[17] But the more usual state of the school funds is shown by the following typical comments in letters to friends:

> The funds of the schools are at present very low, and not adequate to half the expense I am under for this year. (September 1808.)

> I do not find it so easy a matter to procure contributions towards the support of the schools. I have now only £21 to pay £100. (January 1809.)

> The funds are so low that the schools are in my debt considerably. (May 1812.)[18]

A final and most important difference between the two movements is that the schools of Griffith Jones were severely limited in scope. Once they moved on from a locality, education in that locality came to an end. However, from late 1789 onwards, once Thomas Charles had realised the potential and practical value of Sunday schools, a natural development occurred. The increasing number of converts of the Methodist Revival ensured a burgeoning number of scholars of all ages eager to read the Bible. Their local circulating school would strengthen their longings in that it showed to them, in their own village or hamlet, the possibilities and worth of a continuing education.[19]

Some of Thomas Charles's schoolmasters

To his first schoolmasters, in 1785, Charles would pay £8 a year; this rose to £12 by 1787. In 1808 he would complain that he had to pay £15 a year and that at the beginning he could maintain twenty teachers 'at the same cost as ten presently.'[20] An early master was John Davies (1772–1855) who in 1797 kept a school at Llanrhaeadr-ym-Mochnant on the borders of Denbighshire and

[17] DEJ, II, 317.
[18] *Ibid.*, III, 194, 213, 429.
[19] HMGC2, 431-38.
[20] H. J. Hughes in DDM (2014), 23.

Montgomeryshire. It is thought that it was on his recommendation that Charles appointed his friend, John Hughes (1775–1854). Both men became close friends of Thomas Charles. In 1800 John Davies left for Tahiti where he served the London Missionary Society for fifty-four years. John Hughes became one of the leaders of north Wales Methodism, being ordained by them in 1814 and pastoring the cause at Pontrobert, Montgomeryshire, for forty years.[21]

Another of Charles's schoolmasters was Lewis Williams. It is said that his first connection with the Methodists was when he knocked at the door of a dwelling in Cwmllinau, Cemais, Anglesey, the meeting-place of the local society, and stood in the doorway with half-a-crown in his hand, declaring to the one who opened the door to him: 'I want to come to the society, if I may.[22] Here is half-a-crown – all that I have in the world – for me to come; if I may.' Williams was employed at first by Charles at only £4 p.a. because he had not yet himself fully mastered the skill of reading. Charles encouraged him to seek further tutoring and within a year, in 1800, he was the master at Abergynolwyn, Merioneth, where Mary Jones of Bible Society fame, became his pupil.[23]

The necessity of teaching through the medium of Welsh

References have already been made to the use of Welsh as the medium of teaching in Charles's schools. In 1811 a Scottish committee sought his advice before setting up circulating schools among the Gaelic-speaking peoples of the Highlands and Islands and asked particularly for his views on this point. Charles therefore presented his arguments for the necessity of the mother-tongue being the medium of any education. It is fascinating to note that many of the principles that guided him in the late eighteenth century are so similar to those which have underpinned

---

[21] J. E. Caerwyn Williams, 'Roger Edwards,' JHS, 4 (1980), 6-7, quoting R. Owen, *Ysgolfeistriaid Mr Charles o'r Bala* (1898).

[22] E. Wyn James, 'John Hughes, Pontrobert, a'i gefndir,' JHS, 37 (2013), 76-77.

[23] Hughes in DDM (2014), 23.

the eminently-successful Welsh-language education movement of the second half of twentieth-century Wales. What is equally interesting is to note other principles which motivated the godly Thomas Charles and which are so completely different from those advocated by modern secular educationalists. The following are some extracts from his letter:

> At first, the strong prejudice which universally prevailed against teaching them to read Welsh *first*, and the idea assumed, that they could not learn English so well, if *previously* instructed in the Welsh language; this, I say, proved a great stumbling-block in the way of parents to send their children to the Welsh schools, together with another conceit they had, that if they could read English, they would soon learn of themselves to read Welsh; but now these idle and groundless conceits are universally scouted. This change has been produced, not so much by disputing, as by the evident salutary effects of the schools, the great delight with which the children attended them, and the great progress they made in the acquisition of knowledge ...
>
> As to the expediency of teaching young people, in the *first* place, to read the language they generally speak and best understand, if imparting religious knowledge is our primary object, as it most certainly ought to be in instructing immortal beings, it needs no proof, for it is self-evident. However, I beg your attention to the following particulars ...
>
> 1. The time necessary to teach them to read the Bible in their vernacular language is so short, not exceeding six months in general, that it is a great pity not to give them the key immediately which unlocks all doors and lays open all the divine treasures before them. Teaching them English requires two or three years' time, during which long period they are concerned only about dry terms, without receiving one idea for their improvement.
>
> 2. Welsh words convey ideas to their infant minds as soon as they can read them, which is not the case when they are taught to read a language they do not understand.

3. When they can read Welsh, scriptural terms become intelligible and familiar to them, so as to enable them to understand the discourse delivered in the language (the language is generally preached through the Principality) …

4. Previous instruction in their native tongue helps them to learn English much sooner, instead of proving in any degree an inconveniency. This I have had repeated proofs of, and can confidently vouch for the truth of it …

5. Having acquired new ideas by reading a language they understand, excitement is naturally produced to seek for knowledge; and as our ancient language is very deficient in the means of instruction, there being few useful books printed in it, a desire to learn English, yea, and other languages also, is excited, for the sake of increasing their stock of ideas, and adding to their fund of knowledge. I can vouch for the truth of it, that there are twenty to one who can read English to what could when the Welsh was entirely neglected …

6. By teaching the Welsh *first* we prove to them that we are principally concerned about their souls, and thereby naturally impress their minds with the vast importance of acquiring the knowledge of divine truths …[24]

It is an unfortunate fact of Welsh history that these principles were so soon forgotten by the promoters of Victorian state education. The education provided through the medium of English only, coupled with the punitive 'Welsh Not' disciplinary measures to ensure that no Welsh speaking took place in school, not only made the process of learning so much more difficult for generations of monoglot children, but almost succeeded in driving the language to extinction.

Sunday schools

The founder of the Sunday schools movement was Robert Raikes (1735–1811), the owner of *The Gloucester Journal.* He paid a shilling

[24] DEJ, III, 366-68.

a week to 'four decent well-disposed women to gather round them boys and girls that they might teach them to read and repeat the Catechism.' The school first met in 1780 in the Littleworth area of Gloucester. Raikes was not the first man to begin such a school, but it was he, through the pages of his *Journal*, who succeeded in publicizing the idea so as to set in motion a Sunday school movement. Two eminent women, Fanny Burney and Hannah More, encouraged its spread so that John Wesley, writing in his *Journal* in 1784, could say: 'I find these schools springing up wherever I go.' The primary motivations for setting up these Schools in England were educational and moral.

Thomas Charles knew of the work of Robert Raikes and of the establishing of the Sunday Schools Society in England. He would have known also of the subsequent unsuccessful efforts by Dr George Lewis and Morgan John Rhys, for example, to establish Sunday schools in Wales. But at first Charles was not persuaded of the usefulness of Sunday schools. When he began to establish his circulating schools, he commented in the letter to Edward Griffin, dated July 6, 1785:

> ... As to your Sunday schools in England I have heard of them, but it would be impossible to set them up here in this wild country, where the inhabitants of every parish live so distant from each other. Besides the clergy would not join with us in any such thing, for the old enmity keeps its ground in all its malignity among that body of people.[25]

It is not known exactly when Charles changed his mind and began to arrange schools on a Sunday. Most probably it was sometime in 1787. Nor was the step taken in accordance with a well thought-out plan of action. Rather, as was so often the case with Charles's projects, an opportunity to do good arose; he embraced it, willing to see whether it would gain heaven's blessing; it flourished under his hands and, under that blessing, in a few years' time, he was superintending a flourishing movement. One of his strongest

[25] Richard Bennett, 'Llythyrau y Parch. Thomas Charles,' JHS, 5 (1920), 42.

characteristics was his firm belief in the guidance of providence, by which God reveals his will. What must not be forgotten, on the other hand, is the immense amount of labour that Charles was willing to take upon himself in order to ensure that providential openings had every opportunity to reveal themselves. The first instances were of circulating schoolmasters teaching an extra lesson on a Sunday night. It was then found that at these times more pupils turned up than for the week-day schools. More children, but especially more adults, had some hours of freedom from their work on the Sunday that they could use to learn to read.

Eventually, these Sunday schools taught by the employed circulating school-masters evolved into the more familiar voluntary Sunday schools, but the whole process of development occurred over a period of some ten to twenty years. The numbers of schools increased considerably between 1789 and 1798 because the London Sunday School Society took an interest in them and provided funds that enabled more teachers to be employed. Charles became a director of the Society and was appointed its agent for Wales in 1798. As the Sunday schools flourished, the week-day circulating schools declined, but even at the time of his death Charles still employed a few teachers.

Initially, however, there was considerable opposition to be overcome. The first response of the Welsh clergymen to Sunday schools was almost universally negative because of the Methodist connection. Many Dissenters also argued fiercely against the schools. In their sincere desire to keep the Sabbath holy, they remembered the further exposition of the commandment that 'in it thou shalt not do any work.' Even some from among the Methodists themselves were ambivalent in their attitude: the Penrhyndeudraeth society, for example, tolerated a school but would not allow it to meet in the building which they had built, judging that the teaching of children to read was too secular a work to be carried out in a chapel. In Bala also, Charles had to face considerable opposition to his school.[26]

[26] DEJ, II, 144.

Lewis Edwards, principal of the Calvinistic Methodist Theological College in Bala from 1837 to 1887, said of Thomas Charles:

> He suffered moral martyrdom for long years, and that at the hands of his friends. But on he proceeded, quietly and busily, with no fuss and bother. There was a life that would not die in the Sunday schools. And by now that grain of mustard seed has become a great tree.[27]

What Charles longed for was that all might read, in order that they might understand the Scriptures, and then proceed to study and discuss them together. The original Sunday schools were therefore divided into two: the teaching classes, children and adults separately, learning to read; the Bible classes, children and adults separately, learning and discussing the Scriptures. All ages were present. He wrote a report to the committee of the Religious Tract Society describing his work, and this was published in the 1806 issue of the *Evangelical Magazine*:

> Thousands of young people, all over the country, have at this time their attention wholly engaged about divine things. They are learning Catechisms, and chapters out of the Bible, with wonderful facility. It has been my delightful work, since I left London in December last, every Sunday to catechize publicly, and hear them repeat chapters before thousands of people; besides preaching twice generally every Sabbath, and sometimes thrice, in different places. In order to give you some idea of the work, I would just mention some of the following particulars, which are strictly true: Whole families, young and old, the governors and the governed, learn the Catechisms together, and chapters of the Bible; they have appeared together, and repeated alternately what they have learnt. All the grown-up young people, in some of our Societies, have done the same. Boys and Girls, from eight to sixteen years old, learn whole books of the

---

[27] Lewis Edwards, *Traethodau Llenyddol* (Wrexham, 1867), 273.

Scripture; and repeat what time will permit us to hear, such as the whole epistle to the Ephesians, Hebrews, etc; others learn select chapters to an astonishing number, such as 10, 20, 30. One little girl learnt seventy-two psalms and chapters; and another the astonishing number of ninety-two, the list of which I have in my possession.[28]

It might be wondered how the limited time for teaching in a Sunday afternoon or a Sunday evening, after the services of the day, could ever supersede the prolonged teaching of a five-day-a-week circulating school. This is to forget the essential purposes of the schools, namely to teach the pupils to read their Bibles and understand the Catechism, with some also being taught to write. Nothing more was attempted in that no more was judged essential. Once the children had been grounded in this way in their early years, the Sunday school teaching of the ABC gave way to the memorization of scripture verses and the thorough teaching of the content and message of the Bible. The children would then eventually progress naturally to attendance at the adult Bible classes which, for the majority, would become a lifelong practice. Secular education was never a part of the process.

Comparing the Sunday school movements of England and of Wales

The two national movements were to develop very differently so that Lewis Edwards, commenting on the Welsh Sunday school movement in 1867 could state that 'It may be no exaggeration to say that this institution is the pre-eminent glory of Wales, and that this is the greatest of the works of Charles of Bala.'[29]

The differences have been discussed by Beryl Thomas in her survey of Charles's educational work.[30] She makes the following points:

[28] DEJ, III, 136.
[29] Lewis Edwards, *Traethodau Llenyddol* (1867), 272-23.
[30] Beryl Thomas in HMGC2, 444-46.

1. In Wales the schools were open to all, and appealed to all ranks in society. Members were not discriminated against on any basis of social standing. As such the schools acted as unifying elements in the community.

2. They were characterised by a democratic order. Though the schools came within the jurisdiction of the rules of the Methodist society they would be controlled locally by the schoolmaster not the local elders. In England it would be a clergyman or salaried lay-teacher who would generally be in charge, but in Wales the teachers and superintendents were usually appointed democratically on the basis of their skills. They would then provide their services willingly and free of charge.

3. Though classes were not mixed, girls and boys (and men and women) had liberty to attend and the schools were an important factor in providing education for girls and for emphasising equality for women.

4. They provided education regardless of age, and thereby established the important principle that learning is a continuous, unbroken process.

5. The presence of parents together with their children in the same school meant that discipline was never any real problem. Charles emphasised in his *Rheolau Ffurfiaw a Threfnu Ysgolion Sabbothawl* (1813) (*Rules for Establishing and Organizing the Sunday schools*), 'There are many ways of rebuking children without resorting to corporal punishment.'[31]

Literature produced by Charles for the Sunday schools

Charles wrote and published nearly all of the very many pamphlets and booklets, in Welsh and English, used as resources in his schools. His *Crynodeb o Egwyddorion Crefydd: neu Catecism Byrr i Blant, ac eraill, i'w ddysgu* (*A Summary of Religious Principles: or a Short Catechism to be learnt by Children and others*) (1789) was a 67-page booklet. Charles had probably written it, or parts of it, much earlier, perhaps as early as 1785. The parts would then have

---

[31] *Rules for Establishing and Organizing the Sunday schools* (1813), 15.

been copied by hand and distributed to the various schools, different schools receiving different parts in turn. The *Catechism* was divided into the following eleven chapters: About God; the Fall of Man; the Covenant of Grace, and the Person of Christ; the Work of Redemption; the Work of the Holy Spirit; Conviction through the Holy Spirit; the Work of the Holy Spirit revealing Christ to the Soul; the Fruit of the Spirit, and the Christian's Warfare; the Sacraments; God's Government and the Law; the Day of Judgment. He emphasised that the principles taught in the catechism were those of the Church of England, and he quoted from the *Thirty-nine Articles* to prove his point. Charles revised and enlarged this small catechism over the years to reach its final form in 1807 as *Yr Hyfforddwr* (*The Instructor*), probably the most widely-used publication of religious instruction ever produced in Wales.[32] For those whose first language was not Welsh, he wrote and published English translations of his catechisms and an exposition of the Ten Commandments.

Another significant production was *Rheolau i Ffurfiaw a Threfnu yr Ysgolion Sabbothawl* (*Rules for Establishing and Organizing the Sunday schools*) (Bala, 1813). Charles drew up these rules more than twenty-five years after setting up his first Sunday school. They provided detailed instruction on every aspect of Sunday school organization: the venues where they should be held, the classes, the curriculum, teachers, superintendents, visiting the sick and absentees, rewards and punishments. Thus, schools should be held in 'spacious, clean and healthy' buildings; in the summer, barns might be used as long as they were swept and cleaned. A school was to be divided into six classes: in the first, the alphabet was to be taught; in the second, spelling and short exercises; the third class dealt with one and two-syllable words; the fourth with three and four-syllable words; in the fifth class the New Testament was read; in the sixth the whole Bible was read. Men were to teach the boys and women the girls, if not in different rooms then at least in opposite corners of the room. Charles emphasized also that the

[32] See below, pp. 243-46.

aim was to keep class numbers low, so that each pupil might receive adequate attention: 'it is better to keep the number at twelve than for there to be more children in a class.'[33]

It was in the Sunday schools of Thomas Charles that the poor children of Welsh peasantry were first taught social graces and manners, and such were the development of the schools, in numbers and geographical spread, in the next hundred years that it is entirely appropriate that Charles has been described as 'the father of Welsh Christian peasant courtesy.'[34] Beryl Thomas comments: 'To Charles ... order and godliness were not two opposite extremes but elements that were to be combined to ensure continued success,' and she quotes from the *Rules*: 'No means should be excused that would tend to further the salvation of their souls – which should be our main purpose in keeping the schools.'[35]

[33] Hughes in DDM (2014), 28.
[34] Derec Ll. Morgan, *Pobl Pantycelyn* (1986), 85.
[35] Thomas in HMGC2, 452.

9

LEADERSHIP OF THE CONNEXION AND
REVIVAL AT BALA
(1791–95)

If it had to be decided by general ballot who were the three
men to whom the Welsh nation owed most, there might
possibly be disagreement over two of them, but I believe
that the nation would unanimously appoint Thomas
Charles as one of the three. He did not excel in one sphere
but in many. He was a good preacher, very rarely do we
meet his equal as an organizer, and he was an extremely
effective educator through the instrumentality of the various
institutions that he founded and of his published works. He
was not amongst the founders of Methodism … But if he
did not contribute to the laying of the foundation, he had
an enormous part in the building of the superstructure. He,
above all, safeguarded the fruit of the Revival in Wales so
that rather than being a temporary excitement, appearing
and then disappearing, it continued in its permanent influence upon our land.

John Morgan Jones, writing in 1897.[1]

Increasing respect

THERE were two clear indications in 1790 of the increasing respect
being shown towards Thomas Charles, not only by his Methodist
brethren in the north but also by those of south Wales. Though he
had only been a member among them for six years, Charles was

---

[1] Jones and Morgan, *Calvinistic Methodist Fathers of Wales*, Vol. 2 (2008),
239.

entrusted with the drawing up of *Rheolau tuag at Iawn Drefn a Gweddeidd-dra yn y Cymdeithasfaoedd* (*Rules for the Proper Order and Propriety in the Associations or Quarterly Meetings*) at an Association in Bala on 9 June 1790.[2] With these rules Charles established the Northern Association on a formal basis. This was the first of many occasions for him to be responsible for drawing up rules for the organization of various aspects of the Connexion. Through them he began the process of 'Presbyterianising' the Connexion; thus, for example, in the *Rules* the emerging definitions of Minister and Ruling Elder may be seen. A selection from these *Association Rules* illustrates the procedures of these meetings as they had been held in north Wales for some decades previously, and in south Wales for nearly fifty years since the first Association at Watford, Caerphilly, in 1742.

> 3. The preachers, and only the preachers, should gather at ten o'clock the first morning with the purpose of exhorting, training and warning one another in love; that unity and fraternity may be nurtured; and that by this mutual assistance they may become a light to the world, a salt that has not lost its savour.
>
> 6. That everyone should have the right to speak on the matter, or matters, in hand, until these are decided upon; with the avoidance of long speeches ...
>
> 7. That one meeting should be appointed for the consideration of *spiritual matters only*. By spiritual matters is meant the doctrines of the gospel, together with spiritual experience of them; religious exercises, Church discipline, etc. All temporal matters of the Body should be dealt with in the other meeting.
>
> 8. If no particular matter is put forward for the Association's consideration, the Body should converse with an appointed individual with respect to his knowledge of the doctrines of the gospel, his experience of them, and his fellowship with God. These are topics that may not be

[2] HMGC2, 137.

neglected in our meetings without the Body suffering loss, nor will they be neglected whilst the life and power of godliness remain within us ...

9. That every controversial matter is to be decided prudently, according to the wish of the majority of the Body, and let the others, of different opinion, behave peaceably and kindly towards their brethren.

11. It is the ardent and loving desire of the Body in Gwynedd that whoever of the brethren of the South who happen to be present should have the same liberty as ourselves in whatever is being discussed and considered in that we desire to keep the unity of the body throughout all of Wales ...[3]

In contrast to this increasing respect from his fellow-believers, it was during 1790 that Charles experienced one of the very few occasions when he had to endure physical assault. He was preaching in the open air at Corwen, Merioneth. The Methodists had no society there and the inhabitants were determined not to allow such 'enthusiasm' to enter their town. As Charles began to preach, the local blacksmith started beating a drum as a signal for the rougher elements of the town to gather. Stones were thrown, and one struck Charles on the mouth, knocking out a tooth. As a result he was forced to flee the town without having preached.[4]

The following year was to prove a crucial one in Thomas Charles's career. During this year, circumstances outside his control were to place him even more centrally within the relatively small circle of leaders of the Welsh Calvinistic Methodist Associations, both north and south. During this year his spiritual and organizational gifts were to be called upon to lead the movement in the equally stressful situations of controversy and of revival.

Of the five founding fathers of Welsh Methodism, Howel Davies, Pembrokeshire, was the first to die, succumbing at the relatively young age of fifty-four in 1770, when Charles was fifteen

---

[3] *Ibid.*, 137-39; see also Edward Jones, *Y Gymdeithasfa* (Caernarfon, 1891), 3.
[4] DEJ, III, 604-5.

years old. Howel Harris died in July 1773, aged fifty-nine, exactly six months after Charles was converted. There is no record of Charles having met or heard either of these two leaders. On 16 October 1790, Daniel Rowland, Charles's father in the faith and the preacher whom he most respected, died at Llangeitho. At the end of 1790 therefore, the acknowledged leaders of the movement were made up of six clergymen: the two remaining founding fathers, Peter Williams of Carmarthenshire, the Bible commentator, now aged sixty-seven, and William Williams of Pantycelyn, aged seventy-four; two men of the next generation – David Jones of Llan-gan, Glamorgan, aged fifty-five and Nathaniel Rowland, the son of Daniel, aged forty-one; and two relative newcomers – David Griffiths of Nevern, Pembrokeshire, who was thirty-four and Thomas Charles, now thirty-five years old.

The death of William Williams, Pantycelyn

A sequence of five letters sent between 1786 and 1791 by William Williams, Pantycelyn, to Thomas Charles have survived, the last of these being written only ten days before Williams's death on 11 January 1791. In them there is a very tangible sense of the old warrior, the last but one surviving member of the early Methodist Fathers, passing on the baton to a new leader. The letters reveal many characteristic elements of the godly old man and minister. In the first two letters (1786 and July 1787) Williams was merely passing on personal news and maintaining friendship. By the third letter (May 1790) Williams's health was beginning to break down, severely curtailing his itinerating. He was aware that his life was nearing its end and his long, influential ministry with it. It may well be also that he believed that the future unity and order of the two Associations would depend a great deal upon the leadership and wisdom of his correspondent, and so he wrote to warn Charles of the weaknesses that he discerned in the organization in the south.

> … I am glad to see such a demand for preachers in Gwynedd.
> Up to 10 or 12 of them are missing at times from our country,

William Williams, Pantycelyn.

and yet there is no great depletion here, for new ones rise every day and some of them have received spirit and light. May the Lord add to their number. But some have such a desire to go forth that Gwynedd is too small for them, whereas there is no great name for them at home. It would be well for young preachers to give themselves first to read books which have much of Christ in them, to study much more that great salvation which extols the attributes of the Godhead to the highest degree, giving complete satisfaction to the Father for all that His righteousness, holiness and divine truth demand of propitiation and payment of debt from the most miserable sinner …

I fear for some that they come to Gwynedd before they are mature, for many come to you without even asking permission from the Association. It would be well for the Association to give them some liberty before they stand in front of such multitudes of mixed hearers as you have. Do they have the sense, light and spirit that they may undertake such a mighty work without drawing dishonour down upon it? Our Association has become quite careless in this matter; every man being allowed to do as he wishes, without permission, and it has never been in such need of reformation as now.

> I fear for some … that they go forth in order to gain
> a name for themselves … and that you will give encour-
> agement to them so that they return home proclaiming to
> the world that they have greatly prospered. But let me keep
> my peace concerning this matter in the hope that you have
> received the anointing and know all this …[5]

By the time of the fourth letter (25 May 1790), Arminianism and Arianism had gained further support in some of the Dissenting churches of the south. Well aware of this, Williams, who with Daniel Rowland had been the main theologian of the early founding fathers and had fought more than one battle for the orthodoxy of the movement, passed on his concerns to his younger friend.

> … Know, my dear brother, that heresies now, as in the apos-
> tles' time, are conceived and brought forth amongst many
> sects and denominations of people, and boldly preached out
> without shame or fear. But as Methodism so far has been
> kept clear from the so pernicious and destructive tares, I
> hope the Lord will keep us to the end …
>
> The Articles of the Church in England, the Nicene and
> Athanasian Creeds, the lesser and larger Catechisms of the
> Assembly with their Confession of Faith, are some of the
> grandest and most illustrious beauties of the Reformation.
> I think our young exhorters should study such orthodox
> tracts over and over.
>
> There are now heresies and palpable errors brought out
> to light which for a long time have been dead and buried,
> such as the denial of the doctrine of the Trinity, which is the
> foundation of Christianity; the denial of the eternal genera-
> tion and the Deity of Christ. They say that the Baptists deny
> the divinity of our Saviour …
>
> Believe me, dear Mr Charles, the Anti-trinitarian, the
> Socinian, and Arian doctrines get ground daily. Our unwary

---

[5] Gomer M. Roberts, *Y Pêr Ganiedydd*, Vol. I (Aberystwyth: Gwasg Aberystwyth, 1949), 164-66; Eifion Evans, *Bread of Heaven: The Life and Work of William Williams, Pantycelyn* (Bridgend: Bryntirion Press, 2010), 319-20.

new-born Methodist preachers know nothing of these things, therefore pray much that no drop of this pernicious and poisonous liquor may be mingled or privately thrown into the good delicious divine fountain of which the honest Methodists drink …[6]

The last of the series was a long letter (1 January 1791) written ten days before William Williams died. In it, the man who was so skilful in the society meetings in drawing forth the experiences of the saints, now describes his own experiences as he prepares for death. The letter arrived at Bala later in the month but before Charles had heard of his death. The dying man encourages his younger brother-in-arms:[7]

… A visit from some of your preachers is much needed in south Wales. Of the preachers owned of God, six or seven are either dead or afflicted of the Lord, and the north Wales preachers most in favour with the people have not visited us for some time. You yourself are one of them, because your services are called for from every part of south Wales, and the Lord will reward you if you come. My dear, dear brother, work while it is day; the night will overtake you, as it has overtaken me, so that you will not be able to travel nor preach. Nothing would please me so much as to go the round of north Wales as in former days. I would do my utmost not to spend one moment of my time except in speaking about the things of God.

[6] Roberts, *Y Pêr Ganiedydd*, I, 167-68. There is some discrepancy between the exact texts of these fourth and fifth letters as found in *Y Pêr Ganiedydd*, I, 167-68 and 170-72, in Gomer M. Roberts, *Bywyd a Gwaith Peter Williams* (University of Wales Press, 1943), 88, and in DEJ, II, 51-55. The letters were first published by Edward Morgan in *Ministerial Record of W. Williams* (1847) and he was an author who frequently adjusted or omitted sentences from the texts of his subjects' letters, or even merged separate letters together. In addition, when Charles himself published the fifth letter in the *Trysorfa Ysbrydol* (1799, 90) he also omitted sentences, presumably because he considered that they might be offensive to certain parties.

[7] Edwin Welch, 'Letters of Thomas and Sally Charles,' JHS, 1 (1977), 29-30.

A great revival has taken place in many parts of our country – from five to six hundred, to my knowledge, have been added to the number of those who profess religion, during the last two years. Welsh schools are much needed in order to teach the Word of God …[8]

The excommunication of Peter Williams

When William Williams wrote the sentences, 'There are now heresies and palpable errors brought out to light which for a long time have been dead and buried, such as the denial of the doctrine of the Trinity, which is the foundation of Christianity; the denial of the eternal generation and the Deity of Christ,' he was referring to the views of Peter Williams. Almost certainly Charles knew this and knew also that the dying hymnwriter's purpose in drawing these matters to his attention in these last two letters sent to him, was that he, Charles, should do something about the situation.

Peter Williams (1723–96) was younger than the other four men remembered as the pioneers of Welsh Methodism. His upbringing had remarkable similarities to that of Charles but unlike Charles he was appointed to various curacies. His Methodism got him also into trouble, however, and he was never ordained priest. He joined the Methodist society at Newcastle Emlyn in 1747 and continued an itinerant preaching ministry for well over forty years. Of the early preachers no one, except perhaps Howel Harris, endured more occasions of persecution and physical abuse. He eventually settled in Carmarthen where he built a chapel for the society in his own back garden.[9]

In May 1770, Williams had published an edition of the Welsh Bible, with notes and comments on every chapter. Printed in Carmarthen, it was the first Bible to be actually printed in Wales. It proved immensely popular and useful, passing through many reprintings. Tens of thousands of copies were in circulation in the nineteenth century, with very many Welsh households owning a

---

[8] DEJ, II, 51-55; Roberts, *Y Pêr Ganiedydd*, I, 170-72.
[9] Water Street Chapel, Carmarthen.

copy of 'Peter Williams's *Bible*.'[10] By 1791, he was sixty-eight years old. The sad controversy which was to engulf him had its roots in the occasion of the first publication of his *Bible*, more than twenty years previously.

In his notes on the first chapter of John's Gospel, verse 1, Peter Williams had included the following:

> ... God is Father, Son, and Holy Spirit, from eternity, in his own eternal will; not 'in a necessary mode of *existence*, even if no man was to be saved nor one soul to be sanctified,' as some in their ignorance state; but because he willed to save and sanctify; ... some beheld his glory, and believed that Jesus was God! Not 'God by ordination' as some foolishly speak, but that he is the *only* true and living God – for the Scriptures witness that the Man Jesus is the eternal Father; and what Christian would endure the blasphemy of those who deny the Deity of Christ.[11]

These words were sufficient to arouse the suspicion that Williams had fallen into the heresy known as Sabellianism, a belief that originated in the third century, deriving from the teaching of Sabellius a bishop in Africa. He taught that the Trinity does not exist essentially as three different *persons*, but that the one God has manifested himself to us in three different *modes* according to the different function of each mode in the plan of salvation. With what degree of clarity Peter Williams believed or taught this is not known, but what is clear is that neither Daniel Rowland nor William Williams wished to pursue matters against their old friend and brother-in-arms at that time. The controversy quietened down, though not without Rowland at least privately warning Peter Williams of the unorthodoxy of his words. In order to maintain

[10] In his biography of Peter Williams, Gomer M. Roberts lists 39 various editions of his *Bible* up to 1895; see Gomer M. Roberts, *Bywyd a Gwaith Peter Williams* (Cardiff: University of Wales Press, 1943), 199-202. In 1773 Williams produced the first Welsh Bible Concordance to be published in Wales.

[11] Jones and Morgan, *Calvinistic Methodist Fathers of Wales* (2008), Vol. 1, 674.

peace in Zion, Daniel Rowland had also to reprove his own son, Nathaniel, who was bitter in his condemnation of the old pioneer.

Peter Williams's *Bible* was a large quarto volume and its price of one guinea was much more than the poorer people could pay. As the Methodist converts multiplied in the years from 1770 to 1790 the demand for cheaper Bibles became almost desperate. To try to meet something of this need, Peter Williams brought out another version of the Welsh Bible with marginal references and notes, in the form of a pocket-book, and selling for six shillings. The notes were a translation of those in an English edition of the Bible by a Scottish Baptist, John Canne (or Cann), and the Welsh edition was published in full in September or October 1790.[12] Unfortunately, Williams had not been satisfied with a translation only but had added some of his own notes and had also seen fit to change some of the text of the Welsh Bible itself. The nature of some of these notes and changes almost immediately brought down an even fiercer storm upon his head. Thus, in Proverbs 8:25, where it is understood that Christ declares, 'Before the mountains were settled, before the hills was I brought forth,' Williams had put, 'Before the hills was I born.' Also, in a couple of his notes, he was, if anything, more emphatically Sabellian:

> Matt. 1:20. '*that* which is conceived.' Not, '*he* who is conceived,' in order to show that our Saviour's human nature is not a different *person from the Father*, but is in essence God. The mistletoe is not a different tree but a different substance!'
>
> Luke 1:35. 'that *holy thing*.' Not, 'the *holy one*.' Behold, the *Man* Jesus is not a *different person* from the Father, but is in him in essence![13]

In October, William Williams heard of the death of his greatest friend, Daniel Rowland, whose 'armour-bearer' he had been for over forty years. While grieving for his friend he must also have realised that the two of them had not dealt as they should have

[12] The earlier parts of the work had been appearing since 1788.
[13] Roberts, *Peter Williams*, (1943), 85-86.

done with the danger inherent in Peter Williams's thought, which was now bursting out afresh. In the same month he published an elegy to Rowland that included the verses:

If some *Antitrinitarian*	*Os deuai* Antitrinitarian
Came with heresies to allure,	*A rhyw* heres *front ddisail,*
Denying God's essential being:	*Haeru ni fedd Duw bersonau*
Three eternal Persons pure;	*Cynta,' trydydd, nac un ail;*
Daniel there would rise against him,	*Daniel yno safai fyny,*
As a pillar, mighty, strong;	*Fel rhyw golofn gadarn, gref,*
And would prove, to countless hearers,	*Ac wrth'nebai, o flaen cannoedd,*
All his wayward doctrines wrong.	*Ei athrawiaeth ynfyd ef.*
Three confessions gird his teaching,	*Mae ei holl ddaliadau gloyw,*
Founts of wisdom, clear indeed:	*Mewn tair credo i'w gweld yn glir,*
Athanasius and *Nicea*,	Athanasius *a* Nicea,
With the *Apostolic Creed*;	*'Nghyd* â'r *apostolaidd wir;*
So the *Articles* of Cranmer,	*Hen articlau eglwys Loegr,*
So *Westminster's* teachings bright,	*Catecis* Westminster *fawr,*
But, supreme, the holy Bible	*Ond yn benna'r Beibl sanctaidd,*
Shines, on all, its glorious light.	*Dywynnodd arnynt olau wawr.*[14]

These words were as public a reference as possible to Peter Williams without actually naming him. However, it is perhaps possible that Williams, even as he wrote, appreciated the inadequacy of this response. Nathaniel Rowland, Daniel's son, without doubt would eagerly take up arms and return again to fight his old adversary, but Nathaniel was not of the same spirit as his father. He was a proud, selfish man, driven by personal ambition. He might succeed in repressing Peter Williams's views but he might as easily demolish him in the process, and break up the Connexion at the same time, because of his unspiritual and dictatorial attitude. In the very last fortnight of his life, therefore, he turned again to the new, rising power in the north, hoping that Thomas Charles and the younger

---

[14] Thomas Levi, *Casgliad o Hen Farwnadau Cymreig* (Wrexham, 1870), 48-50.

generation might deal with the problem which his own generation had failed to solve. He would have been confident of Charles's orthodoxy on this point having read in the latter's 1789 *Short Catechism*:

> Although it is the Godhead of three Persons that works all things, yet, some works, more appropriately than others, pertain to each one of them … which also clearly shows that there are three Persons … One cannot deny the Persons without also denying their works – which, at a stroke, would pull down the whole plan of redemption. The doctrine of the Trinity is a foundational truth, and any error here would destroy the whole edifice …[15]

The matter was first raised in a meeting of the South Wales Association in Aberystwyth in the spring of 1791 with no conclusions reached, but in the North Wales Association of April 1791 in Llanidloes it was agreed that

> Mr Charles and John Evans, of Bala, attend the Llandeilo Assembly next May to confer with the brethren of the South with regard to the views of Mr Peter Williams respecting the Trinity of Persons, and respecting his work in changing words in the latest pocket Bibles that he has published: with a view to deciding in the next Assembly at Bala what to do in this matter.[16]

The Association at Llandeilo assembled on 24-25 May and, as the representative of the northern Association whose letter was being considered, the opening address almost certainly would have been given by Charles. He would have explained the reasons for their disquietude and their unwillingness to distribute Bibles that contained error. The old commentator defended himself vigorously but the many months of argument and counter-argument had cemented the Association's view. The eventual proposal to excommunicate Peter Williams, and thus to forbid him to visit

---

[15] *Crynodeb o Egwyddorion Crefydd: neu Catecism Byrr i Blant* (1789), 6-7; quoted in Roberts, *Peter Williams* (1943), 89-90.

[16] Roberts, *Peter Williams* (1943), 93.

the societies in the south to preach or to sell his Bibles, was carried unanimously. An almost identical proposition was carried at the June North Wales Association at Bala.

On three occasions, over the next few years, Peter Williams wrote lengthy letters of appeal to his former brethren, pleading for a return to their fellowship. Unfortunately he also still argued the correctness of his views on the Trinity. Thus, in a sermon that he published soon after his expulsion, he argued that 'it is because of the weakness of the human understanding of the work of salvation that we have to sometimes call him the *second Person*, although he is *Alpha* and *Omega*.' The Connexion therefore was given further occasions to consider its action, but the members continued of one mind and his pleas were rejected.

As might be expected, there has been much criticism of this excommunication, and of Charles's part in it, by those who have written on this topic, particularly in the twentieth century: '[PW] was thrown out of the Connexion, excommunicated and accursed, in his seventieth year, and that for no reason in the world' (D. Ambrose Lloyd);[17] 'The cruel treatment meted out to him after his unrivalled services to Welsh Methodism stands out as the darkest passage in the history of that body' (D. Lleufer Thomas);[18] 'What I see, once again, is the folly (and worse) of placing such weight on "right belief," on creedal orthodoxy, as the condition for co-habiting in religion … Persecuting the good, old man to his grave – *and for what?*' (R. T. Jenkins).[19]

These comments, however, are associated with liberal theological viewpoints that had no sympathy for those who took their theology seriously. Others have had a clearer understanding of the issues involved: 'that … the matter had been debated in two or three associations … the doctrine held by him undermined the

---

[17] D. Ambrose Lloyd, *Griffith Jones, Llanddowror*, 104; quoted in Roberts, *Peter Williams* (1943), 114.

[18] D. Lleufer Thomas, *Dictionary of National Biography*; quoted by Roberts, *ibid.*

[19] R. T. Jenkins, *Yng Nghysgod Trefeca* (Caernarfon, 1968), 168, 171.

views of the Body ... the Methodists were unanimous in favour of his excommunication.' (Thomas Charles Edwards);[20] 'In giving such little weight to the importance of doctrine as such to the leaders of the Methodists at the time, is he not, perhaps, doing an injustice not only to Thomas Charles, the chief defender of the orthodox Trinitarians of Llandeilo, but also to Peter Williams, who was just as determined not to deny his beliefs as Charles was not to tolerate them.'[21] Derek Ll. Morgan, commenting on the words of R. T. Jenkins quoted above.)

There have also been attempts to explain the expulsion as if it were an untypical action of a body tyrannized by a few powerful individuals, or to discover speculative personal piques held by Charles against members of Peter Williams's family. All such endeavours impugn the integrity, courage, and godliness of so many of the members of the Methodist Associations: John Evans, Bala; David Charles, Carmarthen; Dafydd Morris, Twr-gwyn; Robert Roberts, Clynnog; Evan Richardson, Caernarfon; John Jones, Edern; John Roberts, Llangwm, for example. By 1791 all these men, and others like them, were in their prime and had experience of many years in the ministry. It is impossible to imagine such men as these being bullied into submission. Ultimately, all such arguments are brought up short by the unanimity of the decision to excommunicate.

Though opposing the Sabellianism taught by Peter Williams (whether the latter did so intentionally or otherwise), Charles respected him greatly. When he came to write a tribute to him in 1813 in his *Trysorfa* he was full of thankfulness and praises for Peter Williams's long, faithful, self-sacrificing service to the cause of Christ:

> He laboured diligently and faithfully in the vineyard of the Lord. He travelled in all weathers, and suffered much for the gospel's sake; he was the means of conferring great blessings on many souls in the dark days in which he lived. He

[20] Roberts, *Peter Williams* (1943), 114-15.
[21] Derek Ll. Morgan, *Pobl Pantycelyn* (Llandysul: Gomer Press, 1986), 37-38.

had been given a strong physique, and a mind unflinching; he could work hard, travel long distances, and put up with indifferent lodgings and poor food. His gifts were most suitable to the dark understandings of the common people …'[22]

A last letter from the Countess of Huntingdon

The first few weeks of June 1791 were the last weeks of the life of Selina, the Countess of Huntingdon. On 12 June the Countess wrote, in a failing, tremulous hand, to Charles:

> My days of suffering not being ended, I avoided (when tolerably able) to add any of those feelings to so kind a heart like yours. You have my faithful love and regard for you and yours. Since we parted I know not a day (but when the Lord smiled) but I was passing the great tribulation and think while this lasts you will not deny me the great pleasure and joy of seeing you here. I am sure dear Mrs Charles will yield her consent while so critical to the poor old widow's importunate request. … could my dear friend be here by Sunday 19th instant or at the latest on Sunday to preach here the 26th? You would be a wonderful comfort to me …
>
> My dear friend, let me have a line to assure me of your kindness. I am weak and low and immersed in the great business of preparing a mission for the South Seas and the Indian nations in America. I wish to die and would do so in my dear and blessed Master's business. I can say no more from weakness but it must ever be to assure you and dear Mrs Charles how appreciative I am.
>
> S. H.[23]

This was to be the last letter that the Countess wrote. Five days later she was on her death-bed. 'Is Charles's letter come?' she asked, on that last morning. She heard that it had. 'It must be opened,' she said, 'to see if he comes.' As Lady Anne Erskine was leaving

---

[22] *Trysorfa* (1813), 483-85; D. E. Jenkins, DEJ, II, 81-82.
[23] Faith Cook, *Selina Countess of Huntingdon* (Edinburgh: Banner of Truth Trust, 2001), 417-18.

the room to fetch the letter, the Countess added, 'To know if he comes – that is the point.' These were her final words. She was assured that the pulpit of her chapel would not be empty: Charles had consented to come. She died on 17 April, 1791, at eighty-three years of age. Charles supplied the Spa Fields pulpit from 24 July to 11 September.[24]

The Countess's work with her Connexion was continued under the leadership of four trustees, two of whom, Thomas Haweis and Lady Anne Erskine (1739–1804), were good friends of Charles. The latter had been the Countess's devoted companion and assistant in her work for over twenty years. She proved as close a friend and supporter of Charles as her noble predecessor had been, and requests for his presence in the London chapels were, if anything, even more frequent. On these occasions he would stay with Lady Anne in her London home.

The Bala Revival of 1791

The Methodist Revival in Wales may be viewed as a season of revival in the country extending over almost a hundred years from 1735 onwards. Looked at in more detail it may be seen as a series of major awakenings for extended periods spread over considerable areas of the country (in 1739, 1762, 1781, 1790, 1805 and 1817, for example), interspersed with more frequent, sudden and powerful visitations confined to smaller localities – a county, a town or village, or even a single congregation. In his first seven years of ministry among the Methodists Charles had experienced and been instrumental in a few of these local awakenings but towards the end of 1791 he was to be at the centre of a major revival.

On the first Sunday in October 1791 an extraordinarily power-ful revival broke out in Bala at the close of the evening service in which Charles had preached on the text, 'May the God of peace be with you all' (Rom. 15:33). Charles had preached in the morning also and nothing out of the ordinary had occurred during the two services. Two months after the outbreak of the revival he wrote to

---

[24] Cook, *Selina Countess of Huntingdon*, 419; DEJ, II, 83.

A Bala Association preaching service on Bala Green
early in the nineteenth century.

a friend, probably Edward Griffin, and gave a detailed description
of events. The letter was subsequently published anonymously in
The Christian's Magazine:

> You enquire about the state of the churches in poor Wales. I
> have nothing but what is favourable to relate. We had, lately,
> a very comfortable association at Pwllheli; some thousands
> attended more than was ever seen there before. And here, in
> our town of Bala, for some time back, we have had a very
> great, powerful, and glorious out-pouring of the Spirit of our
> God, on the people in general, especially young people. The
> state and welfare of the soul is become the general concern
> of the country. Scores of the wildest and most inconsiderate
> of the people have been awakened. Their convictions are
> very clear, powerful, and, in some individuals, very deep, till
> brought for a time to the brink of despair; their consolations
> also, which soon follow, are equally strong.

A wild, vain young woman of this town was a singular instance of this. She had such a deep sense of her lost and helpless estate, as to confine her to her bed for three weeks, where, in the greatest agony of soul-distress, she roared till her strength failed her. She hung, supported only by a slender thread of hope, over infinite and eternal misery, justly deserved. In this distressing situation I found her, on my return from London; and a more aweful case I never saw. The arrows of God stuck fast in her, and his hand pressed her sore, killing her to make her alive. And in his good time, he graciously removed the bitter cup, and filled her soul with strong consolations and joy unspeakable. He set his prisoner free and gave her the garment of praise for the spirit of heaviness. This case struck awe and terror into the minds of many; but still they were able to go on in their usual course, and no visible good effects appeared till the first and second Sundays in October, which are weeks ever to be remembered by me.

This glorious work began on a Sunday afternoon, in the chapel, where I preached twice that day, and cannot say that there was anything particular in the ministry of that day, more than what I had often experienced among our dear people here. But, towards the close of the evening service, the Spirit of God seemed to work in a very powerful manner on the minds of great numbers present, who never appeared before to seek the Lord's face. But now, there was a general and loud crying, 'What must I do to be saved?' and 'God be merciful to me a sinner.' And, about nine or ten o'clock that evening, there was nothing to be heard from one end of the town to the other, but the cries and groans of people in distress of soul. And the very same night, a spirit of deep conviction and serious concern fell upon whole congregations in this neighbourhood, when calling upon the name of the Lord.

In the course of the following week we had nothing but prayer meetings and general concern about eternal things swallowed up all other concerns. And a spirit of conviction spread so rapidly that there was hardly a young person in the neighbourhood but began to enquire, 'What will become of me?' The work has continued to go on ever since with unabated power and glory, spreading from one town to another, all around this part of the country. New conquests are gained every week and new captives brought in. A dispensation so glorious I never beheld, nor indeed expected to see in my day. In the course of the eight years I have laboured in this country, I have had frequent opportunities of seeing, and feeling also, much of the divine presence in the Lord's work and ordinances, and great success attending the ministration of the word; but nothing to equal the present work. Whilst it stirs up the dormant enmity and rage of some, who continue the determined enemies of our God, yet the coming of the Lord amongst us has been with such majesty, glory and irresistible power, that even his avowed enemies would be glad to hide themselves somewhere, from the brightness of his coming.

What number has been savingly wrought upon, time will reveal; there are hardly any here without some concern about their souls; but some feel a much deeper work than others. This revival of religion has put an end to all the merry meetings for dancing, singing with the harp, and every kind of sinful mirth, which used to be so prevalent amongst young people here. And during a large fair, kept here a few days ago, the usual revelling, the sound of music, and vain singing, was not to be heard in any part of the town; a decency in the conduct, and sobriety in the countenances, of our country folk, appeared the whole of that fair, which I never observed before; and by the united desire of hundreds, we assembled at the chapel that night, and enjoyed a most happy opportunity …

Ride on! Thou King of Glory, is the fervent cry of my soul day and night; and in this, I doubt not, but you will join me. I verily believe the Lord means soon to give the kingdom of darkness a dreadful shake; for he takes off the pillars of it. Those who were the foremost in wickedness and rebellion are now amongst the foremost in seeking for

mercy and salvation in the blood of the Lamb. It is an easy
and delightful work to preach the Gospel here in these days;
for many are the fervent prayers put up by the people for
the preacher; and they hear the word for eternity. Divine
truths have their own infinite weight and importance in
the minds of the people. Beams of divine light, together
with irresistible energy, accompany every truth delivered. It
is delightful indeed to see how the stoutest heart bended,
and the hardest, melted down with fire from God's altar;
for the word comes with power, and in the Holy Ghost,
and is made mighty, through God, to the pulling down of
strongholds. I bless God for these days, and would not have
been without seeing what I now see in the land – No, not
for the world ...

All I relate are matters of facts, and have not exaggerated
in the least degree; nor related but a small part of the whole.
The Lord hath done great things for us, and to his great
name be all the praise.[25]

This letter aroused such a response of interest that Charles sent
a further letter, seven weeks later, noting that the work was still
progressing 'with great power and glory.' He then proceeds to list
what he judged to be the particular characteristics of the awakening. It was:

(i) A very *gracious work*: 'Unsought for, unexpected, and
unthought of.'

(ii) A very *powerful work*: 'Convictions are deep and overpowering. All self-confidences and vain hopes are powerfully and
thoroughly demolished, and the sinner is left naked and helpless
before infinite eternal misery ... Their consolations, in general, are
strong consolations, which always proceed from a discovery made
to their souls, of Christ in the divine excellencies and dignities of
his person, and glorious fullness and freeness of his redemption.'

(iii) A '*short work*': 'There is little preparative work preceding.
Convictions fly, like arrows from a strong well-bent bow, and

[25] DEJ, II, 88-91.

fasten at once, not unlike St Paul's when going to Damascus. I mean, this is the case *frequently*, though not always.'

(iv) A *growing work*: 'I do not mean that it spreads wider and wider in the country, though that be the case; but it grows and thrives in the souls of those where it is begun. Indeed, here I have found great satisfaction. It is most pleasing and comfortable to observe, how those whom, at first, we perceived enveloped in great darkness, only full of fear and dreadful apprehensions of futurity, now enlightened in the truths and established in the doctrines of the Gospel. When evangelical truths become the *food* of souls, and they desire them as new-born babes do the breast, they must necessarily thrive and grow. Human, speculative knowledge, even of divine truths, freeze and starve the soul; whilst divine, experimental knowledge, warms, enlivens, and invigorates those, who are blessed with it from above. They then become not truths to *talk* of only, but to *feed* and live upon; and when we *live* on this *living* bread, we cannot but be *lively* and *strong* ourselves.'

5. A *lasting work*: 'I doubt not but it is so on the souls of many; but may the Lord continue in his power and glory still to carry on amongst us, till Satan's kingdom be entirely in ruins! Glorify God on our behalf, dear Sir, and pray earnestly for us, that in such an awfully delightful season as this, we may be enabled so to conduct ourselves, as not to grieve the good Spirit of the Lord, and thereby cause him to withdraw himself from us. I dread that! Lord keep us!'[26]

Two years later, Charles answered a request for more information on the Bala Revival from John Campbell, a correspondent from Edinburgh:[27]

> Here at Bala, through mercy we still go on well, and have much cause for thankfulness; though not favoured with the wonderful scenes we were gratified with this time two years.

---

[26] *Ibid.*, 93–95.
[27] John Campbell (1761–1840) served as a missionary for the LMS in South Africa for some years, before fulfilling some thirty years of ministry at Kingsland, London.

Most of those of whom we had any degree of satisfaction as to a work of deep conviction on their minds, and not only terror for a moment, have stood their ground amazingly well; we have lost very few of them; and many, respecting whom we had no satisfaction at first, have come on well; at first, perhaps, only a little terrified; yet being on in that fright, and brought to attend the preaching of the word, they have been gradually enlightened and wrought upon, and are now hopeful members of our church ...

I must add also, though with sorrow, that a great many who have felt most powerful supernatural workings upon their minds have entirely lost them, and are quite fallen off; they will yet come to hear, but hearing is all. Some even of them have had a second visit from the Lord. More effectual than at first, and we have received them again with joy ...[28]

In his fascinating volume, *Diwygiadau Crefyddol Cymru* (*The Religious Revivals of Wales*), Henry Hughes devotes three chapters to this revival.[29] He describes its spread westward from Bala into Caernarfonshire, and southward into Cardiganshire and Pembrokeshire. In the summer of that same year (1791) the first preaching tour of the Baptist minister, Christmas Evans, to south Wales had brought spiritual quickening to many regions of these counties and these areas were now well prepared for the fresh waves of blessing following on from the awakening at Bala. The intensity and power of the revival in a particular area might wane after a while but then spring up anew some weeks or months later. In this way its effects were experienced in various places throughout 1792 and 1793. As late as March 1794, Robert Jones, Rhos-lan, when writing to his son Daniel in Liverpool, described fresh outbreaks

---

[28] DEJ, II, 101, quoting from Robert Philip, *The Life and Times of the Rev. John Campbell* (1841), 149-51. See also references to Campbell in Alexander Haldane, *The Lives of Robert and James Haldane* (1852; repr. Edinburgh: Banner of Truth Trust, 1990).

[29] Henry Hughes, *Diwygiadau Crefyddol Cymru* (Caernarfon, 1906), 177-201.

in Clynnog, Pentreuchaf and Brynengan in Caernarfonshire and in many places in Anglesey.

Very many of the converts were past or present members of the Sunday schools. Charles commented:

> 'The Charity Schools, which are set up all over the country, are abundantly blessed of God; children that were aforetime, like jewels buried in rubbish, without seeing their worth, now shine with peculiar lustre. They flock in great numbers to hear the word; behave with all decency, and solemn attention; and many, under the age of twelve years, are deeply affected, astonished, and overpowered with divine truths, and their minds filled with nothing else day and night; of these things they talk when they lie down, and when they rise up.'[30]

According to D. E. Jenkins this awakening was to become 'one of the best known revivals of the latter half of the eighteenth century associated with any fixed place or town.'[31] In Charles's view it was, 'the coming of the Lord ... the brightness of his appearing.' It may be argued that these years of 1791 to 1794 were the highest point of the Methodist Revival in Wales: the culmination of fifty years of a gradual leavening of the whole country and a springboard for the fifty years of spiritual, doctrinal, and moral influence to come. In these years some of the most powerful preachers that ever arose in Wales were either called to preach or received new fire in their ministry, men such as John Elias, Ebenezer Richard, William Williams of Wern, John Evans, New Inn, Thomas Richard, William Morris, Cilgerran, William Roberts, Amlwch, Christmas Evans and Ebenezer Morris. One immediate practical result in Bala was that the Methodist chapel in the town, for the second time, had to be enlarged. This work was completed in 1792.

The significance of the Bala Revival with respect to Charles's own influence and career must also be noted. For all his unbounded Christian confidence and assurance, he must occasionally have

[30] DEJ, II, 91.
[31] *Ibid.*, II, 88.

considered his position in comparison to some of the lay-preachers then ministering in Wales. God had been pleased to bless the land with certain individuals whose preaching, at times, would completely overcome the crowds who gathered to hear them. When men such as Howel Harris, David Jones, Llan-gan, Robert Roberts, Clynnog, and, later, John Elias and Ebenezer Morris, visited a locality, a considerable proportion of the population would gather to hear them; a single sermon from them might be sufficient to revolutionise the morals of a whole neighbourhood. Charles was never a popular preacher in this sense. His ministry was very similar to that of John Evans of Bala – balanced, judicious, eminently scriptural – but without the overcoming power that so often accompanied that of some of his contemporaries. By marking him out as his instrument in this revival, God's approval of his service may surely be viewed as a timely, strategic providence. It was a local revival, associated particularly with Bala, and therefore with himself, but proved to be the first-fruits of a widespread period of awakenings from 1791 through to 1794. It was a decided divine seal of approval upon Charles now, at the very outset of his leadership in the Connexion. It certainly confirmed Charles in his view of the importance of revival, which he expressed in 1792:

> I am persuaded that, unless we are favoured with frequent revivals, and a strong powerful work of the Spirit of God, we shall in a degree degenerate and have only a 'name to live': religion will soon lose its vigour; the ministry will hardly retain its lustre and glory; and iniquity will of consequence abound.[32]

The Association at Bala

The two most important early venues for the associations of the Methodists in south Wales were Llangeitho, Cardiganshire, and Llan-gan, Glamorgan, the places connected with the ministries of Daniel Rowland and David Jones respectively. After Jones's move to Pembrokeshire and Thomas Charles's assumption of leadership

[32] DEJ, II, 98.

in the north, it was Llangeitho and Bala that were the two 'Jerusalems,' one for the southern Association, the other for the north. It is not known when the preachers and exhorters in the north began to meet together, in Monthly Meetings locally, and as Associations in quarterly meetings. It is said that an Association met at Llangollen, Denbighshire, in 1768 and at Llanllyfni, Caernarfonshire, in 1769; the first at Bala, as mentioned previously, was about 1760. But from the 1790s and throughout the first half of the nineteenth century, it became the practice that one of the Northern Association Quarterly Meetings would always be held at Bala, and one of the Southern Association Quarterlies always at Llangeitho.

When Robert Jones wrote of the 1767 Association at Bala, he noted that there were scarcely two hundred in attendance. In 1760, it is said that the preachers – Peter Williams, Daniel Rowland, William Williams, and others – spoke while standing in the hollow stump of an old tree in the main street in front of Plas-yn-dre, the home of the Lloyd family. Some years afterwards the site was moved to a position in the High Street in front of the Plas Coch Inn, with the preachers standing on a mounting-block. At the beginning of Charles's time at Bala, the crowds gathered on the street in front of his house with the preachers standing in his first-floor window.

With the numbers attending increasing, particularly after the 1791 Revival, the Association meetings were held for some years in the chapel but with the preachers standing in the front window so that both the packed church congregation and the great crowd gathered in front of the building could hear. One can imagine Charles seated in his chapel, listening to the various Association preachers. He may have sat with Sally and the family, but more probably in his customary seat, next to John Evans, with the other ministers, under the pulpit.[33]

As mentioned, believers from all parts of north Wales would attend.[34] With many tens of thousands converging on the small

---

[33] Goronwy Prys Owen, *Thomas Charles a'r Bala* (Y Bala: Cantref, 2016), 13.

[34] Henry Rees once commented, 'Sometimes, when I read the words of Paul, or others similar, "The earth also and the works that are therein shall be

rural town, the logistics of shelter, feeding, stabling, etc., were considerable. Homes at more than seven miles radius about the town would help to house the pilgrims. By about 1810 the numbers attending the Bala Association were so great that no chapel, even with its forecourt, could hold the crowd. At some point within a year of this date the meetings were moved to the Bala Green. This was an open area of ground to the east of the town. It remained the annual venue up to 1850, and on many occasions thereafter.

---

burnt up," I think to myself, "Well, old earth, whatever your condition after that great conflagration, you will forever be in my memory! I will remember the paths to the old chapel in Llansannan, and the walking over the mountains to the Associations of old in Bala, to all eternity."'

10

SUPPORT FOR MISSIONARY ACTIVITIES, A BRUSH WITH DEATH, AND INCREASING RESPONSIBILITIES (1799–1802)

We look to you, Brother, to be active in your inquiries respecting such as you know we want, and your mountains, I think, can supply. Examine them, and state to me their qualities, age, and occupation, that these may come before the Committee, and such a selection made as may give glory to God, and accomplish the great end we have in view of Heathen conversion. Meekness and humility are among the first qualifications.

From a letter to Thomas Charles
from his fellow LMS director, Thomas Haweis.[1]

The London Missionary Society

In 1792, through the urgent promptings of William Carey, the Baptist Missionary Society was formed. It was limited to Baptists, not particularly because of sectarian reasoning but because Carey and his friends believed that this would be the most effective way of acting. Their action spurred on their paedobaptist brethren to similar action. The Evangelicals of the Church of England, Independents, Presbyterians and the Calvinistic Methodists co-operated to establish a society for sending the gospel, without any denominational emphasis, to the pagan world. After much discussion and publishing of many articles in the *Evangelical Magazine*, meetings

[1] DEJ, II, 196.

were held in September 1795 to launch the London Missionary Society. The launch received an amazing response. The numbers that gathered and the spirit exhibited prompted some to describe the event as a new Pentecost. An immense congregation, including 200 ministers, met in Northampton Chapel, Spa Fields, on Tuesday morning, 22 September 1795, for the first public meeting of the new society. The meeting began with William Williams's well-known hymn:

> O'er the gloomy hills of darkness
>> Look my soul; be still and gaze;
> All the promises do travail
>> With a glorious day of grace:
> Blessed Jubilee! Blessed Jubilee!
> Let your glorious morning dawn.

One of the most encouraging aspects of the meeting was its evangelical ecumenicity. Present were Thomas Haweis and John Eyre (Episcopalians); David Bogue of Gosport (Independent); John Love (Scottish Presbyterian); Alexander Waugh (English Presbyterian). Thomas Charles would have been present also had the meeting been held in August, as was originally intended, for throughout that month he was in London, ministering in that same Spa Fields Chapel. By May 1797, both he and David Jones, Llangan, were directors of the society. This was a natural development as both men were close friends of Thomas Haweis (1734–1820), one of the founding fathers of the Society. Haweis was an evangelical clergyman from Cornwall and one of the Countess of Huntingdon's chaplains.

Charles described the missionary longings in the hearts of many at the time when he wrote in his periodical for April 1799:

> The Lord, in all probability, had been making all preparation for this work for some years past, by impressing the condition of poor pagans upon the minds of many people in the British Isles. As they considered their case and grieved for them, they saw that there was no hope for expecting the

gospel to be proclaimed to them unless some Christians put forward the means and effort to that end. Therefore, when friends conversed together, many perceived that the same fire burned in the bosom of their friend as in their own.[2]

In 1796 the Society bought a ship, *The Duff,* which sailed to the South Sea Islands with thirty missionaries on board. The choice of this first missionary field for the society was influenced particularly by the great interest in the voyages of Captain James Cook in the Pacific Ocean. After *The Duff'*s return, while it was harboured in London, Charles went on board to speak to and dine with Captain William Wilson, who was to be the captain for the second trip. He was the nephew of James Wilson, the original captain, and had sailed with his uncle on the first voyage. Charles therefore received an account of that maiden voyage from an eye-witness. He wrote it up and sent it in a long letter, dated 9 September 1798, to Thomas Jones, then at Mold.[3] With Charles's permission, and the blessing of the Caernarfon Association of October 1798, Thomas Jones translated the letter into Welsh and, by the end of that year, it was published as a pamphlet. The following are some paragraphs from it:

> I dined on board one day, and I cannot but confess that I felt great joy and thankfulness on the occasion. While I could see, at one glance, many hundreds of vessels trading to different parts of the globe, engaged in conveying the perishable treasures of this world from one nation to another, I could see ONE (and that, perhaps, the first solely so employed) trading for heaven, the great cause of the gospel, and the salvation of immortal souls. I thought this no little honour to our nation, as well as to the faithful and active men who have undertaken the task ...
>
> The Directors have been pleased to elect me one of their number: and I was present at some of their special meetings.

---

[2] *Trysorfa Ysbrydol* (1799), 52. For this periodical see pp. 205-10.
[3] Dewi Arwel Hughes, *Meddiannu Tir Immanuel* (Bridgend: Evangelical Library of Wales, 1990), 45-46.

I heard some of the young men, who are candidates as missionaries, under examination; and I felt proud of them. I could not but judge them to be spiritual men, suitable in the matter of knowledge and understanding, and devoted to the work. There is need of still more missionaries; and there is need of money. An earnest request is also made for the prayers of all on behalf of this most important task ...

Have we none in our midst of suitable qualifications and willing to consecrate themselves to God and his work as missionaries? Godly, spiritual men, enlightened by the gospel, are acceptable whatever be their calling. Carpenters, blacksmiths, tillers, or any kind of craftsmen are very suitable to send out. It will be in the power of such men to be of service to the poor inhabitants in various ways to win their affections by many an act of kindness.[4]

Charles's letter also clearly demonstrates the theology that lay behind so much of the optimism and zeal of the nineteenth-century missionary spirit:

It might well be thought that the promises are about to bring forth in an extraordinary way – that the secret wheels of Providence are hasting the fulfilment of the prophecies. We see a shaking of the nations and as a consequence, 'the desire of all nations shall come,' in some particular way, in the lengthening of the bounds of the Kingdom and the gathering in of the elect. If we look closely at the prophecies we find three important tasks and their consequences, yet to be fulfilled; and the time of their fulfilment is, it may be, soon to be upon us. It is probable also that if one of these is fulfilled, the fulfilment of the others will not be long delayed. The glorious tasks to which I refer are *the destruction of Antichrist; the Calling of the Gentiles; the Conversion of the Jews*. Then the kingdoms of this world shall become the kingdoms of the Lord and of his Christ; and he shall reign forever and ever ...

[4] DEJ, II, 188–90; a translation by D. E. Jenkins of the Welsh letter published by Thomas Jones.

> It has been, on many occasions, no small comfort to
> my weak mind, to be able to believe, on the basis of the
> Scriptures, that we labour in a work that is *certain of success*.[5]

That optimism was sorely tried in the LMS annual meeting of
28 July 1799. Charles was supplying the pulpit at Spa Fields at the
time, and was therefore almost certainly present and would have
heard of the sad history of *The Duff*'s second voyage. She had sailed
from London in December 1798 with thirty missionaries on board
intended for Tahiti, but had been captured by a French privateer
off the coast of Brazil in February. The ship, crew, and missionaries
were allowed to leave Montevideo in May but were then captured
again, this time by the Portuguese, in June. It was noted in the
meeting, 'that, as a consequence of the capture of *The Duff* the
funds of the Society have suffered very considerably, a subscription
be opened for repairing the loss.' The loss of the ship cost the LMS
£10,000. As ever, Charles's fund-raising skills were set to work. The
society's treasurer acknowledged contributions of £167.9.3 sent in
1799, and £180.7.2 in 1800 – the sums of his collections amongst
the Calvinistic Methodists of north Wales for those years.

John Davies, Tahiti

Charles's influence may also be seen in the departure in 1801 of the
very first Welshman to serve the missionary cause. John Davies
(1772–1885) was the son of a Montgomeryshire weaver. Probably
his only education was a term in one of Madam Bevan's circulating schools, but he had made sufficient use of that education for
Charles to employ him as one of his schoolmasters in Montgomeryshire. Possibly, as was his custom, he gave Davies some personal
tuition for a period at Bala before sending him on to the schools.
Through his regular contact with his teachers, Charles would have
informed Davies of the activities of the evangelical brethren in
London. In this way it transpired that sometime about January
1800, the following letter from Charles was being read in the LMS
office in London:

[5] Hughes, *Meddiannu Tir Immanuel*, 48-49.

Top: Thomas Haweis.
Bottom: The London Missionary Society ship, *The Duff*.

The bearer of this is John Davies, whom I recommended and you accepted last summer for a missionary … I still heartily recommend him as a young man who has been useful as a teacher in our circulating schools and has hitherto honoured his profession by a consistent walk and conversation. It is with regret I part with him, though, when I consider the vast importance of your undertaking and the noble end you have in view, I wish I had many more such to recommend to you, though our poor people are slow in offering themselves for missionaries (from a sense of their insufficiency more than from their indifference I believe), yet I can assure you, they heartily pray daily for the success of the missionary cause, and are very inquisitive about the transactions of the Society and of the prosperity of the missionaries …[6]

Davies was accepted for service in Tahiti and sailed on 9 May 1801 to the South Seas. His ship, *The Royal Admiral*, was transporting convicts to New South Wales, Australia, and he wrote to Thomas Charles from the Isle of Wight as they waited for favourable winds: '… if I speak my own opinion, I have much more favourable thoughts of the convicts than of the ship's company. They are all of them, officers and sailors, only the captain, surgeon and ship's carpenter excepted, a set of the most wicked and ungodly characters.'[7]

John Davies never left Tahiti again, remaining there for fifty-four years. He was the author of a dictionary and a grammar of the Tahitian language and translated *The Pilgrim's Progress*, a large portion of the New Testament and of the Psalms, the *Westminster Shorter Catechism*, and many other smaller works, into Tahitian. Although blind for the last ten years of his life, he continued to minister to the churches he had established, and kept up his correspondence with John Hughes, Pontrobert, the leader of the Methodist society at Llanfihangel-yng-Ngwynfa and once a fellow-master in Charles's schools.

[6] DEJ, II, 197-98.
[7] *Ibid.*, II, 199-200.

A death in the family and a brush with death

In the autumn of 1799 Charles was completing an exhausting two-month pulpit supply at Spa Fields Chapel, London. His increasing responsibilities and the wider recognition of his abilities resulted in further and further demands being made upon him during his visits to the capital. The amount of preaching involved was almost the least of his burdens. Inquirers and visitors would call upon him, demanding much of his time; his directorship of the various societies would require meetings, appointments and correspondence; the Welsh society,[8] with its chapel in Wilderness Row, called for a good deal of his time and counsel. He was 'the one man in universal demand wherever Welshmen were concerned with divine affairs. Yet his very humility made him unconscious of the strain that was put upon him.'[9]

It was a very weary man therefore who returned to Bala in September, 1799. Charles had sent his son, Thomas Rice, and orphaned nephew, David Thomas, to Shrewsbury for their education. That year the boys were both fourteen years old. In December the weather was bitterly cold. Charles was again away from home on a preaching itinerary which he intended to terminate at the winter Association at Llanrwst, Denbighshire. David Thomas contracted a cold at Shrewsbury. This developed into an inflammation on his lungs and he, under Thomas Rice's care, was sent home hurriedly to Bala. His great disappointment at not finding his uncle at home resulted in an urgent message being sent to Charles for his immediate return. The messenger caught up with him at Caernarfon on a Monday afternoon, 16 December, and he immediately hurried for home, more than fifty miles away, 'as fast as his little mare could carry him.'[10] On a bitterly cold day and in a freezing wind, he passed through Rhyd-ddu, on the lower slopes

---

[8] That is, the Welsh Calvinistic Methodist society, first formed in London in 1774 and with its first chapel built in Wilderness Row, near Blackfriars Bridge, in 1785.

[9] DEJ, II, 240.

[10] *Ibid.*, II, 242.

of Snowdon, through Beddgelert and Tan-y-bwlch, and began the climb over Migneint mountain. It was on this part of the journey that his left thumb, continually gripping his horse's reins presumably, became frostbitten. His eventual arrival at home brought him only bad news. David's condition had deteriorated and he died on the Wednesday morning. Charles wrote to inform David's older brother, Joseph, of the sad news:

> My dear nephew,
>
> … We parted with him with much regret – we loved him next to our own children. However, it is our great joy and comfort that we trust he died in the Lord. He knew Jesus as the Saviour and friend of sinners, and looked to him solely as the refuge and sole hope for salvation. Having cast his anchor into this rock, we may confidently rest assured that his poor little shattered bark got safe into the desired haven …[11]

What must have further complicated his mixed feelings, even as he put pen to paper, was the knowledge that he could not have written such a hopeful letter had he been describing his own son, Thomas Rice. In a letter to a friend, written over thirteen years later, he mentioned that he could not be sure of any 'real change' having taken place in his son.

The frostbitten hand became infected and resulted in attacks of intense pain, causing much lack of sleep and weariness. For the next eleven months, a time when he had a great deal of work on his hands, there were frequent periods when he was unable to work, or when Sally had to be called upon to act as an amanuensis. Eventually he became so broken in health, either through continual weariness due to the pain, or because of the spread of the infection, that there were fears for his life. Many doctors had been consulted during these months with varying counsels but it was now agreed that his only hope was an amputation of the thumb. There was considerable concern for him and prayer offered on his behalf at

---

[11] *Ibid.*, II, 243.

this time in the societies throughout Wales, but none more so than in the Bala society. A member of that society who kept a diary, a man called Richard Jones, recorded a famous occasion:

> On the first Sunday night after I came to Bala, they were holding a prayer meeting in the big loft of Mr Charles's house, previous to the amputating of that renowned man's thumb, because it was amputated the next day. I had the privilege of being there with them, and I remember that one old man was praying very earnestly for the saving of Mr Charles's life, and crying out, 'Fifteen, Lord; wilt thou not give him to us for fifteen years? For my brethren's sake, this prayer is made, and for the sake of my neighbours too.'[12]

The old man was Richard Owen, a shoemaker in the town and a deacon in the society. He repeated his request many times. It is presumed that he was thinking of the promise made to Hezekiah in similar circumstances, 'I will add unto thy days fifteen years' (2 Kings 20:6). The earnestness and simplicity of the prayer so impressed the others at the meeting, that there was a general conviction that it would be answered. The operation took place at 1 Abbey Green, Chester on 24 November 1800.[13] It was successful and slowly, over a period of a year, Charles recovered. However, he never regained his previous strength, and though he was to travel much again, it was not until 1805 that he again undertook a major itinerary of more than two weeks. It is worth noting that when Charles died, on 5 October 1814, he had lived all but seven weeks of the added fifteen years and it is generally accepted that these were the most fruitful fifteen years of his ministry.

On more than one occasion Charles was to describe his spiritual experience during this ordeal in letters to friends. Thus, in a letter to John Mayor (25 March 1801):

---

[12] DEJ, II, 245.

[13] The Georgian house, 1 Abbey Green, Chester, where the operation was carried out, still stands. It was restored in the early 1990s as part of the Rufus Court development. DEJ, II, 246.

… During the whole of my indisposition I had daily proofs of the Lord's great faithfulness in fulfilling his promises graciously made to us in the word. As my day of trial or suffering was, so was my strength. Soon after the commencement of my complaint, when I understood the very serious consequences likely to follow, he graciously favoured me with such glorious views of HIMSELF as produced a comfortable, calm frame of mind and *joyful* resignation to his will. I never had such views before (I mean in the same degree of clearness and continuance) of his sovereignty, and justice, of his goodness and tenderness. It was impossible for me to believe, that he, who gave his life a ransom for me, would do me ultimately any harm, but the greatest good. It was an amazing sight, by faith, of a crucified Saviour, that conquered all the rebellions of my will, and banished all my fears. Under whatever character I viewed the Lord, I could not help loving him, and having confidence in him, and rejoicing with joy unspeakable and full of glory.

The loveliness of his character as set forth in his word, the infinite dignity of the Person of Jesus, the fullness of his salvation, the immutability of his councils, were brought before my view with such overpowering evidence and glory, that my feeble nature could hardly support itself under it. I found a nearness in my mind to the eternal world, which I never experienced before; and heaven was almost in view …

After all the vain talk that is in the world, Jesus is everything to a lost sinner. He is *all* and in *all*. I could hardly bear bestowing a thought on any other subject.[14]

Liverpool

The Irish migration to Liverpool from the year of the great famine of 1845 onwards, with tens of thousands being drawn to the town by the prospect of work, is well known.[15] But long before this, from 1760 onwards, the Merseyside shipping industry provided work

[14] *Ibid.*, II, 338-39.
[15] Liverpool was granted city status in 1880.

for the sailors of Anglesey and Caernarfonshire. By 1815 a Welsh township existed within Liverpool, and areas such as Everton and Anfield were Welsh-speaking. Indeed, by 1900 there were around ninety Welsh churches, chapels, and mission halls ministering to the Welsh communities of the city. Thomas Charles had been involved in this work almost from its beginning. The first Calvinistic Methodist cause had been formed in the town in 1782, two years before Charles joined the Methodists, but with his many links and frequent journeys over the Welsh border to Shrewsbury and Chester it was not long before the fledgling society asked for his support. In 1787, as previously mentioned, he helped the members to raise their first chapel at Pall Mall, collecting £400 for it in Wales.

Charles visited the town often. On one occasion he had a very narrow escape. The ferry over the River Mersey from Cheshire was usually supplied by comparatively small boats and could involve some danger in stormy weather. On this occasion Charles had settled into his seat on a particular boat but then discovered that his luggage had been placed in another boat. He immediately rose and transferred to the other boat. It was fortunate he did so because the first boat capsized on crossing, drowning all its occupants.

For thirty years the cause at Liverpool was very dependent on three north Wales clergymen. For the seventeen years between 1785 and 1802 they received the sacraments in their own building only on those occasions when Charles was with them.[16] Simon Lloyd also began to make visits from 1802 onwards and William Lloyd, Nefyn, from 1806. Charles would visit at least once a year, and when he came there would be a number of babies awaiting baptism – between 1798 and 1813, for example, he baptized 77 children. His visit on 26 May 1806 was in order to open the second Welsh chapel in Liverpool, Bedford Street Chapel.

Thomas Rice, Charles's oldest son, had always suffered from weak health, and in 1805 his father had obtained a position for

---

[16] Apart from one visit by David Griffiths, Nevern, during a tour of north Wales in May, 1802.

him at the business of Major Blundell and Co., drapers and warehouse-men, Holborn Bridge, London. Blundell was almost certainly a member of (or was acquainted with) the congregation at Spa Fields Chapel. Soon after, in December 1806, Thomas Rice married and moved to Liverpool, opening a drapery and hosiery shop there. This stay in Liverpool was not long because he had returned to partner his mother in the Bala business by December 1808.

Philip Oliver (1763–1800)

Charles's English connections led to another friendship that was to increase his responsibilities considerably. Philip Oliver was born in Chester in 1763 to a prosperous family of Puritan background. He was ordained as a curate at Churton Heath Church, Chester, in 1787, and later converted through reading evangelical books lent to him by a parishioner. His health deteriorated from 1791 onwards due to a disease of the lungs which was probably tuberculosis. In the hope of improving his health he obtained a curacy at St Mary's Chapel, Birmingham. A friendship with John Newton increased his evangelical zeal and he began to regret the limitations placed upon him by the rules of the Church of England with regard to preaching outside his own parish. At this point he was introduced to Thomas Charles and visited him at Bala. Here, 'he made full use of the example set by Mr Charles in defying the ban of the bishops, and of going to the people who would not go to the churches.'[17] When he returned to live in Chester, his bishop refused to allow him to preach in the town and he resorted to private services at Broughton Lodge, his mother's residence in the town. A barn at the Lodge was converted into a chapel and it soon had to be extended to include the adjoining areas of a coach-house. Later a small garden had to be included and then a gallery superimposed over the complete area. Eventually the building held almost a thousand worshippers. Charles preached there often and urged his friends to do so also. His brother David Charles, Carmarthen, David Jones,

[17] DEJ, II, 219.

Llan-gan, and Thomas Jones, Denbigh, were all to officiate at Broughton Chapel from 1796 onwards. Oliver established another preaching station at Tarvin, then, as demand for his services grew, others at Kelsall, Saughall, Saighton, Handbridge, Delamere, Cotebrook, Two Mills, Waverton, and even over the border in Rossett, Denbighshire, all within an area of about twenty miles radius of Chester. These would meet at private houses and other premises. The work began to be known as 'Philip Oliver's Connexion.'[18] A further legacy of the co-operation between Charles and Oliver was their joint publication in 1800 of the works of Walter Cradock (1606?–59), in a volume of 532 pages. Cradock was one of the earliest Welsh Puritans and is remembered for his part in helping to establish and pastor the first Nonconformist church in Wales, at Llanfaches, Monmouthshire, in 1639.

During his many visits to Chester, Charles befriended three orphaned sisters, Elizabeth, Mary, and Ann Stringer, members of Broughton Chapel. He often stayed at their home, 1 Abbey Green, Chester. It was there that the operation to remove his thumb took place, and he remained with them a further two months until well enough to travel home. Most of what is known of Charles's dealings with the Connexion is derived from the correspondence over many years between the Charles family and the three sisters.

Philip Oliver died on 10 July 1800, at thirty-seven years of age. His funeral took place on Monday 14 July, and more than five thousand people attended. Charles officiated at a memorial service on the following Sunday. The previous year, Oliver had written to Charles:

> I wish you could take charge of our place. My present inten-
> tion is to leave it after my death to be continued on the
> present plan and I should be much satisfied if it could be
> made your care and in any way connected with your other
> churches.[19]

[18] G. Llewellyn Griffiths, 'Philip Oliver and his Connexion,' JHS, 56 (1971), 68-77; 57, (1972), 3-12..

[19] G. Llewellyn Griffiths, JHS, 57 (1972), 9.

Oliver's reference to 'your other churches' was to the Welsh Calvinistic Methodist societies. He subsequently made over his house and chapel to three trustees, Charles being one of them, and added that Charles 'shall have the entire rule and government of the religious interests and concerns.' After his death the members of his Connexion asked Charles to direct the work. He began his directorship by arranging regular supplies to Broughton Chapel and the Connexion. This was a pattern with which he was familiar from the example of Spa Fields, namely, an independent connexion ministered to predominantly by clergymen and operating within the liturgy and practices of the Church of England. But Chester and Philip Oliver's Connexion did not have the same draw as London and the Countess of Huntingdon's Connexion. Several clergymen came to his aid for the remainder of the year, but when he found himself incapacitated following the frostbite, and not able to fill the periods between visitors, he judged that a permanent resident minister was the only solution. In June 1801 he sent a letter to David Griffiths, Nevern, asking him if he could supply the pulpit for a term and if he knew of anyone ('he must be a clergyman') who would take the place as a resident minister.

Though various men served the churches for periods of some months no one was found who was willing to take on the position permanently and the responsibility for arranging a supply for the Chester churches was to remain with Charles for the rest of his life. In the years from 1801 to 1804 particularly, very many of his Sundays would be spent in the Chester area. He would travel the forty-mile journey from Bala to Chester on the Friday or Saturday, preach in two or three of the various stations of the Connexion and then return to Bala on the Monday or Tuesday. During these years he very frequently had to refuse requests to visit other churches on Sundays in order to maintain the ministry at Chester. He relieved himself of some of the burden by forming a committee in Chester who were able to make arrangements with local men. After the ordination of ministers by the Calvinistic Methodists in 1811 matters became easier. Eventually, over a period of forty years, Philip Oliver's Connexion (involving the six chapels at Chester, Waverton, Tarvin, Delamere, Cotebrook and Saughall) was absorbed into what was by that time the Calvinistic Methodist Church of Wales.

The Rules and Designs of the Private Societies (1801)

A letter to Charles from Thomas Jones, Denbigh, dated 4 August 1801, contained the following postscript: 'I have sent the *Rheolau* some time since to the printer and desired him to send a proof to you, that you might have an opportunity of amending, etc – since then have not heard how far they have gone on.'[20] The reference is to *Rheolau a Dybenion y Cymdeithasau Neillduol yn mhlith y Bobl a elwir y Methodistiaid yn Nghymru* (*The Rules and Designs of the Religious Societies amongst the people of Wales known as Methodists*). The two men had been asked by the North Wales Association to draw up such a document and it had been accepted by the Association at their Bala meeting in June 1801. It was printed as a 32-page booklet.[21]

This was not the first occasion that the Welsh Methodists had seen the need to distribute rules to the societies in order to exercise oversight and to regularize their practice. An early association at Ystrad-ffin, Carmarthenshire, in 1741 had produced a few pages of directions which were then copied by hand and circulated to all society leaders.[22] A similar set of rules (written almost certainly by Daniel Rowland), drawn up in 1742, was printed, and this 'remained the standard code of practice for the societies until the appearance in 1777 of William Williams' *Drws y Society Profiad* (*The Experience Meeting*).'[23]

The *Rules* of Charles and Jones are different in tone and content to these earlier directions. The 1742 rules were warm, pastoral exhortations, with the main theme of 'the ministry of believers to

[20] DEJ, II, 352.
[21] An English translation was published in 1802.
[22] Eifion Evans, *Daniel Rowland*, 123.
[23] *Ibid.*, 181.

one another in their need, a ministry of honesty, encouragement and exhortation.'[24] The tone of the 1801 document is best appreciated by noting some of the rules for members:

> That they be, in a measure, convinced of sin by the Holy Ghost, poor in spirit, sorrowing for sin after a godly sort, and seeking to be delivered from it…
>
> That they hunger and thirst for Christ and his righteousness, and, consequently, show all diligence to make the right use of the means of grace – the hearing of the word, the ordinances of the Gospel, and the assembling of themselves together, to the end that they may grow in the knowledge of Christ and in likeness to him …
>
> That they hold family worship at least twice a day, "rule well their own house," and bring up their children "in the nurture and admonition of the Lord" …
>
> That they, and all who are under their care, keep holy the Sabbath day, by abstaining on that day from worldly business … not shortening the day by indulging in too much sleep …
>
> That they have no fellowship with the vanities of the world, and the unfruitful works of darkness; such as gatherings for foolish pleasure, wakes, dances, plays, banquettings, revellings, carousals, and other things of like nature …
>
> That they be men of few words in buying and selling, not contentious, not unduly praising what they sell, nor saying "it is naught, it is naught" of what they buy, not taking advantage of others …
>
> … At the beginning of every meeting a portion of the word of God should be read in a thoughtful and intelligent manner; then let all unite in prayer and praise to the Lord. After this, let them speak upon a doctrinal truth, or other profitable subject, that has a bearing upon their spiritual condition or experience, making known their fears, their doubts, their trials, and their consolations (*yet no further than is proper to spread the heart before men*) … Still it is not

[24] *Ibid.*

THOMAS CHARLES OF BALA

well to protract the meeting to undue length. Two hours'
length is enough for any meeting, except when special circumstances require that it should be prolonged.

All matters of dispute or doubt, that may arise in any
society, should be discussed and settled, if possible, by the
members among themselves. If that cannot be done, the
matter should be referred to the Monthly Meeting; and if it
cannot be settled there, it should be referred to the Quarterly Association; and let the judgement of the brethren there
assembled be a final decision.

A comparison of these rules with those produced in the 1740s
reveals an evident change of emphasis. 'There is no mention of
assurance or the witness of the Spirit, and the majority of the rules
have a more legalistic outlook.'[25] An appreciation of the political
and ecclesiastical climate of the times is needed in order to understand the motives of the two authors in writing the *Rules*.

Persecution and politics

'Though well abreast of the politics of his day, he never busied
himself with politics as such.'[26] D. E. Jenkins considered this
description to be so evidently true of Thomas Charles that he noted
it on the very first page of his biography. Its truth is indeed borne
out on most occasions when Charles's life comes into contact with
political matters. Thus, when writing from London in August 1793
to friends at Milborne Port, Charles noted:

Well, perhaps a little account of what is going on in this
miserable world may not be unacceptable to you. Here in
London a considerable deadness seems to overspread the
religious world. The empty noise of Politics has had its
influence in promoting it. A fresh outpouring of the Spirit,
another Pentecost, is wanted to revive his drooping cause.[27]

[25] Eifion Evans, *Fire in the Thatch* (Bridgend: Evangelical Press of Wales,
1996) 120.
[26] DEJ, I, 1.
[27] Marion Löffler, 'Thomas Charles a gwleidyddiaeth y Methodistiaid,' in
DDM (2014), 96.

At a time, therefore, when his fellow-Welshmen in London were exuberantly engaged in the discussions on political and social reform that arose in Britain during the first years of the French Revolution, Thomas Charles saw only the 'considerable deadness' that this produced in religious circles.[28] He clearly considered an interest in politics as being entirely of the world and exerting a negative effect on any believer engaged in it. Eight years later, however, he was forced into a closer involvement with the politics of the day because of the way in which local, national, and international events began to touch upon the Methodists.

The Bala Revival of 1791–93 had increased the numbers of Methodists in Merioneth, and north Wales generally, to such an extent that the Anglican Church, sensing a threat to its order and authority, was roused to a further wave of opposition and persecution. In Bala, as previously mentioned, the main instigator of actions against the Methodists was the Rev. Rice Anwyl, the rector of Llanycil, the parish church, but he was only the more active representative of the majority of the clergy. They were supported by many of the local landowners and squires: men such as William Price, Rhiwlas, Bala; Sir Watkin Williams Wynn, Wynnstay; the Vaughans, Corsygedol; and the arch-persecutor, Edward Corbet, Ynysymaengwyn, Tywyn. The influence of these men lay in their being justices of the peace, and among the various tools of harassment open to them were the use of press-gangs, allegations of breaching the Toleration Acts, and ruinous fines.

In the wartime conditions prevailing in the 1790s, an 'ever present menace was the activity of press-gangs who went about roping in persons at random for service in the army or navy.'[29] Itinerant preachers, travelling far from home and with no influential sympathizers on the local magistrates' bench to whom they

---

[28] *Ibid.* Such Welshmen in London included Jac Glan-y-gors (1766–1821), Thomas Roberts (1765–1841), Llwynrhudol, and the members of the Gwyneddigion Society.

[29] E. D. Evans, 'Methodist Persecution in Merioneth in the Late Eighteenth Century,' JHS, 28 (2004), 28-29.

might appeal, were particularly vulnerable. A few Methodist exhorters were forced to serve periods in the navy, and the fear of being 'pressed' led to many of them taking out licences under the Toleration Act. While this protected them from being treated as vagrants and therefore from being press-ganged, it was also an act of last resort because to be licensed was to be considered a Dissenter, whereas most Methodists at this time still maintained a degree of allegiance to the Established Church.

A more direct way for the justices to harass the Methodists was by accusing them of technical breaches of the Toleration Act and, on finding them guilty, fining them heavily. Exhorters would be arrested for 'preaching against the peace,' and householders for 'allowing preaching to take place in their houses.'[30] Describing the situation in Merioneth during this period, Charles wrote:

> Many suffered considerably by imprisonments, fines and confiscations … One of our preachers, a poor, inoffensive, godly man was very unlawfully imprisoned at Dolgelley, for six months. Our steady attachment to the Established Church cost us, in fines, in one year, near one hundred pounds; for we scrupled to have our places of worship recorded and our preachers licensed as dissenters.[31]

Such sums were far too great for the individual members of the societies to pay, but as a result of its increasingly organized structure the Association was able to raise the funds to pay off the fines. Eventually, however, the increasing persecution forced the Methodists to register their chapels and to build more of them so as to be less dependent on preaching stations in barns and houses.[32]

Of even greater danger was the reaction in the country to the political turmoil and violence of the French Revolution. The Methodists were being suspected of subverting the social order by 'encouraging an enthusiastic hot-headedness and allowing

[30] Evans, 'Methodist Persecution in Merioneth,' JHS, 28 (2004), 96.
[31] DEJ, II, 379.
[32] E. D. Evans, JHS, 28 (2004), 35-36.

untrained laymen to preach in unconsecrated places … There were attempts to put a stop to the work of the Methodists by applying the Conventicle Act of 1664 to them, forcing them to register as Nonconformists, and … by a campaign of public slander.'[33]

The Calvinistic Methodist Connexion in Wales could very easily be portrayed as a most dangerous, insidious movement. Its two Associations, north and south, operated as a centralized authority, co-ordinating the various provincial Monthly Meetings and, through them, the hundreds of local cells which were the societies. It constituted the largest indigenous national movement in the country. Furthermore, the democratic element in their activities was unusual in eighteenth-century Britain and could be perceived as a dangerous precedent politically. Once the comparison was made between the structure of the Connexion and that of the National Convention in France which directed the Revolution, a whole host of suspicions and accusations might be directed against them.[34]

One of the reasons therefore for the publication of the *Rules and Designs of the Religious Societies* was as a first step to counteract these slanders. The emphasis of the specifically moral and social rules was intended for public consumption as much as for Methodist discipline. The country needed to know that Methodists were 'faithful subjects of the government, honouring the king and all that are in authority under him'; nor were they Dissenters in disguise, planning rebellion against the Established Church. In the *Preamble* to the *Rules*, the authors go out of their way to clear themselves of this suspicion, and do so in terms and style which very clearly reveal that the document was not in any way intended merely as an internal *aide-de-memoire* for society leaders:

> We do not designedly dissent or look upon ourselves as dissenters from the Established Church. In doctrine we exactly agree with the Articles of the Church of England; and

[33] Loffler, in DDM (2014), 96-97.
[34] E. D. Evans, '"They Turn the World Upside-down": Methodist Attitudes to Politics in Eighteenth Century Wales,' JHS, 37 (2013), 50-51.

preach no other doctrines but what are contained and fully and clearly expressed in them … Whatever appears in our proceedings as in any degree tending towards a separation from the Established Church, takes place from *necessity* and not from *choice*. Making a sect or forming a party is not the object we are aiming at – God forbid!

… The Methodists have taken refuge under the protection of the Toleration Act from necessity – they wish to cleave to the Established Church, and by no means desire to consider themselves as a separate body.[35]

The Welsh Methodists Vindicated

The relatively limited distribution of the *Rules*, however, could do very little to counteract the myriad pamphlets and letters that surfaced in periodicals such as *The Gentleman's Magazine* and *The Anti-Jacobin Review* alleging that the Calvinistic Methodists were revolutionary Jacobins. The Methodists responded, in private letters, in Association minutes, and in their sermons, by urging their members to be obedient to all authorities and not to interfere in matters of government. One of the most influential responses was an eight-page pamphlet produced by Thomas Jones, Denbigh, in 1798, *Gair yn ei Amser at drigolion Cymru* (*A Word in Season to the inhabitants of Wales*). In it Jones appeals to all citizens to 'stand or fall with the religion of Christ, with the King and our two Houses of Parliament, with our Laws and Liberty, and with the true Cause of our Country and Kingdom.'[36]

Thomas Charles mentions that ten thousand copies of this pamphlet were distributed throughout Wales, and no doubt it greatly influenced the Methodist believers and provided arguments for them to withstand the radical views of the period. The *Word in Season*, however, was an exhortation written by an individual rather than a defence of a specific organization, and as such it did not succeed in stopping the rumours and attacks against the Methodists.

[35] DEJ, III, 299.
[36] *Ibid.*, II, 368.

Support for Missionary Activities, a Brush with Death, etc. (1799–1802)

Some of the accusers were Welsh clergymen concerned about the large numbers of their parishioners who were flocking to the Methodists. One of the most strident publications was the anonymous pamphlet *Hints to Heads of Families* (1801), whose author was later found to be the rector of Llandyfrydog, Anglesey, Rev T. E. Owen. In it he stated:

> I have [no hesitation] in declaring that they are the most dangerous, because *the most secret, the most wary and most persevering of our enemies,* that their numbers have astonishingly and incredibly increased of late, that their hostility to the Church has proportionately increased and that unless some method is adopted to put a stop to their proceedings, the safety of the country will be endangered.[37]

The Methodist order and rules he saw as nothing but 'freemasonry and illuminism in disguise' and he complained that:

> They pursue the same means to attain the same ends with their fraternized J[a]cobins of France … two of their most violent and most ignorant preachers, Elias and Lloyd, from Wales, went over to Ireland for the vowed purpose of preaching to the Welsh regiments. Preaching what? Not loyalty, you may be sure, for that was unnecessary, as the unshaken loyalty and good conduct of those regiments were, till then, unimpeached. I have heard complaints of some of them since; and if these soi-disant missionaries did not endeavour to withdraw the soldiers from their allegiance, there is no question but they wanted to withdraw them from the Church. How long a soldier may retain his allegiance to the King after his apostasy from the Church, I shall not pretend to calculate?[38]

The large crowds gathering at Associations were an indictment of the moribund condition of so much of parish life and religion.

---

[37] Frank Price Jones, *Radicaliaeth a'r Werin Gymraeg* (University of Wales Press: 1977), 25-26.
[38] DEJ, II, 375-76.

[197]

The accusers therefore began also to make use of reported anecdotes of bad conduct during Association meetings to blacken the
Methodist character. It is at this historical juncture that so many of
the well-known complaints against the Methodists congregations
as 'Jumpers' began to arise in the English press. It had become fash-
ionable for leisurely English gentlemen to make tours of Wales, of
north Wales in particular, and the visit to an Association meeting
became a feature of the tour not to be missed. It could then be
written about in articles to periodicals, or in the travel-books of
tours that were popular at the time. Thus an anonymous author,
'D,' wrote in *The Gentlemen's Magazine*, 21 July 1799:

> Though excursions through Wales have of late become fash-
> ionable, yet I do not recollect ever seeing an account in any
> publication of the religious sect at Caernarvon called *Jumpers*
> ...
>
> At six in the evening the congregation assembled ... we
> observed ... a man, in appearance a common day-labourer,
> holding forth to an ignorant and deluded multitude ...
> The preacher continued raving, and indeed foaming at the
> mouth, in a manner too shocking to relate. He allowed
> himself no time to breathe; but, seemingly intoxicated,
> uttered the most dismal howls and groans imaginable,
> which were answered by the congregation, as occasionally
> to drown the voice of the preacher. At last, being nearly
> exhausted by continual vociferation, he sunk down in his
> seat. The meeting, however, did not disperse; a psalm was
> immediately sung by a man, who, we suppose, officiated as a
> clerk, accompanied by the whole of the congregation. In the
> middle of the psalm, we observed part of the assembly, to
> our great surprise, jumping in small parties of three or four
> together, and lifting up their hands, beating their breasts
> and making the most horrid gesticulations ...[39]

'D,' of course, obviously having no knowledge of Welsh, could
not provide instances of the ignorant and delusional comments

[39] DEJ, II, 360-61.

being made. On occasion, both types of allegation, Jacobinism and fanaticism, might be made in the same letter.

To be thought guilty of treasonable motives and unseemly conduct was more than Thomas Charles could endure without protest. He therefore very gladly agreed to a request from the North Wales Association to answer the charges, and eventually published a book of eighty-five pages, entitled, *The Welsh Methodists Vindicated*, with the sentence on the frontispiece, 'Signed in behalf, and by order of the association, held at Llanrwst, February 25, 1802 … Thomas Charles.' The book was predominantly an answer to *Hints to Heads of Families* and he considered first what he viewed as the most grievous accusation, that of political treason and argued that the Methodists were fully loyal to the Crown, the Government, and the Established Church. They were not in any way a threat to the country:

> [We] behave in all things as becometh loyal, faithful, and obedient subjects. We therefore according to the apostle's injunction, *daily*, both in private and public, *pray* 'for the King …' We believe the Bible, and bow implicitly to its divine authority: In that best of books we are enjoined to 'fear God and honour the King' (1 Pet. 2:17); nor do we believe the first can truly subsist in the mind without the other being a fruit of it.[40]

The danger to the country was not from Methodists but, rather, from sin, in all its various forms. Charles then proceeds to refute the various specific accusations made against them in *Hints to Heads of Families*:

> We peremptorily deny any designed privacy or secrecy observed by us in our private societies, as alleged against us by the author. No secrecy is observed any further than what is requisite for peace and quietness, and to prevent the intrusion of those who may wish to disturb us, as often we have been …

---

[40] Thomas Charles, *The Welsh Methodists Vindicated* (Chester: 1802), 11.

Our regulations are now before the world, and let the
impartial public judge of our designs and of the evil tendency of our societies, if they can perceive any ...

Another charge against us is that we hold our private
meetings in the dead of night. This also is not true; many
societies, in country places, meet at ten or eleven o'clock
in the forenoon; and where they meet in the evening, the
general rule is to begin at six o'clock in the winter, and at
seven in the summer, and the meeting to continue *only* for
two hours.[41]

A brief comment on this period by John Elias in his *Autobiography* describes how the booklet was put to use by the Methodists
and the eventual outcome: 'The Rev. Thomas Charles wrote an
excellent defence of the Connexion, entitled *The Welsh Methodists
Vindicated*. We sent a copy of the book to every gentleman in the
country; the storm subsided.'[42]

In 1802, Thomas Edwards, *Twm o'r Nant*, (1731–1810), the
satirist and celebrated author of interludes, entered the fray by
writing a biting satirical poem of 112 stanzas, *Cân ar Berson Paris*
(*A Song to the Parson of Paris*). Parys Mountain, Anglesey is within
T. E. Owen's parish, Llandyfrydog. When Thomas Charles happened to meet Edwards he remonstrated with him for the rough
and mocking language that he had used. Edwards, who never had
much time for parsons, replied, 'You look after the sheep, Mr
Charles, and I'll look after the wolves!'

In all his actions and writings, Charles was displaying the
typical political conservatism both of the Established Church and
of the Methodism of his day. Indeed, he would not only display it
but emphatically prescribe it so that there might be no shadow of
doubt as to the loyalty of the Methodist body. An irony inherent
in his life and work is that one by-product of his religious and educational efforts was the development and increase of those skills

[41] DEJ, II, 380.
[42] Edward Morgan, *John Elias: Life, Letters and Essays* (Edinburgh: Banner
of Truth Trust, 1973), 91.

and attitudes that were to result in the political activism of the Nonconformist conscience of a later generation:

> ... he was leading the peasant membership of an evangelical church that was 'saturated with a democratic spirit in all its internal activities.' While Charles was at the helm, unordained men of low social class were allowed to preach, members were taught to read, write and discuss the Scriptures, they were taught that to live in obedience to God's Word should have priority above everything (including all worldly authority), and the societies of the movement were organized to be self-governing, for example, to decide 'every controverted matter ... prudently by the majority of the body,' i.e. by vote.[43]

---

[43] Loffler, in DDM (2014), 105.

Joseph Hughes, secretary both of the Religious Tract Society
and the British and Foreign Bible Society.

11

BIBLES FOR WALES AND THE WORLD
(1802–06)

The Bible is a friend to all who love him, and can give them consolations, strong, divine and eternal. You can never change him for a better friend; he is a *tried* one. Thousands have found him faithful and sufficient in all straits and difficulties.

You can converse with him at any hour of the day or night, silently and privately. And his advice is that of the highest wisdom and goodness, and may be safely relied on and followed …

On the bed of languishing, there is no such sympathising and supporting friend to be found for love or money … he will accompany you through death, as far as you need him, and will point out a brighter world before you, as an everlasting inheritance; where you will want him no more, but shall eternally enjoy all the rich promises therein made to you …

As I trust you already love him sincerely, you will not be sorry to receive your beloved friend in the best clothing that can be put on him, such as worms cannot affect; which well suits eternal and unchangeable truth. I will detain you no longer from his pleasing company by my poor tale.

Part of a letter from Thomas Charles, written in 1814, presenting a gift of a new Bible.[1]

[1] *Memoir*, 384-85.

The scarcity of Bibles in Wales

THE Protestant Reformation had been slow to arrive in Wales and its influence, when it did so, was considerably less, proportionately, than in England. Similarly, the strength of Puritan beliefs in Wales in the seventeenth century was very much weaker than in England. As a direct consequence of these differing influences the development of the publication of Bibles in the two countries proceeded at very different rates. Estimated figures suggest that the number of Welsh Bibles produced in the sixteenth century (1588–1599)[2] was one thousand; in the seventeenth century, 27,500; in the eighteenth century (up to 1770), 70,000. A total of about 98,500 Bibles had therefore been printed in two hundred and eighty-two years to serve a Welsh population which by 1770 was nearing 500,000. This must be compared to the figure of 30,000 English Bibles that were already being produced *annually* in England by the seventeenth century.[3]

There had been no printing of a reasonably priced Welsh Bible since the SPCK edition of 1769, and by 1787 this edition was very nearly sold out. The revivals of the last quarter of the eighteenth century along with the increasing number of circulating schools and Sunday schools were producing tens of thousands of newly-converted believers eager to possess the word of God for themselves, so that they might read it in their own homes rather than only during school hours. A letter from Charles in the spring of 1787 to Thomas Scott reveals something of the situation:

> … You ask me 'whether a parcel of Welsh Bibles would be acceptable?' You could think of nothing more acceptable, more wanted and useful to the country at large. I have been often, in my journeys through different parts of the country, questioned, whether I knew where a Welsh Bible could be bought for a small price. And it has hurt my mind much to be obliged to answer in the negative. There are none to

[2] The first Welsh translation of the Bible was produced in 1588 by Bishop William Morgan.
[3] Eryn M. White, *The Welsh Bible* (Stroud: Tempus, 2007), 70, 75-76, 155.

be bought for money, unless some poor person pinched by poverty is obliged to sell his Bible to support himself and family. Mr Williams' Bible,[4] with notes, are some of them unsold; but the price, 18 shillings, is too high for the poor to command …[5]

Through the instrumentality of John Thornton (1729–90) of the 'Clapham Sect,' London, Charles obtained a hundred copies from the SPCK. At this time also, Dr John Warren, the bishop of Bangor, requested and obtained more than one shipment of Bibles at cheap prices from the SPCK. But these small numbers of copies were thoroughly inadequate to meet the demand in Wales. Charles himself, who had suggested that one to two thousand Bibles were needed in his own locality, had greatly underestimated the true state of affairs. Hopes were raised when Peter Williams agreed to prepare a new edition of a pocket, and hence a cheaper, Welsh Bible. The subsequent controversy over its errant notes, and the Methodist prohibition against its use, meant that, to his great disappointment, Charles could not make use of the copies available. By 1792, all the SPCK stock of the 1769 Bible had been sold.

One new source, though short-lived, came to light when Charles persuaded one of the trustees of Madam Bevan's Trust that it would be sensible to sell a stock of five hundred and twenty Bibles and fifty Testaments that had remained in her house for thirteen years since her death in 1779 because of the complications with respect to her will. He obtained these for £122.[6]

Mary Jones and her Bible

In 1794, Mary Jones, the poor weaver's daughter from Llanfihangel-y-Pennant, Merionethshire, was ten years old. She had come to faith in Jesus Christ two years previously. She regularly helped her widowed mother by carrying a lantern before her as her mother attended society meetings in the evenings. For this

[4] The second edition of Peter William's annotated Bible.
[5] DEJ, I, 566-67.
[6] *Ibid.*, II, 122-23.

reason, although she was only eight years old, she was allowed to remain for the meeting, effectually becoming a society member at an age that was extremely unusual. She had therefore become far more acquainted with the message and content of the Bible than most children of her area at that time. Her experience, between the ages of ten and fifteen (1794 to 1800), and especially her longings to read God's word, were typical of many at the time:

> Apart from the copy of the Bible in the parish church, the only Bible in the vicinity at that time, it would seem, was the one at Penybryniau Mawr, a farmhouse about two miles from Mary's home. The Bible was kept on a table in the small parlour, and Mary was given permission by the farmer's wife to go and read it, on condition that she removed her clogs before venturing in. It is said that Mary would walk there every week, whatever the weather, over a period of some six years in all, to read the Bible and commit portions to memory.[7]

By 1795 the bishop of Bangor had managed to persuade the SPCK of the need. In February 1796 they agreed to print 10,000 copies of the Bible and 2,000 copies of the New Testament. By December 1799 they had sent out letters to all the members of the SPCK informing them that these were available at 2s. 9d per Bible and 6d per New Testament. Charles now had to ensure that those who looked to him for copies might get access to them. He was not a member of the SPCK himself, nor was there any possibility of his becoming so, being 'a notorious sectary' according to one member of the committee. He therefore had to discover indirect routes for obtaining Bibles and dispersing them where they were most needed. One way was by advising people to send in their requests to their local clergyman; another was for Charles himself to use his friends who were members of the society to obtain copies for him. He particularly made the most of Thomas Scott's efforts and good will. The latter's contact with the SPCK was Charles Grant

---

[7] E. Wyn James, 'Bala and the Bible: Thomas Charles, Ann Griffiths and Mary Jones,' www.anngriffiths.cardiff.ac.uk/bible.html.

(1746–1823), another member of the 'Clapham Sect,' an important officer in the Indian government, and a close friend of William Wilberforce. Grant obtained five hundred copies for Charles to distribute. Another five hundred copies were obtained in a similar fashion through the instrumentality of Edward Parry, Swaffham, Norfolk, one of the directors of the East India Company.[8]

It is at this point, perhaps just before Charles had received any copies of the new impression, that the well-known story of Mary Jones reached its climax. In the words of E. Wyn James:

> The story of her walk to Bala, barefoot for most of the way, in order to purchase a Bible from Thomas Charles, is well-known in Christian circles world-wide. That was in 1800, when she was fifteen years old. It would have been a round journey of about fifty miles. However, the heroic effort on her part was not so much in walking to Bala as in the sacrifice and perseverance involved in saving to buy a Bible. Walking that sort of distance to Bala was not at all unusual among Methodists of the period, and walking barefoot was quite normal among the common people at that time; but for someone as poor as Mary Jones, saving enough money to buy a Bible was a great sacrifice. Bibles were very expensive in those days, and she would have had to have scrimped and saved every penny for years before succeeding to accumulate the little over seventeen shillings she would have needed to buy a Bible – a huge sum for a poor girl like Mary.[9]

There are a number of uncertainties concerning the details of Mary Jones's story. When exactly did she make her journey in 1800? Was it, as described above, in the spring, before the arrival of the new Bibles? If so she would have received whatever Bible Charles happened to have available – a large Peter Williams Bible perhaps, or one of the last of the SPCK 1769 stock. If it was either of these, that would explain the price of 17s mentioned above. Or did she arrive in the late summer of 1800, and receive one of the

---

[8] RTJ (1979), 23.

[9] E. Wyn James, www.anngriffiths.cardiff.ac/bible.html.

last of the new Bibles before they were all dispersed? This is D. E. Jenkins's belief, and he calculates that in this case she would have paid about 3s.6d for a Bible.[10] This version of events is confirmed by the strong tradition that the Bible kept in the British and Foreign Bible Society's archives in Cambridge University Library (which is a 1799 SPCK edition) is the very copy that Mary Jones received from Charles. Written within, in Mary's handwriting, are the words:

> Mary Jones was born 16th of December 1784
> I bought this in the 16th year of my age. I am daughter of Jacob Jones and Mary Jones His wife. The Lord may give me grace. Amen.
> Mary Jones His The True Onour of this Bible. Bought in the Year 1800. Aged 16th.[11]

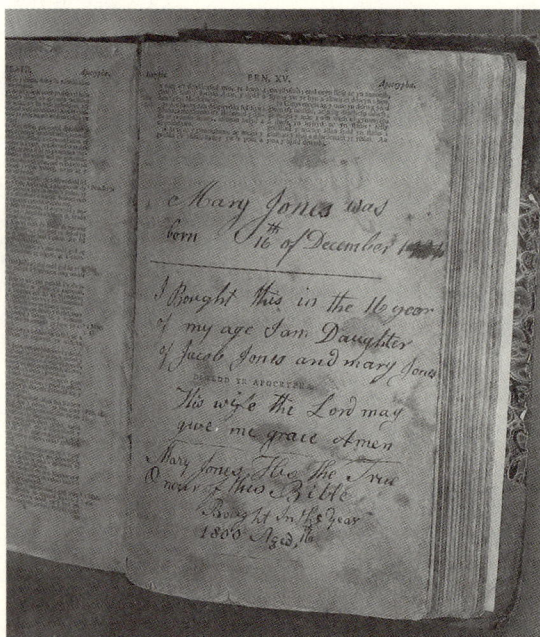

Mary Jones's Bible.

[10] DEJ, II, 492-94, 519.
[11] *Ibid.*, 493-94.

Top: The plaques to Thomas Charles and Mary Jones
on the wall of his home in Bala.
Bottom: Grave of Mary Jones, at Bryncrug, Tywyn.

THOMAS CHARLES OF BALA

Then there is the question of the number of Bibles she received. One source states that it was one copy only, received as a gift from Charles, or paid for with her slowly accumulated halfpennies. Another, more probable account, refers to three copies, two paid for and one received as a gift. Whatever the details of the story, and accepting the fact that it is impossible now to be certain of them given the lack of any contemporaneous record, it is still the case that the familiar tale is broadly true.

The SPCK, advised primarily by the Welsh bishops, had considered ten thousand copies to be more than adequate for the demand in Wales. The inadequacy of this advice is seen in a letter received by Charles from Thomas Jones, Creaton, a friend and fellow Welshman who was vicar of Creaton, Leicestershire. The letter was dated 23 April, about a month before Charles had even received his quota. In it, Jones noted, 'The Welsh Bibles are sold, every copy. I applied through the interest of a friend in London for 300 copies; but too late: the Bishop of St Asaph applied on the same day in vain.'[12]

Others, as well as the SPCK, began to publish editions of the Welsh Bible.[13] But the demand was still increasing and the need was so much greater than the supply. Charles's vision was actually wider still: he hoped that sufficient Bibles might be printed that they could even be placed in those homes where as yet there was no demand for them.

The British and Foreign Bible Society

The Religious Tract Society (RTS) was founded in 1799 as a non-sectarian publisher of Christian literature intended initially for evangelism, and including literature aimed at children, women, and the poor. It had the support of Established Church bishops but the driving spirits behind it were David Bogue (Independent),

[12] DEJ, II, 262.
[13] Another edition of John Canne's Bible was produced in 1796 and an edition of John Evans's Bible appeared in 1802 along with Titus Lewis's New Testament.

Robert Hawker (Anglican), Joseph Hughes (Baptist), as secretary, and Joseph Reyner (Independent), as treasurer. These four men were involved in the foundation of the London Missionary Society in 1795, and they would all become involved in the establishing of the British and Foreign Bible Society in 1804. Another officer of the society was Joseph Tarn who, as a member of the Spa Fields Chapel committee and of its congregation, was already a close friend of Charles. The RTS's existence was mainly due, however, to the labours of George Burder (1752–1832) of Coventry, secretary of the LMS and editor of the *Evangelical Magazine*. Thomas Charles was 'a country member' of the RTS, i.e. a member not resident in London. In the autumn of 1802, Charles was again supplying at Spa Fields and was therefore able to be present at a meeting of the RTS on Tuesday morning, 9 November. D. E. Jenkins comments: 'It was no part of the business of the RTS committee to discuss anything in literature more weighty than tracts, but the committee consisted of the very men who were most likely to show him practical sympathy.'[14] Charles made no mention of his great burden for more Bibles that afternoon, but later discussed the subject fully with Joseph Tarn at Spa Fields. Both men were aware of the delicacy of the situation in that many of the philanthropists present on the committee were also very involved in the work of the SPCK. The printing of Scriptures by any institution other than the SPCK could have been interpreted as setting up in competition with that Society.

At the next meeting (Tuesday, 23 November) of the RTS committee therefore, Charles was absent (possibly deliberately so) and Tarn himself, well-known and well-respected by the various members, raised the subject of the dearth of Welsh Bibles and of his friend's great concern. He did so during an informal discussion after the business of the committee was concluded, and succeeded in obtaining an invitation for Charles to present his concerns at their next session (7 December). The morning before this meeting, Charles was rehearsing in his mind what he would say

[14] DEJ, II, 502.

to the committee and how best he could secure subscriptions and donations for printing a further few thousand Bibles. It then struck him that should he succeed in his object, and a further printing be obtained, he would soon find himself again in exactly the same predicament. To proceed in such an *ad hoc* manner, appealing to one charity after another, was not the answer. What was needed was a single society dedicated solely to the work of producing Welsh Bibles – a Welsh Bible Society.

On Tuesday morning, 7 December 1802, the committee of the RTS met in their usual venue at the business premises of Hardcastle and Reyner, by the Old Swan Stairs, not far from London Bridge. Matthew Wilks[15] chaired the meeting. Once the regular business of the committee was disposed of, Charles explained the need in Wales, using as his main arguments his own personal knowledge of the scarcity of Bibles throughout the country, and the fact that a new edition of 10,000 Bibles had seen all its stock sold in less than four months. His comments being very favourably received, tradition has it that some member of the committee then remarked, 'If a Society for Wales, why not also for the Empire and the world?' Whether this was the case or not, the minutes of the meeting record:

> Mr Charles of Bala having introduced the subject, which had been previously mentioned by Mr Tarn, of dispersing Bibles in Wales, the Committee resolved that it would be highly desirable to stir up the public mind to the dispersion of Bibles generally, and that a paper in a Magazine to this effect may be singularly helpful …[16]

In various meetings during the next few weeks, at all of which Charles was present, this was one of the main topics. On 21 December, the secretary, read a paper on 'the importance of forming a Society for the distribution of Bibles in various languages.' On 28 December, it was decided that the aim of the new society would

---

[15] Matthew Wilks (1746–1829) was minister of Whitefield's two churches in London (the Tabernacle and Tottenham Court Chapels) for fifty-five years, and one of the directors of the LMS for thirty-four years.

[16] DEJ, II, 506.

be 'to promote the circulation of the Holy Scriptures in foreign countries and in those parts of the British Dominions, for which adequate provision is not yet made, it being understood that no English translation of the Scriptures will be gratuitously distributed by the Society, in Great Britain.' The reference to 'gratuitous distribution' was again a guarding of the interests of the SPCK. No actions were being considered that could be understood in any way as an attempt to undercut the prices of SPCK publications.

The RTS committee meetings continued throughout 1803. That of 19 April was the first in which the name of William Wilberforce appears among those present. He, however, proved to be typical of so many of the more influential individuals of the evangelical establishment in that many months and many letters were required before they were convinced of the very real need and were willing to sign a circular letter expressing their support. A new title was agreed upon on 10 January 1804: 'That the Title of the Society be: "The British and Foreign Bible Society,"' and the announcement eventually made that the society would be launched publicly in the London Tavern, Bishopsgate Street, London on Wednesday, 7 March 1804. About three hundred people were present at that inaugural meeting.

On the day of the inauguration of the Society, Joseph Tarn wrote to Charles:

> We cannot, dear brother, but rejoice together, when we consider that this work had its beginning in a conversation which took place between us two, one week-day morning that is ever to be remembered. Hence I was induced in the next meeting of the members of the Tract Society to mention the scarcity of Welsh Bibles; and then was kindled that flame which has now burst forth, and which, I trust, will burn brighter and brighter until that brightest day of universal knowledge, when we shall no longer teach our brother, saying 'Know the Lord,' for all shall know him, from the least to the greatest of them. To the Lord be all the glory.[17]

[17] *Ibid.*, II, 517.

There had been some thirty meetings of the RTS committee during the fifteen months of planning which had been necessary up to the inauguration. Joseph Reyner, at whose business premises the committee met, was present for all thirty meetings, Joseph Tarn and Joseph Hughes present at all but two. They were the labourers who brought the society into being – a society which was, according to Edward Morgan, Charles's biographer, 'the noblest institution ever set on foot by human beings'[18] – but the initial trigger for their actions was the suggestion put forth by Thomas Charles. As a recent study has concluded, 'By pleading the need of Wales, Charles opened a window upon the need of the world. In this narrow sense, Charles was the founder of the Bible Society.'[19]

Mary Jones and the Bible Society

According to tradition, it was the recounting by Charles of Mary Jones's visit to him that produced such an electrifying effect on the members of the RTS committee that they were convinced of the urgent need to establish a Bible society. Twentieth-century historians have questioned the truth of this tradition because there is no contemporary evidence for it. The minutes of the relevant meetings do not mention any such account. D. E. Jenkins states that the story was never heard of as the cause of bringing the Bible Society into being until after 1862, fifty-eight years later.[20] E. Wyn James, on the other hand, argues that 'from a fairly early period, there is regular mention that one girl had made a particular impression on Thomas Charles; and all the evidence suggests that Mary Jones was that person, and that a special rapport had developed between her and Thomas Charles following her visit to Bala to purchase a Bible.'[21] It is not now possible, however, to prove one way or the other whether her story was mentioned or not. What is certainly true is that she was but one of many and, surely, as Charles strove

---

[18] *Memoir*, vii.
[19] R. Watcyn James, in DDM (2014), 42.
[20] DEJ, II, 518.
[21] E. Wyn James, www.anngriffiths.cardiff.ac/bible.html.

to convey to that gathered collection of London businessmen and philanthropists the deprived condition of the peasantry of the hills and valleys of Wales through the utter unavailability of Bibles, he would have mentioned, as he did in a letter to Tarn, soon after the formation of the society, that '[y]oung females, in service, have walked over thirty miles to me with only the bare hope of obtaining a Bible each; and returned with more joy and thanksgiving than if they had obtained great spoils.'[22] Mary Jones, therefore, was not unique: there were other Mary Joneses, and also, no doubt, John Joneses, who had walked along their various routes to Bala in the hope of obtaining a Bible from '*Charles of Bala.*' Mary Jones will always be remembered, however, as the one member of those godly Bible-seekers whose name has survived.

The BFBS, Thomas Charles and the Welsh Bible

It has been noted by R. Watcyn James that, from the beginning, there were two elements in the philosophy of the Society that would have appealed strongly to Charles.[23] The first was the eclectic nature of the membership of the committee. He expressed in his periodical his disappointment that a similar attitude of co-operation was not prevalent in Wales:

> I grieve in that churchmen and the noblest of our country are, as yet, very sluggish and lacking in effort in their support … the various religious parties in our land are very far from one another; they should unite in this task, after the English plan, where they might meet and confer despite their differing views on other matters. Perhaps a general meeting in the various localities … might draw them together and warm them towards one another and lessen the party spirit which so disfigures Christianity.[24]

James suggests that Charles would have been glad to have had

[22] DEJ, II, 517-18. The letter was subsequently published in the *Evangelical Magazine* (1804), 524-25 (misprinted as 554-55).
[23] R. Watcyn James, in DDM (2014), 45-46.
[24] *Ibid.*

the opportunity to publicize such sentiments in favour of unity, at a time when the groundswell for separation was increasing strongly among the Methodists.

The second element was the emphasis of the Society on distributing the Scriptures 'without notes or any other additions.' The directors insisted that it was only the text of the King James Version and nothing else that would be printed. With the scars of the battle over the excommunication of Peter Williams in 1791 still fresh upon him, Charles would have welcomed such clarity. A further delight to Charles in all his relations with the Society was the opportunity it gave him to strengthen his ties with Joseph Tarn. They were already friends, drawn together by similar hopes and beliefs, but the years of co-operation on Bible Society business would bind them and their families closer together.[25] Writing to Tarn as a friend and writing to him as the assistant secretary of the committee of the BFBS were, however, two very different things, as evidenced by the following polite request (21 July 1804) from Tarn:

> I am directed to request that in your communications to me in my official capacity you will avoid any *extraneous* matter, which I presume is on account of the variety of persons composing the committee, many of whom, though zealously pursuing the object would look very shy on measures which *we* deem highly important to the welfare of Zion. But as I should be extremely unwilling to lose the benefit of your friendly communications I have devised the present method, which if you would have the goodness to adopt by writing on this sized paper and *folding it as I have done*, I can then cut off the postscript and leave a complete letter on the size of a large Post paper to show the committee.[26]

[25] Joseph Tarn's eldest daughter, Maria (*c.* 1803–1846) married Samuel Dyer (1804–1843). They became LMS missionaries to the Chinese, working from Malaya. Both died young, leaving three orphaned children. Their youngest daughter, also Maria Dyer (1837–1870), married James Hudson Taylor, the founder of the China Inland Mission.

[26] DEJ, II, 536-37.

It had been agreed that half the membership of the BFBS were to be Churchmen and half Dissenters. Joseph Tarn was a Calvinistic Methodist, a member of the Spa Fields congregation in the Countess of Huntingdon's Connexion. There would have been much that he and Charles discussed which other members would have 'looked very shy' upon.

The first task of the BFBS was the printing of Welsh Bibles, and it was to Thomas Charles that the committee turned to supply the information needed in order to make the correct technical, editorial and linguistic decisions required of them. Between April and October 1804, numerous letters passed back and forth between Charles and Tarn. The most important question concerned the previous edition upon which a new one would be based. On 19 July 1804, the Society directed Tarn to ask Charles if there was any objection to the use of the latest SPCK edition, namely the 1799 Oxford edition. He was also asked to prepare the copy for the press.[27] By mid October 1804 he was at work, being helped, as he described in a letter to the committee, via Joseph Tarn, by 'two gentlemen best acquainted with the ancient British tongue[28] in all the country.' These were Robert Jones, Rhos-lan, and Thomas Jones, Denbigh. He continues:

> My assistants are from distant parts of the country, one twenty miles off, the other fifty. They live with me in my house, and we are together at work night and day … If the gentlemen of the Committee should think it proper, perhaps it will not be amiss to offer a few guineas towards the travelling expenses of my kind and pious assistants.[29]

It is worth pausing to imagine the scene: Thomas Charles, Robert Jones, and Thomas Jones, the three notable leaders of the Methodists in north Wales – certainly the three most able – sitting at their separate desks, or perhaps sharing a large table, each concentrating over his apportioned Scripture, passing around the

---

[27] DEJ, II, 536.
[28] That is, Welsh; the language of the Celtic Britons, or Ancient Britons.
[29] *Ibid.*, II, 541.

Hebrew dictionary, or an old rare edition of the Welsh Bible, with Sally, or more probably Shani or one of the other maids, providing periodic refreshment. By 1 November 1804, Charles could write to Tarn:

> I have sent you one part of the Bible as correct as I believe as I can make it. My assistants left me last week, since then I have gone over it myself the second time, and have made some additional corrections which escaped our notice the first time. ... I have really bestowed up every attention in my power and spared no pains or labour to send the Committee a correct copy. I have particularly examined every word, every letter and every stop. I have compared 8 different impressions together in the Welsh language and 3 in English, deemed correct ones, to help me to fix the stops, the placing of which, in some instances, materially affects the sense. I found some words omitted in this impression [1799] which have been replaced; others were changed through carelessness, which have been duly restored. The stops, in general, we found properly placed, more so than in other impressions. Those we have altered, we had the English copies for our guides ...
>
> The remaining parts shall be corrected uniformly with this and I hope every part will be ready long before it is wanted ...
>
> I have paid one of my assistants 2 guineas toward his time and expenses, the other gentleman refused to accept anything.[30]

He himself also refused any payment for his work. He was bearing an immense work load at this time. In a letter to friends in Chester he noted 'I am in my study eight or ten hours every day. I go as far as I can on Sunday, and back again sometime Monday.'[31]

---

[30] DEJ, II, 545-46.
[31] *Ibid.*, II, 547.

Mistakes and delays

When Charles wrote, on 1 November 1804, 'The remaining parts shall be corrected uniformly with this and I hope every part will be ready long before it is wanted,' he could hardly have imagined that three more years of intense labour would be required of him before the Bible would be printed. Mistakes, his own and those of others, were to mean that on two occasions he had virtually to start his work from scratch.

The first mistake, and one that might easily have proved disastrous had its consequences not been pre-empted, was due to an error of judgment on Charles's part. The man appointed to superintend the printing of the Welsh Bible in London was William Owen (later to be known in Wales as Dr William Owen Pughe). Pughe believed that the work of a grammarian was to describe a language as it ought to be. Instead of seeking to understand the forms, syntax, and idioms of the Welsh language from the classic texts of its past and from the instinctive and natural forms of the spoken language, he devised erroneous theories of syntax, spelling, and accentuation, and coined numerous neologisms based on these theories. He was not alone in this; indeed, he was only applying current ideas to the Welsh language. Unfortunately, Charles was convinced of the correctness of this approach and had introduced some orthographical changes in accordance with Owen's views. Thus, in the letter of 1 November, he wrote to Tarn:

> The alterations in the spelling consist mostly in the omission of one of the two letters where one was quite sufficient, as *hyny*, instead of *hynny*, etc. We found the negative *di* often put where the praepositive *dy* ought to have been, this error we have corrected in very many instances.[32]

When these alterations became known in Wales, objections to the changes began to be raised. The Rev. John Roberts, vicar of Tremeirchion, Flintshire, the man who had supervised the original publication of the 1799 SPCK Welsh Bible, sent a letter to the

[32] *Ibid.*, II, 545.

SPCK informing them that the BFBS was preparing a new Welsh Bible and that, 'The orthography of the copy prepared for the press, is very much changed and altered, and makes the language a different dialect from that of the Bible in present use.'[33] Roberts was very much opposed to the new ideas on orthography. There is also a hint of mischief-making in other phrases in the letter: 'The whole care of the edition in question, I understand, has been committed to two leading characters among the Methodists'; 'Pocket Bibles are not so much wanted as Bibles with large types. This new edition seems more intended for the use of children and itinerant preachers than that of Christian families.'[34] The ranks of the SPCK directors, which included a number of those who were also directors of the BFBS, were aroused. Those concerned raised the matter in the BFBS meetings and Charles was asked to prepare a detailed memorandum listing the extent of the mistakes in the 1799 edition and explaining what orthographic changes he had introduced.

By early February 1805, however, the BFBS had more or less accepted Charles's approach to the work.[35] It was difficult for those who knew not a word of Welsh to adjudicate on such questions. They clearly trusted Charles but, in order to be seen to act impartially, they requested the Rev. Walter Davies, vicar of Llanwy-ddelan, Montgomeryshire, an antiquarian and literary critic, to act as moderator and comment in detail on the proposed corrections. Unknown to them, this was an inappropriate appointment in that John Roberts and Walter Davies were close friends.

This complication was soon pre-empted, however, by the announcement in March 1805 that the SPCK had decided that they would themselves prepare and publish a new edition of the Welsh Bible. This would, of course, be a family Bible of large type, as all of their editions had been. When the BFBS heard of this, again from those who were members of both committees, they decided in May 1805 that for convenience of use their new edition would have to be of the same orthography as that of the

[33] DEJ, II, 556.
[34] *Ibid.*
[35] *Ibid.*, II, 571-72.

SPCK. The BFBS therefore now asked Charles to prepare a copy of a new edition requiring him only to note 'any typographical errors' in it. That is, he was only to correct mistakes and not adapt the orthography in any way. Putting aside all his detailed changes, Charles was perfectly willing to agree. He knew that the success of the BFBS venture was the only way that Wales would receive a cheap edition of the Bible and, moreover, that the BFBS intention was 'to keep the types always standing which will afford a *constant* supply of Welsh Bibles.' On his own this time, the eight- to ten-hour-a-day shifts in his study continued, as he began again to work through the Bible.

But a further mistake had been made, and it would result in even further unnecessary labour for Charles. He had been told that the new edition was not to be based on the 1799 Bible, as first decided, but on an earlier SPCK version of 1746. He worked on the New Testament of this version therefore for three or four months, only to be told, in mid-August, that he had been misinformed. The version that the SPCK had decided upon was in fact the 1752 edition. In December 1805, therefore, Charles began afresh, for a third time, to prepare a corrected copy.

By September 1806 the New Testament was ready. The first load of five hundred Testaments (of what would eventually be a print run of 20,000) arrived at Bala on 25 September 1806. A description of the event was published in the *Christian Observer* for July 1810 and has been retold often since. D. E. Jenkins supplies one of the livelier accounts:

> By the Thursday ... the whole country was wild with excitement, and people began to pour into Bala from the neighbouring villages and hill-slopes at an early hour. When the time came for the carrier to be at no great distance from the town, the people went out in crowds to meet him; the old mare, which had ever before been obliged to struggle with her load as best she could, was now relieved of it, and muscular farm-servants pushed themselves for the first into the shafts. Ropes were adjusted and manned and maidened,

and the cart was literally swarmed on all sides; then the joyful procession proceeded towards the town, where they were hailed by crowds which blocked up the streets. Mr Charles, who had only arrived home from his tour with the Rev. Rowland Hill the night before, had no time to examine the contents – the impatience of the people hardly gave him time to unpack the boxes – for even his dignity, and the reverence in which he was held, could not prevent the people from snatching the first copy they could reach. How quickly the supply vanished … The first Scriptures of the British and Foreign Bible Society reached Bala, then, on September 25, 1806.[36]

Along with his own request for a further five hundred Testaments, Charles enclosed orders from a list of shopkeepers, amounting to 913 other copies. Among these was 'Mrs Foulkes, Shopkeeper, Machynlleth, Montgomeryshire.' Lydia was not to be forgotten.

Another year was to pass before the complete Bible was ready. As with the New Testaments, 20,000 copies were to be printed. The first dispatch from the printers in September 1807 was, naturally enough, addressed to Bala. When a copy was put into Charles's hands he examined it keenly. To his immense disappointment he found that the eighth chapter of the book of Judges was missing altogether, and that there were numerous other flaws. On 7 September the BFBS had passed that twenty-five of the best copies 'handsomely bound, accompanied with a respectful Letter from the Secretaries of acknowledgement of the essential services which he had rendered to this Institution' should be presented to him.[37] To his embarrassment, in the same letter that he expressed his thanks for their generosity, Charles also had to inform them of these serious defects in the new edition. Joseph Tarn wrote a fierce letter to William Owen rebuking him for his carelessness in proof-reading. The letter began with the following paragraph:

[36] DEJ, III, 68-69
[37] Ibid., III, 89.

Sir – It is extremely unpleasant to me to complain of inattention in the correction of the Welsh Bible; but such flagrant instances of neglect have already appeared, as to induce me to acquaint you that the credit of the British and Foreign Bible Society and of the University of Cambridge, are materially affected by them, the errors being so glaring as to be evident even to the country people; and we are informed that, unless they are corrected, the Bible will not sell for any money …[38]

Charles undertook the task of what amounted to a second proof-reading of the edition. He discovered scores of other mistakes, some of them involving the omission of whole verses. The printers produced errata slips which were sent out to the purchasers of the initial copies and the type was corrected for future impressions.

This appearance of the first Welsh BFBS Bible was soon followed by the publication of the new SPCK edition. The latter was called the '*1809 Bible*' but in fact it was 1810 before it was printed. Here again Charles had given substantial help; it was he who had corrected the proofs.

Fund-raising for the Bible Society

Long before the first Welsh New Testament arrived at Bala, the name of the British and Foreign Bible Society was very familiar in the country. As soon as the Society was formed in 1804, Charles began raising funds and establishing interest in it. The returns for the first collection made on behalf of the Society throughout Wales were included in an account published by the Society in August 1805. They suggest something of the enormous extra load of correspondence and book-keeping involved for Charles, on top of his ongoing duties, and this was acknowledged by the committee of the BFBS who passed a vote of thanks to Charles for his great efforts on their behalf.

[38] *Ibid.*, III, 95.

But Charles could not continue to give so much of his time to fund-raising. What was needed was for others in their own localities to commit themselves to this work. He had been helped by the establishing of local branches in one or two places with respect to the Sunday school work but for the Bible Society, with its international vision, any continuing progress would require a multiplicity of groups committed to the long-term support of the work. By letter and on his preaching journeys, Charles encouraged all to take up the work of establishing such auxiliary branches of the Society in their localities. For some years, the response was disappointing: many auxiliaries were springing up in England but none in Wales – a situation that seems quite inconsistent with the success of fund-raising in that country. The explanation lay in the fact that the Bible Society had agreed that the committees of any auxiliaries should be composed of both Dissenters and clergymen, as was that of the parent society. This condition raised no problems in England; sufficient clergymen there had some experience of co-operating with the old Nonconformist denominations. In Wales, however, the two north Wales bishops were strongly opposed to the society. Ostensibly, they argued that they could not be associated with the distribution of Bibles that did not contain the *Book of Common Prayer*. According to Charles, 'they do themselves no credit by asserting that the prayer book must go along with the Bible to the hands of the common people, *to guard it from doing them harm*.'[39] This argument, however, did not seem to have caused any problems for English clergymen. In reality, the problem was that the one man in Wales associated with the Bible Society was Thomas Charles – the Methodist. Though many individual north Wales clergymen were sympathetic to the BFBS they were bound by their bishops' opposition from taking a leading role. The only way that Charles could proceed was by bypassing the bishops and clergy and approaching individual Churchmen of influence and asking them to be chairmen and patrons of the auxiliary branches. On 7 January 1811, he chaired the meeting in which the first BFBS branch was

[39] DEJ, III, 455-57, 461.

formed in Wales at Llangollen, Denbighshire. It was not without considerable effort on his part that eventually a chain of branches was established throughout Wales.

HYFFORDDWR

YN EGWYDDORION Y

GREFYDD GRISTIONOGOL.

GAN Y DIWEDDAR

BARCH. THOMAS CHARLES, B.A.

" Bod yr enaid heb wybodaeth nid yw dda."—SOLOMON.

THE SEVENTY-EIGHTH EDITION.

CYHOEDDEDIG DROS Y PERCHENOG

GAN

HUGHES & SON, HOPE STREET, WREXHAM.

Title-page of a late nineteenth-century edition of Charles's *Hyfforddwr.*

12

FEEDING THE FLOCK OF GOD
(1800 ONWARDS)

WHEN weighing up Charles's life as a whole, what immediately strikes one is the immense volume of work which he accomplished in the various spheres of his activity. His life was one continual round of travelling, preaching, organizing, administering, studying, writing, and publishing. That he was enabled to fulfil all this work was due to various factors, four of which were particularly significant.

Firstly, his own physical strength and stamina: up until the critical illness of 1799 he was capable of seemingly inexhaustible labours. When itinerating, he could travel on horseback for up to a few hundred miles in a week. Even in the last fifteen years of his life (when he cut down on the number of journeys he undertook) his powers of concentration enabled him to work at his desk for long hours. This was the case until only a few months before his death. Rising with Sally at five in the morning, as she prepared for the day's business in the shop, he would spend the early hours of the day in his study, leaving the remaining hours for public duties.

Secondly, the greatest factor, humanly speaking, was the joy and emotional support which he derived from Sally. Their letters demonstrate the unfailing nature of their love for each other throughout their years together.

Thirdly, and most importantly of all, his confident, Christian assurance and his firm belief in the goodness of God's providence, meant that he continued with his labours from day to day, and from week to week, with no unnecessary debilitating worries and anxieties as to the rightness of his purpose and methods, or his popularity or otherwise amongst his peers.

A fourth factor was the helping hand that he gained from the contributions of his friend, Thomas Jones of Denbigh, to so many of his projects. In their intellectual abilities, their theological understanding, and their zeal for and faith in the gospel, the men were two of a kind. Their joint undertakings were strengthened by the complementary nature of the skills and abilities which they brought to the task.

Thomas Jones (1756–1820)

Like Charles, Jones was of gentry stock, but of a wealthier family; his father owned the freehold of the family home, Penucha, Caerwys, Flintshire. His formal education ended when he was fifteen years of age but he had by then learned to read Latin and Greek fluently and gained an interest in classical and antiquarian literature that was to remain with him all his life. In sharp contrast to Charles was the fact that throughout these years Jones was in contact with the Welsh-speaking culture and poetic tradition of the locality. His grasp of Welsh grammar, vocabulary, and idiom was far sounder than Charles's in the first years of their joint endeavours. The two young men had been converted at about the same time, and by the preaching of the same man: Charles, as already described, while listening to Daniel Rowland preaching in January 1773, and Jones, a few months earlier, in September 1772, at the Caerwys society, on hearing an account of a sermon by Rowland from a fellow-member. Within a month of Charles's settlement at Bala (August 1783), Jones preached for the first time for the Methodists at Caerwys. Charles introduced his friend to the theological treasures of the classical Reformed tradition, and with his acute intellect and habits of study as diligent as those of Charles himself, Jones eventually became the leading theologian of the Welsh Methodist movement. The seniority within the friendship, however, never changed: 'Reverend brother,' Jones wrote at one point, 'or rather should I say, my father.'[1]

---

[1] John Humphrey and John Roberts, *Cofiant y Parch. Thomas Jones* (Denbigh: 1820), 7; quoted in Andras Iago, DDM (2014), 176.

As they approached the beginning of a new century, the two men became increasingly aware of the frustrated desires (brought about by their own activities) of their Methodist flocks. Having been taught to read, and now meeting regularly to study and discuss the teachings of the Bible, the believers were naturally longing for more Christian literature. Greatest of all, of course, was the longing for their own personal copy of the Bible. But this in turn led to a demand for all kinds of Christian literature – commentaries, sermons, works on theology and church history, practical and ethical teaching, news of the progress of Christianity at home and in foreign parts. The hunger of the thousands of spiritually reborn men and women constituting the Methodist societies had somehow to be met.

Thomas Jones, Denbigh.

THOMAS CHARLES OF BALA

Trysorfa Ysbrydol (*Spiritual Treasury*)

Charles and Jones decided to produce a Welsh Christian periodical, based on the English magazine with which they were so familiar: *The Evangelical Magazine*. The first notice of their intention appeared, appropriately enough, in the pages of that magazine. In a note in the issue of March 1799 describing the success of their distributed letter about *The Duff*, Charles added:

> We are commencing a Magazine in the Welsh language in which an account of missions and other religious intelligence will be regularly published every quarter. Whilst you supplicate the Throne of Grace for our brethren in the distant islands, don't forget the poor Britons among their barren mountains.[2]

This would be the first periodical of any kind associated with the Calvinistic Methodists (and one of the very first periodicals published in the Welsh language). The editing, translation of articles into Welsh, proof-reading, and all dealings with the printers were the responsibility of Thomas Jones, whereas Charles gathered most of the material.

The first issue, entitled *Trysorfa Ysbrydol* (*Spiritual Treasury*) with a circulation of six hundred, appeared in April 1799, comprising sixty-four pages and costing sixpence. Six numbers were produced: April, June and October 1799; January and October 1800; December 1801. It was initially intended to publish every three months but the illnesses of one or other of the editors put paid to these hopes. These illnesses, together with the rising cost of paper and difficulties over distribution, brought the venture to a halt at the end of 1801. Eight years later, when his own health was considerably improved, Charles re-established the periodical with an issue in March 1809. By this time Thomas Jones had very heavy writing commitments of his own and Charles was therefore the sole editor. This second series, with the shorter title of *Trysorfa*, ran for twelve issues, from March 1809 to November 1813.[3]

---

[2] *Evangelical Magazine*, 1799, 260; DEJ, II, 192.
[3] Simon Lloyd edited a third series from 1819 to 1822. Then in 1830 the

The contents of the *Trysorfa Ysbrydol* show clearly the compilers' belief in the responsibility of every Christian to give glory to God for every aspect of his creation. Christ's pre-eminence is to be recognized in the life of the believer, in his lordship over his church and his universe, in culture, in history, in all the ways of providence, as well as in every teaching of his word. One modern historian has written:

> The reader of the *Trysorfa* ... was expected to pay attention to the work of the nurture of the soul and to follow the development of the British war against Napoleon. In the October issue of 1799, for example, he is called upon to meditate on Creation on one page; on another he may study the history of William Wroth; he may then work through a discussion on Calvinism; he will be entertained by proverbs, a poem, and 'Selected Sayings'; he may receive the minutes of various Associations, stories of 'godly' events, and the history of the four persecutions of the early Christians; he may then digest a lengthy sermon on 2 Cor. 2:15-16. And this list comprises only a little over half the contents of the issue![4]

Most issues would contain one or two short articles, letters or quotations from eminent writers of the past: Martin Luther, Lady Jane Grey, Robert Rollock, Walter Cradock, Edmund Calamy, Daniel Rowland, George Whitefield, James Hervey, John Newton, Philip Doddridge, for example. The periodical also became the means by which future well-known Welsh authors first began to discover their writing gifts, men such as Robert Jones, Rhoslan, Richard Jones, Wern, Llanfrothen, Simon Lloyd, Bala, and Thomas Jones, Creaton.

One of the longest sequences of articles (one chapter in the first series and six others in the second series) drew upon the memories

---

Calvinistic Methodist Church of Wales produced a denominational periodical entitled *Y Drysorfa* on the same pattern as the original *Trysorfa Ysbrydol*. Its circulation in the 1870s was over 7,000. It continued for over a hundred years, the last issue appearing in 1968.

[4] Derec Ll. Morgan, in HMGC2, 482.

of John Evans, the leader of the Bala society. The *Ymddiddanion rhwng Scrutator a Senex* (*Conversations between Scrutator and Senex*) are a primary source of information on the early history of Methodism in the districts of Bala, Dolgellau, Barmouth, and Anglesey from 1739 onwards. The *scrutator* ('questioner') is Charles and John Evans is the *senex* ('old man').

The other major historical contribution from Charles was the inclusion of the minutes he had taken of many of the private sessions of the North Wales Calvinistic Methodist Associations.[5] In these meetings the clergymen, ministers, and exhorters would consider '*spiritual matters only*. By spiritual matters is meant the doctrines of the gospel, together with spiritual experience of them; religious exercises, Church discipline, etc.'[6] The developing nature of these discussions reveal something of Charles's leadership and pastoral care of the Methodist preachers of the northern Association. These minutes were to prove immensely valuable to the denomination later in the nineteenth century, during times of theological controversy and when considering the possibility of publishing a confession of faith. In the absence of any creed or confession drawn up by the founding fathers and early exhorters, the nineteenth-century leaders studied these minutes in order to arrive at an accurate picture of the theological emphases and balances of their predecessors. The minutes of the Bala Association of June 1809, for example, in which the meeting had discussed their understanding of the doctrine of redemption, were very important in 1823 when deciding on the form of words of Article 18 of the *Confession*, 'On Redemption.'[7]

Both Charles and Jones recognized the need for converts to grasp something of the historical development of the faith, especially the history of the gospel in their own country. Many issues

[5] Morgan provides a translation of five of these *Minutes*, and describes the route by which the impressions made by these discussions permeated down through the various monthly meetings by word of mouth to the individual chapels and societies. *Spiritual Counsels*, 437-77; xl-xli [325-55; xxxiii-xxxiv].

[6] See Rule 7 on p. 150 above.

[7] See below, pp. 343-44.

of the *Trysorfa* therefore included a short life of an eminent Christian, particularly Welsh Christians. The lives of the following were included in the eighteen issues: William Wroth, Llanfaches; Walter Cradock; Griffith Jones, Llanddowror; Thomas Gouge; Stephen Hughes; John Penry; William Lloyd, Carmarthenshire; Howel Harris; George Whitefield; Edmund Prys; Peter Williams. The January 1813 issue contained the first brief biography published of William Williams, Pantycelyn. At the time of Charles's death, John Williams, Pantycelyn, the hymn-writer's son wrote to his brother, 'He published, on my request, the history of our father's life; I gave him the skeleton, and he covered it with skin; I sent the materials, and he raised the edifice.' The biography provides an example of the homely and informal style used by Charles in this type of article. When mentioning Williams' prolific literary works he included the following note:

> *He was very guilty of that unhealthy practice of staying up late at night to study and write. Rarely did he go to bed before two* o'clock in the morning. I am certain, from experience, that two hours of sleep before twelve o'clock is better for one's health than four or five hours after twelve; and for any work that requires labour, attention and mental concentration, it is far better to study from four to eight in the morning, without eating but little in order to keep the stomach comfortable, especially in the summer. Only lazy, unemployed fools sleep in the day rather than in the night. There is nothing that sweetens as well as prolongs life more than rising early – nor more advantageous for pressing on with God's work in the world. In this, it must be confessed, the old servant of the Lord was amiss.[8]

Gomer M. Roberts comments that, 'Williams was not lazy or unemployed, and as for prolonging life – well, Williams lived to see his three score years and ten, but Charles, the defender of early rising, died before reaching sixty.'[9]

[8] *Trysorfa Ysbrydol*, Series II (1813), 448.
[9] Gomer M. Roberts, *Y Per Ganiedydd*, Vol. 1 (1949), 193.

The following, an abridgement of an unsigned article which may have been written by Thomas Charles, from the second series (December, 1809), is typical of the practical emphasis on which he so often insisted in his contributions to the magazine.

Indications of Pride

Pride causes a man to blame the actions of his leaders too readily and makes him uncomfortable under their rule.

A proud man would rather rule than obey.

If any office is vacant, a proud man judges that he is the most capable of filling it.

When a proud man views the actions of his leaders he judges that he would do better.

The proud always remembers all that he knows rather than all that he does not know.

Pride prejudices a man in his judgement of his own virtues and failings when compared to the virtues and failings of others.

It is hard to satisfy a proud man.

A proud man loves to have the pre-eminence.

He expects all the good that he has done to be remembered by others.

His flatterers are his best friends.

When a proud man gains the upper hand, he is dictatorial and rude.

He finds it unbearable to be corrected.

Wherever he is, he is unsettled unless he gets his own way.

He tends to be argumentative and easily provoked.

Though he may avoid it in public, yet secretly he is a great boaster.

A proud man is cynical and unkind: few are honest, true and faithful in his opinion, not even those who truly are so.

He is very ready to reprove and convict others, but hates being reproved himself.

When he is convicted, he denies or belittles his fault.

The proud are talkative: readier to talk than to listen, to teach rather than be taught.

The proud man is ashamed to move to a lower position; he is unwilling to submit to such a providence.

He finds it hard to forgive whenever anyone trespasses against him.

Lastly, the proud man is immoderate in his longing that he should be honoured after his death. Many a gravestone has been raised by pride; many books written; many good deeds done (deeds good in themselves, but worthless when measured by that which motivated them); many hospitals, charities and schoolrooms are raised by pride.[10]

It has been generally accepted that the *Trysorfa*, especially in its first series, became the model for all subsequent Welsh denominational periodicals.[11]

The Arminian Controversy

Some years later, in the period between the publications of the first two series of the *Trysorfa*, Thomas Charles had another reason to be grateful to Thomas Jones. The Arminian controversy arose in Wales from 1800 onwards when missionaries were sent by the Wesleyan Conference to north Wales. The issue would have affected Charles personally because of the affiliations of his much-respected step-father-in-law, Thomas Foulks. As has been mentioned, Foulks maintained his membership and paid his subscription to the Chester Wesleyan church throughout his life, while at the same

[10] *Trysorfa*, Series II, (1813), 110-12.
[11] DEJ, II, 211.

time ministering with great acceptance, firstly to the Bala society and then to the society in Machynlleth.

Foulks was himself embarrassed when, about 1791, he received a letter from the Wesleyan Conference asking him if he would like them to establish a mission in north Wales. A further embarrassment might have arisen some time later when Owen Davies and John Hughes, the two Wesleyan missioners in north Wales, called upon him at his home in Machynlleth. At that time the literature controversy had not begun and the Wesleyans were being invited to preach in the pulpits of their Calvinistic brethren. Owen Davies actually preached very acceptably to the Machynlleth society. Within a fortnight, Thomas Foulks had died and thus was removed from all awkwardness and embarrassment.[12] It was not long after his death, however, that the climate changed. More extreme presentations of Arminianism were published, misrepresenting the doctrines of grace. Calvinists responded with equally extreme language and soon a Calvinistic/Arminian pamphlet war was waging in north Wales which was to continue intermittently for some thirty years.

In this situation, Thomas Jones proved to be an even more capable author than Charles, as he set out in clear, logical, forthright Welsh, the arguments of the Fathers, of the schoolmen of the Middle Ages, of the Protestant reformers and the Marian martyrs, and of the creeds and confessions, for the sovereignty of God's actions in salvation, and the scriptural reasons underlying those arguments. He did this initially with two productions: a booklet of seventy-two pages, *Y Drych Athrawiaethol* (*The Doctrinal Mirror*), in 1806, and a book of four hundred and fifty pages, *Ymddiddanion Crefyddol rhwng Ystyriol a Hyffordd* (*Religious Conversations between Two Neighbours, Mindful and Instructed*), in 1807. Then, in 1808, in response to an answer from Owen Davies he brought out a further book of 144 pages, entitled *Sylwadau ar Lyfr gan Mr Owen Davies* (*Comments on a Book by Mr Owen Davies*). It is significant that these three major productions have the imprint,

[12] DEJ, II, 429.

'Published by R. Saunderson,' which indicates they were produced on Thomas Charles's press in Bala.[13] Indeed, when sending his final draft of *Y Drych Athrawiaethol* to the press Thomas Jones requested Charles, 'Look them over and alter, add or abridge as you shall see occasion.' In the book he assured his readers that the contents had been authorized by Charles and John Evans, and also that it appeared with the blessing of the Association. The volumes are as much a delineation of Charles's doctrinal views therefore as of those of Thomas Jones, as in fact was everything that came from the pens of this productive two-headed literary factory during the years of their co-operation. Andras Iago makes the significant comment:

> These volumes have not been greatly read by later historians and as a consequence our understanding of the thought of the Methodist leaders of the period is all the poorer. Together with the more famous *Scriptural Dictionary* they are amongst the most ambitious and brilliant of Welsh Methodist productions since the works of Pantycelyn. They are not mere apologetic essays but confident statements of the position of the Methodist movement in God's saving plan. They present a glorious vision of a church history that equates Calvinism with the true Catholicism of the ages. This was the creed of the apostles and the Early Church Fathers and it will flourish whenever the Holy Spirit is poured out powerfully upon the Church. Jones acknowledges the long years of darkness from the reign of Constantine to the Protestant Reformation. He blames this on the attitude of mind springing from a spiritual rebellion, Arminianism, that arose against the true faith.[14]

It may have been a comfort to Thomas Charles that his step-father-in-law had passed away without having to live through the bitterness that arose from the Wesleyan controversy.

---

[13] See the paragraphs on the Bala Press, on pp. 238-40 below.
[14] Iago, in DDM (2014), 179-80.

The Bala Press

Charles and Jones viewed their publications as the products of a partnership, not only between themselves but also between them and the Methodist body as a whole. This is seen in the letter from Charles to Robert Jones in January 1799, following the Denbigh Association in December 1798:

> I am eager that [the *Trysorfa*] should be truly serviceable to the Connexion and to the country in general. But I do not think it will be so unless it be one in spirit and heart with the Connexion. The Connexion has adopted it.[15]

Similarly, as has been mentioned, the *Rheolau a Dybenion y Cymde-ithasau Neillduol* (*Rules and Designs of the Religious Societies*), 1801, was agreed and accepted by the Bala Association of that year. All their writings, apart from Jones's early poetry, were, 'in all practical senses connexional publications.'[16]

In nearly all their dealings with various presses the two authors experienced difficulties. The presses were far from Bala, resulting in transport problems which caused long delays before proofs and shipments arrived. The printers were so slow in completing orders that their cash flow problems meant they were pressing for payment almost as soon as the contract was delivered, and before any income from sales had been generated. The same problems also slowed down the distribution side:

> Mr Charles was as capable an organizer as Wales had ever seen, yet even he found some of his publications delayed until subscribers had all but got tired of waiting ... and Sunday Schools were sometimes kept for several weeks without supplies of books.[17]

The only solution, it appeared, was for the two men to establish their own press at Bala. On one of his visits to Chester, Charles

[15] DEJ, II, 202.
[16] Brynley F. Roberts, JHS, 16/17 (1992-93), 15.
[17] DEJ, II, 444.

mentioned to the Stringer sisters the possibility of establishing such a press, and asked them if they knew of anyone to whom the work could be trusted. They mentioned a young man, Robert Saunderson who had worshipped with them at Broughton Chapel while learning his trade at the Chester press of W. C. Jones. Having completed his apprenticeship he was now working as a printer in Liverpool. He agreed to move to Bala, and Charles wrote to him explaining the plans for the press:

> I shall be very glad to see you any day you may come. We have employment enough for some years for you if we live. Indeed we have more work at present than we can get forward in time. I wish to call it the Lord's press and to be subservient only to the great Redeemer's cause. There is no other cause worth supporting or troubling ourselves about. I have several English books in contemplation. Remember me very kindly in the Lord to all my dear friends at Chester, Tarvin, etc.[18]

A Blaeu flatbed press was bought in 1802, new Greek and Hebrew type bought from Caslon and Catherwood, type-founders of London, and a number of works were brought out. All of these bore the imprint *Jones & Co., Bala*, i.e. Thomas Jones, with Sally Charles as the '*Company*.'[19] As an ordained clergyman Charles did not believe that his name should be associated with 'lay dealings.'[20] Also involved at this point was John Humphreys (1767–1829). He had been converted during the 1791–94 Revival and was employed by W. C. Jones at Chester to superintend the Welsh orders, as Jones himself was not a Welsh speaker. He was taken into the Bala company because he had begun to compile and publish a Welsh Bible dictionary and Charles had joined him in this work. This was the origin of Charles's *Geiriadur Ysgrythyrol* (*Scriptural Dictionary*), discussed in the next chapter. The *Jones & Co.* partnership was

[18] *Ibid.*, II, 446.
[19] Brynley F. Roberts, JHS, 16/17 (1992-93), 16.
[20] DEJ, II, 473.

dissolved by September 1804, with Sally Charles continuing, in name at least, as the sole director.[21]

> Under the management of the remarkable printer Robert Saunderson ... [i]t flourished and became a crucially important printing house for Methodists in north Wales, publishing (sometimes under its imprint Cambrian Press) some 55 titles ... up to Charles's death in 1814. It continued even afterwards ... under the ownership of Robert Saunderson ... The titles are a roll-call of the seminal instructional works and catechisms of the second Methodist generation ...[22]

The old Bala patriarch, John Evans, was heard to say in 1813 that there had 'never been so much buying of spectacles in the country as now.'[23]

Ann Griffiths

In 1806 the Bala Press published *Casgliad o Hymnau* (*A Collection of Hymns*), compiled and edited by Charles, with the help of Robert Jones, Rhos-lan. The name of the author of each hymn was not provided; indeed, it has been shown that some of the hymns were made up of verses by different authors. But among the collection, in print for the first time, were about twenty hymns by one of Wales's greatest hymn-writers. The name of Ann Griffiths (1776–1805) is held in greater respect by Welsh Christians even than that of Mary Jones.

Ann Thomas was born in Dolwar Fach Farm, Llanfihangel-yng-Ngwynfa, Montgomeryshire, some twenty miles from Bala, and converted when about twenty-one years old. She joined the local Methodist society, superintended by John Hughes, Pontrobert,

[21] Thomas Jones went on to establish his own press, firstly at Rhuthun in 1808, and then at Denbigh in 1809. He eventually sold the business to his manager, Thomas Gee, in 1813, and it prospered, under the name of *Gwasg Gee*, as one of Wales's leading printers of Welsh books until its demise in 2001.

[22] Brynley F Roberts, JHS, 16/17 (1992-93), 16-17.

[23] E. Wyn James, 'Pererinion ar y Ffordd: Thomas Charles ac Ann Griffiths,' JHS, 29/30 (2005-06), 81.

one of Charles's schoolteachers. John Davies, the young man who was recommended by Charles to the LMS and who was sent by that Society to Tahiti, was also a member at Llanfihangel-yng-Ngwynfa, and was a close friend. They would often have joined their fellow-believers in walking over Berwyn Mountain to Bala to hear Thomas Charles preach and to receive the Lord's Supper from his hands. As they returned homewards, all would listen to Ann Thomas, with her remarkable memory, repeating the sermons which they had heard that day. Before her conversion she had been a frivolous, careless girl, looking forward only to the next village dance, but as she rapidly matured under the preaching, and her own reading, of the word, she spent long hours in meditation on the wonders of the person and work of Christ. Ann would express

The grave of Ann Griffiths at Llanfihangel-yng-Ngwynfa.

her experiences by means of poetry. Her verses are called hymns today, but they were never intended for public singing; indeed, they were not meant to be seen by anyone but herself, except for members of the family or the occasional close friend in the society. 'Her hymns are a kind of spiritual diary, therefore, recording and crystallising her experiences and her spiritual insights.'[24] No more than thirty of them have survived, and the story of their survival is fascinating. A maid, called Ruth Evans, came to work and live at Ann's home. She was also a believer and had a good singing voice. Ann would repeat a new verse to her and ask her for a hymn tune with which to sing it. Ruth would sing the verse until she had memorized it.

Ann married a farmer, Thomas Griffiths, but she died ten months later soon after giving birth, aged twenty-nine. Though her married life was so short, she is always known as Ann Griffiths. Ruth, her maid, married John Hughes, Pontrobert, and his close friendship with Charles meant that Ruth met the clergyman often and would recite Ann's verses from memory to him. Charles asked John Hughes to write down all that Ruth could remember, and in this way the precious verses found their place in his hymn-book. They are amongst the most solidly doctrinal hymns written in Welsh, with every verse full of direct and indirect Scriptural allusions. Their form, however, is of the most personal confession and devotion, revealing how the young farm-girl had explored exhaustively the great truths concerning Jesus Christ and his salvation and had assimilated them fully in her own spiritual experience. Charles's theological teaching had directly influenced Ann through his own preaching and through the preaching and conversation of his two school-masters, John Davies and John Hughes, both of whom had kept school at Ann's home in Dolwar Fach on different occasions.

The theology of both Charles and Ann was founded on belief in the covenants – the covenant of works and that of grace. Charles's

---

[24] E. Wyn James, *Rhyfeddaf Fyth ...*, *the hymns and letters of Ann Griffiths* (Gregynog Press, 1998), 105.

Yr Hyfforddwr (*The Instructor*) has a chapter 'On the Two Covenants' and his entry on *Cyfamod* ('Covenant') is the longest in his *Scriptural Dictionary*. Similarly, the words 'covenant,' 'law,' 'commandment' and 'image' (*cyfamod, cyfraith, deddf* and *delw*) are foundational in Ann Griffiths's hymns. Their view of the Bible was also identical; they viewed it as a single, organic work of divine revelation, with Christ the key to the understanding of the whole. They saw in the Old Testament shadows or types of the person of Christ and of the salvation obtained through him, and in both Old and New Testaments, pictures of the ways in which Christ would relate to his people throughout the centuries.[25] His help in preserving the thirty hymns of Ann Griffiths, seventy-three stanzas in all, is not the least of the many kindnesses which Thomas Charles bestowed upon his countrymen.

Yr Hyfforddwr (*The Instructor*)

The reason for Charles's firm belief in the necessity of catechizing was the same as that of Griffith Jones before him. Both men had experienced the disappointment of discovering that many who had attended their preaching for a considerable period were yet still lacking in spiritual and doctrinal understanding. For new converts, the sermon needed to be supported by frequent catechizing, so that the believers had a clear framework in their minds of the main biblical teachings. As more and more Christian families were being raised, with more and more of the children becoming literate, the catechizing of children became a standard Calvinistic Methodist practice.

In writing catechisms Charles was influenced by Griffith Jones's *Catechism* (1752), which was itself an extension of the *Catechism of the Church of England* (1662), and he was also very familiar with the *Shorter Catechism* (1648) of the Westminster Assembly. His first catechism was published in 1789 and it passed through various editions as he supplied the changing needs of his schools. By 1807 he had over twenty years' experience of teaching and catechizing

[25] E. Wyn James, 'Pererinion ar y Ffordd,' JHS, 29/30 (2005-06), 86-88.

children. His final complete version was the *Hyfforddwr*, printed by the Bala Press in 1807. Its full title was *Hyfforddwr yn Egwyddorion y Grefydd Gristionogol* (*An Instructor in the Institutes of the Christian Religion*) which reflects, of course, the title of John Calvin's *Institutio Christianae Religionis*. It became for Calvinistic Methodist Welshmen what the *Shorter Catechism* of the Westminster Assembly was for Presbyterian Scotsmen. The first printing was of 17,000 copies and the demand for it was exceptional. Eighty editions were to be brought out in the nineteenth century (each running to many thousands of copies) along with a host of pirated versions in America.[26] Lewis Edwards believed that it was by learning the *Hyfforddwr* that Wales was enlightened.[27]

The first few questions and answers of the *Westminster Shorter Catechism* are justifiably famous, but those of Thomas Charles's *Hyfforddwr* have their own unique directness (the Scripture references are omitted):

1. *Who made you?*
   God.

2. *What is God?*
   God is a spirit.

3. *Is there more than one God?*
   There is only one God.

4. *Is there more than one Person in the Godhead?*
   'There are three that bear record in heaven; the Father, the Word, and the Holy Spirit.'

5. *Is each one of these Persons true God?*
   Yes; co-eternal and co-equal.

6. *Is not this a great mystery?*
   Yes, a great mystery to be believed, and not to be comprehended.

---

[26] DEJ, III, 180; 656-60.
[27] Lewis Edwards, *Traethodau Llenyddol* (Wrexham, 1867), 277.

7. *What are the works that are appropriated to each one?*
   Creation and Election to the Father; Redemption and
   Intercession to the Son; and Sanctification to the Holy
   Spirit.

The *Hyfforddwr* is a longer work than the *Shorter Catechism*,
with 271 questions within sixty-two pages, compared to the latter's
107 questions in thirty-two pages. This is only to be expected in that
it is a work aimed mainly at children; many of the individual questions and answers are shorter and simpler than the multiple clauses
of the answers of the latter. However, there is still considerably more
material in the *Hyfforddwr* than in its counterpart. Yet, as with
the *Shorter Catechism* in Scotland and America, many thousands
of Welsh children learnt all its sixty-two pages, with their proof-
texts, by heart. Both of them differ 'from the catechisms of the first
generation of Protestants, in that they are particularly interested in
man and in his experience of salvation. The objectivity of the earlier
catechisms is striking: the emphasis is on God. But after the first
generation a subjective element is more evident, and this emphasis
was deepened by the Methodist Revival.'[28]

One aspect of the *Hyfforddwr* that has often been noted is
Charles's achievement in producing a Christo-centric catechism in
which both the objective elements of the gospel and its subjective
elements are interpreted in the light of the person of Christ.[29] Thus,
for example, when discussing justification (Q. 133), in response to
the question, 'How does the righteousness of Christ become our
possession?' Charles answers: 'By its imputation of God, and our
union with Christ.' Or when discussing sanctification (Q. 149), the
question, 'How does the Holy Spirit produce this transformation?'
is answered: 'By uniting the soul to Christ; because it is by our
union with Christ that every grace and privilege flows towards us.'
According to Lewis Edwards,

[28] R. Tudur Jones, in Geraint Bowen (ed.), *Y Traddodiad Rhyddiaith* (1976),
339.
[29] D. Densil Morgan, in HMGC3, 117. This reference contains a useful
synopsis of the *Hyfforddwr*, 112-18.

The imputation of Christ's righteousness to all who believe is a truth; but the greatest truth, that which is the scriptural reason for this imputation, is the spiritual union between the believer and the person of the Lord Jesus Christ. The believer is in Christ, and Christ in him. They are one in the eyes of the Law: therefore all the merit of the Infinite Person, in all he did and suffered in the place of sinners, is accounted to the transgressor.[30]

One evident difference between Charles's *Hyfforddwr* and the *Shorter Catechism* is their treatment of the covenants. In the *Shorter Catechism*, they are referred to briefly, in passing, in Questions 12, 16, 20, and 94. In Charles's work, however, a whole chapter is given to 'The Two Covenants,' and their nature is described in twelve questions (66 to 77). The chapter lies between that on the person of Christ and the one on the offices of Christ, and it provides the starting point from which Charles proceeds to discuss the nature of redemption.

Fresh awakenings (1805–08) and Children's Associations

George Burder, the secretary of the London Missionary Society, wrote to Charles to ask if he would preach at the Society's Annual Meeting in May, 1806. The inter-denominational nature of the Society necessitated a degree of diplomacy when it came to the choice of speakers on these occasions. 'Mr Fleming of Kirkaldy in Scotland, Mr Bradley of Manchester (Independent) and Mr Day of Bristol (Clergyman)' had been asked, and, 'We wish also to have one who has moved more particularly in the Methodist Connexion (Lady H's), and there is no one with equal satisfaction we can invite. Do not then my dear Sir refuse.' But Charles did refuse at first, pleading insufficiency. Burder therefore pressed him more forcibly so that Charles consented to this second request. At the insistence of Rowland Hill, he preached the first of the anniversary services on Wednesday morning, 14 May 1806, at Surrey Chapel, Hill's church in London.[31]

[30] Lewis Edwards, *Traethodau Duwinyddol* (Wrexham, 1871), 628.
[31] DEJ, III, 138-39.

Rowland Hill

More than a year before this date, in April 1805, Charles had written to Burder on a different topic entirely. A further spiritual awakening had begun in a Sunday school meeting in Aberystwyth, Cardiganshire, conducted by two seventeen year-old boys. As they read and prayed with their charges the Holy Spirit fell upon them, the children and the other adults present. Before they concluded the meeting a great crowd of people had gathered about the house. Charles described the progress of this revival in his letter to Burder and it was subsequently printed in the *Evangelical Magazine*, of which Burder was the editor:

> Sir, I am happy to inform you, there is a very pleasing revival in some parts of Wales. At Aberystwyth, and in the adjacent parts, there are general and powerful awakenings among the young people and children. Some hundreds have joined the religious societies in those parts. I was there lately, at an Association of the Calvinistic Methodists, held at Aberystwyth.

The concourse of people assembled on the occasion was computed to amount at least to 20,000. The sight to a religious mind was pleasing beyond expression! A stage was erected in an open common for the conveniency of addressing this vast multitude. Ten preachers in the course of two days, delivered very animated and impressive discourses to the most solemn, attentive and affected congregations I ever saw. The preaching was evidently in the demonstration of the Spirit and with power. Hundreds of children, from eight years old and upwards, might be seen in the congregation, hearing the word with all the attention of the most devout Christian, and bathed in tears. This work first began at Aberystwyth, in the Sunday-School there, in which two young men, under twenty years of age, were the teachers.[32] Soon after the commencement of the school, both teachers and scholars came under serious impressions. The work prevails at present over a large district, fifty miles by twenty. In travelling the roads, it was pleasing to hear the ploughman and the driver of the team singing hymns whilst at their work. Nothing else was heard in all these parts. This I can testify, with satisfaction and joy.[33]

So striking was the number of young people convicted in this awakening that it became known as 'The Children's Revival.' This 'time of refreshing' was given a new impetus by the arrival of the first shipment of New Testaments to Bala in the autumn of 1806, as described earlier. The appetite of the young people for the word was so strong, it is said that they spent whole nights reading it. Labourers would take a copy with them to the fields so that they might read them during any breaks in the work.

---

[32] The 'two young men' were cousins. One was Owen Jones, who was afterwards to help William Owen in correcting the first Welsh Bible of the BFBS; the other was Robert Jones, a grocer in Aberystwyth, who became an elder of the Aberystwyth society and who married Thomas Charles's niece, the daughter of his brother, David. At their home, eighteen years later, the *Calvinistic Methodist Confession of Faith* of 1823 was drawn up.

[33] DEJ, III, 114; *Evangelical Magazine* (1805), 235.

In 1808 Charles began to arrange Sunday school Associations, or *Children's Associations*, as they were called. The first was held at Blaenannerch in Cardiganshire at Whitsun, 1808, with William Morris, Cilgerran, and Ebenezer Richard, Tregaron, leading. Ten Sunday schools joined together on the day. Each school was given a topic and questioned upon it. The children from each school would gather together and then walk, up to perhaps ten miles, to the appointed venue where a day would be spent catechising; each service was some three or four hours in length. The first held at Bala was on the 12 November 1808. The following report is from a letter written by Charles to Joseph Tarn, and published in the *Evangelical Magazine* for 1809:

> Last Sunday fortnight, we had an association of children here at Bala … Our large chapel overflowed, and the effects of the work of that day are very evident and beneficial in the town and neighbourhood; and they are everywhere, in different parts of the country, anxious for similar meetings …
>
> I never knew any means as successful to bring all the grown-up young people to engage in the work of learning the Scriptures. Their whole attention is at present engaged in preparing for another meeting; and nothing else is talked of but the Bible, and consulting together what Scriptures are applicable to the points in hand. The points are: The Duties of Parents and Children; Husbands and Wives; Masters and Servants; Pastors and People; Magistrates and Subjects; Buyers and Sellers. They are to find out Scriptures that are to direct us in all these important points. We have already treated on the first principles and most fundamental points of Christianity.[34]

In the *Christian Guardian* magazine of the same year a fuller account of the Associations, taken from a personal letter by Charles to an interested supporter, was published:

[34] DEJ, III, 200.

... As no place of worship is spacious enough to contain the immense concourse of people which attend on those occasions, we have been obliged to erect stages out of doors in the field – one, very large, for the children to stand upon, two or three schools at a time, and the other for the catechists opposite to that for the children, at fifteen or eighteen yards distance; the place between is for the congregation assembled to stand to hear. We begin the work early in the morning, and the whole day is spent in these public examinations; every opportunity lasts three or four hours, and is generally concluded with short and appropriate addresses to the children and the congregation. We have had on these occasions from fifteen to twenty schools assembled together.[35]

In many neighbourhoods, these associations were greatly instrumental in removing prejudices against the Sunday schools. Their public nature also provided an opportunity to address local problems. Thus, for one association, Charles told the teachers of the Sunday schools to ask the children to look for verses that condemned the evils of drunkenness, prostitution, and dancing:

The children's topic became known, and it caused considerable disturbance and discussion. The day before the fair he arrived according to his promise. The children had gathered together and a large crowd had come to hear. After singing and praying, the catechizing began. Mr Charles asked;

'Is dancing a sin, my children?'

'Yes,' said one boy, with emphasis, 'because of the dancing of Herodias's daughter, the head of John the Baptist was cut off.'

'Does Scripture condemn it?'

'Yes,' he answered, and then recited the verses, 'Woe unto them that rise up early in the morning, that they may follow strong drink; that continue until night, till wine inflame them! And the harp, and the viol, the tabret, and pipe, and

---

[35] DEJ, III, 196-97.

wine, are in their feasts: but they regard not the work of the
Lord, neither consider the operation of his hands.'

In a similar manner, various vices were discussed, one
by one. Mr Charles warmed to the task of questioning; the
children answered with much relevance; and soon the guilty
hearers began to feel ashamed and to drop their heads. At
the end, he exhorted them, with great tenderness, to leave
their ways and to seek higher pleasures. The effect was overwhelming. The next day, the fair was transformed. Once
their trade was over, the people returned home sober and
serious; the musicians were left to themselves in the public
houses, and there was no one to hear the harp. Soon, the
harpists were seen leaving the place in disappointment,
cursing 'the priest with the black cap' who had bewitched
the people.[36]

The effect of these Associations was to increase still further the
focus and influence of the Revival. The Baptist and Independent
churches, learning from the Methodists, had taken up the same
methods and were similarly blessed.

Through all his years as a minister, before and after joining
the Methodists, we find Thomas Charles involved in work for,
or among, children. During his innumerable preaching tours
throughout all areas of Wales he would look out, or plan ahead, for
opportunities to meet with the pupils of Sunday schools. A typical
comment in one of his letters reads,

I am just returned from Montgomeryshire, where I have
been for two days, highly gratified with my dear children
everywhere. They meet me with cheerful countenances,
greet me with chapters without number, and stand up cou-
rageously before the whole country to answer anything I
may think proper to ask them. This is my heaven on earth.[37]

[36] Jones and Morgan, *Calvinistic Methodist Fathers*, Vol. 2 (2008), 292-93.
[37] *Memoir*, 414-15.

Journeys in Wales and Ireland

The infection and illness resulting from his frostbitten thumb had kept Charles from all long preaching tours for over four years (September 1799 to mid 1805). By 1806 he was again undertaking longer periods away from home. Charles's close friendship with the Rev. Rowland Hill (1744–1833), founder and pastor of the independent Surrey Hill Chapel, Blackfriars Road, London, dated from the beginning of his visits to London and from their service together as directors of the LMS and the RTS. They had agreed on a preaching tour together through north Wales.[38] They met in Shropshire at the home of Sir Richard Hill, Rowland's brother, and departed on Monday, 1 September 1806, preaching at Wrexham, Chester, and Denbigh, and reaching Bala on 8 September. After a day's rest they continued to Llanrwst, Anglesey and Caernarvonshire. They also preached in Dolgellau, Corris, Machynlleth, and Llanidloes. Altogether their tour was only two days short of three weeks.

Charles was also appointed with others to tour Ireland and report on the state of religion and education in that country on behalf of the *The Hibernian Society, for the Diffusion of Religious Knowledge in Ireland*, which had been established in 1806. Charles rode on horseback to Holyhead where he met the other members of the party, David Bogue (Gosport), Joseph Hughes (Battersea), and Samuel Mills (London), and they crossed to Ireland on 24 July 1807. He wrote to his son, Thomas Rice, describing the first few days of the visit:

> We arrived at Dublin July 26 and stayed there till the 31. The Sunday I preached twice in a church, and Mr B. and H. in different Dissenting chapels. The congregations were comparatively small. The religious people are sadly divided; hardly two persons think alike, and some persons often change their sentiments; forever disputing with each other instead of labouring to promote the general cause of religion among them. Cooperites, Walkerites, Haldanites, Kellyites,

[38] DEJ, III, 142.

dispute with one another with great uncharitableness. This has given great offence, and people in general become very indifferent to all religion.[39]

The party then split up into two groups, with Charles accompanying David Bogue. They travelled some 600 miles in all, preaching where they were offered pulpits, speaking to as many clergymen and Dissenting ministers as they could, and questioning the Irish peasants whom they met on the journey. From Dublin they passed through Waterford, Limerick ('They were afraid of admitting me into their pulpit – my irregularities are known even here, it seems.'), Newmarket, Gort, Athenry, Tuam, Castlebar (where the town was being occupied by an army of 900 French troops who, taking advantage of the last throes of the Irish Rebellion, had landed on the island), West Port, Sligo, Armagh, Dundalk, Drogheda, and back to Dublin. In the capital they stayed at the home of Thomas Kelly (1769–1855), the hymn-writer.

In the next meeting of the committee of the Bible Society in September 1807, Hughes and Mills were in attendance to present their report, and a letter from Charles was read. The report and the letter expressed completely opposite views on the specific point of publishing Irish Bibles. In the opinion of Hughes and Mills the arguments against this were too great: 'the general impression among, even the most zealous Protestants, is unfavourable to the measure. Scarcely an individual was met with … who did not consider the measure, under present circumstances as altogether nugatory.' They noted that all who could read Irish, though these were very few in number, could also read English; that the opposition of the Catholic priests was general; and that the subjection of the people to the priests was far greater than any attachment of theirs to the language.

Charles's conclusion, stemming from the same observations but with the additional knowledge of historical developments in Wales, was very different:

[39] *Ibid.*, III, 166-67.

The Irish are, in general, exactly in the same state as the Welsh were about 250 years back, without the Bible among them in the language they generally understand, and without being able to read it ... They have been lamentably neglected, and their amelioration is impossible without Divine knowledge; and Divine knowledge cannot be conveyed to them without teaching them to read their own language, and furnishing them with Bibles and preaching to them in the same ... I have the fullest conviction in my mind, therefore, that they ought to be instructed in their native Irish tongue.[40]

Charles's judgement was eventually followed, at least to the extent of producing and distributing 7,500 Irish New Testaments in 1811. The party's more general report to the Hibernian Society, on the other hand, was unanimous with the four members of the deputation joining to condemn the unchristian and dishonouring behaviour of the various Protestant communions which they had observed. 'The Protestant Episcopalians, Presbyterians, Seceders, Methodists, Quakers, Baptists, Independents, and the Marked Separatists – all came under their review, and were candidly dealt with.'[41]

Two months after returning home from Ireland Charles was travelling again, and he spent the whole of November 1807 on a preaching tour in south Wales.

The Rev. Edward Morgan, Syston

At some time in this period, possibly during the November 1807 tour, Charles made the acquaintance of a young man with whom he was to correspond often and who, after Charles's death, became his first English biographer. Edward Morgan (1783–1869) was born in Pyle, Glamorgan. He had been converted under the ministry of David Jones, Llan-gan, and, after graduating from Jesus College, Oxford, in 1806, was convinced of a call to the ministry. Charles's attachment to the young Edward Morgan was no doubt

[40] DEJ, III, 176-77.
[41] Ibid., III, 179.

strengthened by the similarity between Morgan's experience as a curate in several parishes in England and his own during his early labours at Bala. In one parish, the vicar had not allowed Morgan to preach for many months, and Charles wrote to comfort him:

> I feel for your perplexity. But I have no doubt, that if you look up simply to the Lord, he will graciously direct you in the way you should go. But it is not for me to determine. Providence, I am fully convinced led me in the way in which I move … and the Lord will guide you safely; and in his own good time, you will see the way clearly before you.
>
> I feel cautious in advising the servant of another. The Lord only knows what he has designed and fitted for you. Many formerly were ready to advise me: but the most forward were widest the mark.[42]

Many of the letters that passed between Charles and Morgan were on the subject of preachers, preaching, and the preparation for preaching. The following are extracts from Charles's side of the correspondence:

1812

> First of all think over the matter yourself – arrange it in your mind – enlarge upon it; and then consult authors who have best written on the subject. By this means you may correct your own ideas, or be more satisfied with them. Never be discouraged, or admit the doubt, that you cannot go through any thing you take in hand. If all appear darkness to you on the subject, earnestly apply to the Lord for the light of his Spirit, who *most assuredly* will be given to those that ask for him …
>
> Conjoin also the active with the contemplative. You have the young, the aged, the poor and the sick, to converse with about eternal things. We should never forget, that sinners are perishing for lack of knowledge all around us; and all our time must not be in our studies, however profitably spent there. We profit ourselves by endeavouring to profit others.

[42] *Ibid.*, III, 347.

Some of the most luminous and profitable views I have ever had of divine things, I have obtained instantaneously by preaching, or by conversing with others about divine things.

Above all, pray earnestly and constantly for the teaching of God's Spirit; and avoid indulgence, sloth and idleness ... We have an eternity to rest; let us be active here.[43]

18 January 1814

I now proceed to answer your important questions:

1. There may be *false*, I would rather say, *natural* or unholy animation in a carnal man, and also at times even in a spiritual man, when speaking publicly about divine things. A spiritual man knows the difference evidently in their different effects on his mind. There are holy effects and the workings of grace accompanying the one, and none the other, except self-complacency, pride, and self-sufficiency, which are very unholy effects. There is a vast difference between the free and ready exercise of gifts, natural and supernatural, in prayer and preaching, and the holy excitement of the several graces of the Spirit in those exercises; and to take the one without the other, and be satisfied with it, is most dangerous, and the readiest way to self-deception. For the sake of others I have been thankful for the free use of gifts, at the same time most deeply grieved and humbled because God hid his gracious face from my own soul ...

2. Your second question requires no particular reply, as the nature of the question contains the answer. No zeal, or boldness, or confidence, can be *holy*, if not connected with humility and self-abhorrence, as there can be no holiness without humility and repentance for sin. I have never been more shocked by anything than by this carnal and irreverent boldness, or rather presumption, when men speak about divine truths, especially the decrees of God. It is unsufferable to a humble and ingenuous mind that fears God. In our best frame, we are, the best of us, very far from what we ought to be. I have never been more tempted to despise the

---

[43] *Spiritual Counsels*, 389-90 [289-90].

doctrines of grace, than when I have been so unfortunate as to hear them so treated.

3. Your third question, the answer to it is also clear. Speaking of the terrors of the Lord to sinners with firmness, and at the same time without feeling compassion for them, shows the want of the fear of God and love to man in the speaker. We ought to weep over them as Jesus did over Jerusalem. The words in 2 Cor. 5:19-20 are particularly descriptive of the true ambassador of Christ, to whom the ministry of reconciliation is *given* – is *committed* – δόντος θέμενος [*dontos themenos*]. 'We *beseech* – we *pray* you in Christ's stead – δεόμεθα ὑπὲρ Χρίστου [*deometha huper Christou*], be ye reconciled to God. Knowing the terrors of the Lord, we *persuade* men. O my dear friend, our trifling with the souls of men about eternal concerns, is shameful – is most exceeding sinful; it is beyond measure shocking! May God convince us of it, and make us able ministers.[44]

28 May 1814

Do not bring any intricacies into your sermons or catechetical instructions. They will do your hearers no good, and it is only trifling with their souls. Let our instructions be clear, solid and important. We should not so much aim at being ourselves great divines or making others so, as to be, and to make others, *real Christians … Catechizing the children has taught me more divinity than any other means whatever.*[45]

In the event, Morgan was appointed in 1814 to the living of Syston, Leicestershire, and remained there until his death, serving as vicar for fifty-five years. In 1831 he published his *Memoir* of Charles, based on his own personal knowledge of him and on the brief Welsh biography that had been produced by Thomas Jones, Denbigh, in 1816. Then in 1836 he brought out Charles's *Essays and Letters.*[46] He also wrote lives of other Welsh Calvinistic Methodist

---

[44] DEJ, III, 508-10; *Spiritual Counsels* (1993), 394-97 [293-95].
[45] DEJ, III, 527; *Spiritual Counsels* (1993), 399-400 [297].
[46] *Spiritual Counsels* (1993, 2021).

leaders: Daniel Rowland (1840); David Jones, Llan-gan (1841); Williams, Pantycelyn (1847); John Elias (1847);[47] Howel Harris (1852). In this way he was able to narrate for English readers 'the whole story of Welsh Methodism from its beginnings down to the author's own day.'[48]

[47] Morgan, *John Elias* (1973).
[48] See under Edward Morgan, (DWB).

Edward Morgan, Syston.

13

THE FIRST WELSH BIBLE DICTIONARY
(1803–11)

ON 24 November 1804 both Sally and Thomas Charles had written to their friend, Mary Stringer, at Abbey Green, Chester. Charles's note had included the following:

> I am indeed very sorry I could not see you before I set out for London; but I believe it is impossible. I want to finish a number of my Welsh Dictionary before I go; and that I cannot do if I go from home at all. Besides this, I have to prepare a correct copy for the Bible Society in London, which is 'wanted immediately.' I am in my study eight or ten hours every day. I go as far as I can on Sunday, and back again sometime Monday. My dear Miss Ann knows how close I kept in my study when she was here; I am now much more so.[1]

Three men, from three different centuries, each a leading expert in the literature of the Welsh Calvinistic Methodists, have commented on the significance of Charles's *Geiriadur Ysgrythyrol* (*Scriptural Dictionary*). According to Lewis Edwards in the nineteenth century:

> It is hard to describe the benefit that this book provided for the Welsh nation, in so many ways. If it is considered as it relates to the Welsh language, there is perhaps no other book, other than the sacred volume in its authorized translation, that has done more to keep the language alive.[2]

[1] DEJ, II, 547.
[2] Lewis Edwards, *Traethodau Llenyddol* (1867), 278.

R. Tudur Jones, in the twentieth century, commented:

> That which George Lewis's *Corph o Ddiwinyddiaeth* (*Body of Divinity*) is to the Congregationalists and *Gwelediad y Palas Arian* (*A View of the Silver Palace*) of John Jenkins, Hengoed, is to the Baptists, Thomas Charles's *Geiriadur* is to the Methodists, with the three of them expressing, with a little variation, the strength of that evangelical Calvinistic theology that was so influential in nineteenth-century Wales.[3]

And in the twenty-first century, E. Wyn James notes that: 'Thomas Charles's *Geiriadur Ysgrythyrol* is one of the books that most influenced the Welsh mind in the nineteenth century.'[4]

Three issues of a work entitled *Geirlyfr Ysgrythyrol* (*Scriptural Word-book*) had appeared by 1802, printed by the press of W. C. Jones, Chester. It was mainly the work of John Humphreys who worked for the Chester press. Thomas Charles had been involved in the enterprise from its beginnings, however, and by 1804 had taken over full responsibility. In that year his Bala Press issued a revision of the work bearing Charles's name alone. He had greatly expanded the size of the original issues and they appeared under a new title: *Y Geiriadur Ysgrythyrol* (*The Scriptural Dictionary*). The first volume (Parts I to VI) was completed and printed in 1805; the second volume in 1808; the third in 1810 and the fourth in 1811. The first one-volume edition was produced in 1853. Six other editions appeared in Wales, and two others in the United States, before 1900. A reprint of the seventh edition in 1904 on the occasion of the centenary of the founding of the BFBS, and sold for twelve shillings and sixpence, included a short biography of Thomas Charles. It contains 960 double-columned royal octavo sized pages of small print.[5]

[3] RTJ (1979), 39-40.
[4] E. Wyn James, 'David Charles (1762–1834), Caerfyrddin: Diwinydd, Pregethwr, Emynydd,' JHS, 36 (2012), 35.
[5] DEJ, II, 462-77; Brynley F. Roberts, 'The Connexion in Print,' JHS, 16/17 (1992-93), 16-17.

SCRIPTURAL DICTIONARY.

GEIRIADUR YSGRYTHYROL:

YN CYNNWYS

HANESIAETH, DUWINYDDIAETH, ATHRONIAETH, A
BEIRNIADAETH YSGRYTHYROL.

GAN Y DIWEDDAR

BARCH. THOMAS CHARLES, B.A., BALA,

(GYNT O GOLEG IESU, RHYDYCHAIN).

Y SEITHFED ARGRAFFIAD.

WREXHAM:
ARGRAFFWYD A CHYHOEDDWYD GAN HUGHES AND SON, HOPE ST.

MDCCCLXXXV,

Title-page of a late nineteenth-century edition of Charles's
Geiriadur Ysgrythyrol.

The title-page of the revised second part, i.e. the first publication completely under Charles's charge, noted the following intentions:

> The work contains, the meaning of untranslated Scripture words; short expositions of all the chief subjects of the religion of Christ; explanations of many Scripture passages; an account of the fulfilment of prophecies; the histories of the various nations, kingdoms and cities; their positions and surroundings mentioned in the Scriptures ...
>
> In explaining Jewish ceremonies and prophecies, we endeavour to pursue the *via media* of good judgement, avoiding everything imaginary and groundless: but 'comparing spiritual things with spiritual,' paying due deference to the criticisms of the latest scholars who have written on the Scriptures, as well as to the languages in which they were originally written; the constructions of which have special value in rightly understanding many passages and expressions in the Bible.[6]

But Charles's intention was to impart more than just biblical knowledge. As the missionary fields expanded, more and more information on the peoples, religions, and customs of other lands became known. Charles would pass on, within the context of a Bible dictionary, whatever he thought was appropriate for the minds of Welsh readers hungry for knowledge. 'His Dictionary was a kind of encyclopaedia for generations, introducing them to knowledge of every kind of subject, from how to keep bees to the best method for catching crocodiles.'[7] But the provision of new knowledge imposes particular responsibilities on the provider, and Charles was well aware of these. In the closing paragraph of the preface to the first volume he voiced concerns which have been familiar to many who, over the years, have sought to enlarge the literary provision available in Welsh, or in any other minority language for that matter:

---

[6] DEJ, II, 474.

[7] E. Wyn James, 'Pererinion ar y Ffordd,' JHS, 29-30 (2005-06), 83.

Since the field before me is so very extensive and full, it is no wonder the work swells under my hands. The lack of books in our language, on most branches of knowledge, has induced me to enlarge on some subjects, about which, at the outset, I had no intention of saying much. Necessity, from the lack of more suitable ones, made me use some words which are not intelligible to the generality of men; but, by usage, every word will soon become intelligible.[8]

Thomas Charles's scholarship

Charles's scholarship is at its most evident in the pages of *Geiriadur Ysgrythyrol*. It would be interesting to know more of Charles's sources in drawing up his list of entries for the dictionary. Many concordances and Bible dictionaries would have been available to him and would have been the sources for most of his references. Other entries, presumably, would have occurred to him during his own reading of the word. As mentioned already, and as Charles's letter to Mary Stringer shows, his work for the BFBS and the SPCK on the Welsh text of the Bible continued concurrently with his work on the dictionary, He was occupied with both projects during the whole period (1804 to 1811) when the *Geiriadur* was being written. There must surely have been countless occasions, as he worked on the biblical text, of his being struck by a word, phrase or verse making a connection in his mind with a comment lately written on some *Geiriadur* entry or other. Would he have had a notebook by his side in order to scribble down a brief memorandum so as to expand the thought later in the day when he changed his field of study? There must have been considerable interplay between the two fields of work.

It is clear also that he made special use of two biblical dictionaries in particular: those of Calmet and Brown. Antoine Augustin Calmet (1767–1757) was a Benedictine monk and abbot of Senones Abbey in the Vosges region of France. He published his *Dictionnaire historique, critique, chronologique, géographique et littéral de*

[8] DEJ, II, 477.

la Bible in two folio volumes in 1720. An improved and enlarged edition in four folio volumes was published in 1730. The English translation was by Samuel D'Oyley and John Colson (1732). It was revised, with additions, by Charles Taylor in 1795 and this was the edition used by Charles. The *Dictionary of the Holy Bible* of John Brown of Haddington (1722–87) is a more familiar, two-volume work published in 1769 and often reprinted in the nineteenth century. D. E. Jenkins shows that Charles used these dictionaries, particularly for entries of a factual nature, but that he identified the sources not mentioned in these two works, following them up, providing quotations from them, and giving fuller explanations.[9]

In 1969 R. Tudur Jones published an illuminating article entitled, '*Diwylliant Thomas Charles o'r Bala*' ('The Culture of Thomas Charles of Bala'), in which he analysed the literary sources used by Charles in his *Geiriadur*.[10] Jones emphasized that one of Charles's main qualifications for the work was his interest and fluency in languages, based on that foundation of linguistic knowledge laid down so effectively by his tutor, Dr Jenkin Jenkins, during his years at Carmarthen Academy. Charles was thoroughly fluent in Latin, Hebrew, and Greek, could read French adequately and possibly Italian also. He had some knowledge of Dutch and German. The majority of the more than 5,000 entries in the *Geiriadur* provide the Greek or Hebrew words or phrases for the topics being discussed. Many of the pages have longer Latin quotations as footnotes. In the *Geiriadur* Charles quotes from, or mentions, the works of no less than five hundred different authors. He refers to about forty classical authors,[11] mainly for providing factual information.

[9] DEJ, II, 480-81.

[10] In J. E. Caerwyn Williams (ed.), *Ysgrifau Beirniadol*, Vol. IV (Denbigh, 1969), 98-115.

[11] They are listed by Jones as Ammianus Marcellinus, Anacreon, Aristotle, Cicero, Columella, Cornelius Nepos, Ctesias, Diogenes Laertius, Didorus Siculus, Dio Cassius, Dioscorides Pedanius, Florus, Galen, Herodotus, Homer, Horace, Josephus, Julius Caesar, Juvenal, Lucan, Lucian, Livy, Longinus, Martial, Ovid, Pausanias of Lydia, Plato, Pliny, Plutarch, Propertius, Ptolemy of Alexandria, Solinus, Sophocles, Strabo, Suetonius, Tacitus, Terence, Virgil, Xenophon.

Thus he made much more use of Pliny, Strabo, Herodotus, and Josephus, for example, than of the more literary writers. His manuscript (kept in the National Library of Wales, Aberystwyth) shows that he was in the habit of adding many of these classical references in the margin of the text sometime after having written the entries. That is, he was not merely duplicating the references of Calmet or Brown but discovering relevant quotations in his own reading of the Classics and noting them down.

Charles made much use of the Greek and Hebrew dictionaries of John Parkhurst (1728–1797), the Greek-Latin dictionary of Johann F. Schleusner (1759–1831), and the seven-volume *Ancient History* and the ten-volume *Roman History*, both by Charles Rollin (1661–1741). His most frequent references are of course to theological works. He has few quotations from the Early Church Fathers but includes brief references to Justin Martyr, Tertullian, Irenaeus, Athanasius, Hilary, and Chrysostom. Origen and Jerome are mentioned more often, and Eusebius and Socrates are mined for historical purposes. With Augustine, however, he is clearly very familiar. From the medieval period he quotes very little of Aquinas, but holds Anselm in greater respect. His more frequent references are to Thomas Bradwardine (1290–1349) whose *De Causa Dei contra Pelagium* is often quoted. The Protestant Reformation is represented by a few citations from Luther, Peter Martyr, Bullinger, and Bucer; more so by Beza; surprisingly, the references to Calvin are comparatively few.[12]

R. Tudur Jones considers that:

> The writers of the next generation are Thomas Charles's true teachers. He reserves an honourable place for the Puritans – William Perkins, John Ball, Joseph Caryl, Jeremiah Burroughes, Thomas Goodwin, William Gurnal, Samuel Cradock, Roger [Stephen?] Charnock, William Ames, John Howe and Richard Sibbes. Dr John Owen is frequently complimented – though he can at times disagree with him. And there is one reference to John Bunyan … And this was

[12] D. Densil Morgan in HMGC3, 124.

not only an English influence. As far as their theological system was concerned Continental authors were just as important. Edward Morgan had asked Charles's advice on purchasing the works of some divines. In his answer Charles wrote: 'Some of the old German and Dutch divines I judge preferable; such as – Jerome Zanchius, Musculus, Vertringa (sic), Venema, Witsius, Cocceius, etc. I think Turretin's works would be very useful to you. It is an excellent body of divinity.' These authors are all referred to constantly in the *Geiriadur*.[13]

Wolfgang Musculus (1497–1566) of Bern, Hieronymus Zanchius (1516–90) of Heidelberg, and Francis Turretin (1623–87) of Geneva were eminent for their volumes of systematic theology and dogmatics. Of more significance for Charles was the Dutch school of Covenant or Federal Theology established by Johannes Cocceius (1603–69). Cocceius was professor of theology at Leyden in the Netherlands. His exposition of redemption as an activity of God founded upon divine covenants (*Summa Doctrinae de Foedere et Testamento Dei*, 1648) was the first attempt at a biblical theology. His work was refined and expanded by two of his followers: Hermann Witsius (1636–1708), professor at Utrecht, and Campegius Vitringa (1659–1722), professor at Franeker. Herman Venema (1697–1787) was Vitringa's student, and his successor at Franeker.

All of these continental works mentioned were known to Charles in their original Latin, except perhaps a work by Witsius which was translated into English (*The Oeconomy of the Covenants between God and Man*) in 1763. Cocceius had opposed the analytical doctrine-by-doctrine approach of the systematic school and 'had worked out in detail what we would call today a biblical-theological, redemptive-historical perspective for presenting covenant theology.'[14] It has long been recognized that systematic theology

[13] In J. E. Caerwyn Williams (ed.), *Ysgrifau Beirniadol*, Vol. IV 108-09; quoting *Spiritual Counsels*, 385-86 [287].

[14] Peter Golding, *Covenant Theology* (Fearn, Ross-shire: Christian Focus: 2004), 47.

and biblical theology are not contradictory, as Cocceius argued, but are completely complementary; both are needed for a full understanding of biblical teaching. What is interesting is that Charles, by choosing to present his thought in dictionary form, was able, to a considerable extent, to pass on the benefits of both approaches to his readers. An anthology of his strictly theological entries, presented in a logical order, would result in a full and profound systematic theology. Consider, for example, three of his entries, taken almost at random: the 2,600-word article on 'redemption' (*'prynedigaeth'*), has seventy-five scriptural references taken from twenty-six different biblical books, nine from the Old Testament and seventeen from the New; the 2,300-word article on 'three' (*'tri'*), which includes Charles's treatment of the Holy Trinity, has ninety-one citations taken from thirty-one different biblical books, fourteen from the Old Testament and seventeen from the New; for the 6,500-word entry on 'covenant' (*'cyfamod'*), the sixty-one citations are taken from twenty-six different biblical books, fifteen from the Old Testament and eleven from the New. That is, he surveys the whole of the biblical testimony on the topic under discussion in order to present the truth in its fullness. His presentation of a biblical theology, on the other hand, is admittedly much less evident, but a careful selection from entries such as 'sacrifice' (*'aberth'*), 'covenant' (*'cyfamod'*) and 'prophecy' (*'prophwydoliaeth'*), for example, and from his many biographical entries, reveals his understanding of the developing nature of God's special revelation and of the various agents of revelation. Thus, for example, in his entry on 'tree' (*'pren'*), Charles discusses the principles of life and of probation revealed in Eden, as symbolized by the tree of life and the tree of the knowledge of good and of evil. His entry on Joseph has been described as 'a great sermon on Providence,'[15] and in his article on 'prophecy' (*'prophwydoliaeth'*), he notes:

> As we consider the holy Scriptures we see that prophecy has a great range; beginning at the fall of man and reaching out to the end of all things. In primitive ages its light was

[15] R. Tudur Jones, in *Ysgrifau Beirniadol*, Vol. IV, (1969), 114.

comparatively dim, and illuminated only a few. There were long intervals between one prophecy and the next. But as time passed it became brighter and more frequent, and developed progressively amongst one race of people, who were set apart primarily, amongst other reasons, for this one purpose of being entrusted with the Word of God. With only a few intervals a spirit of prophecy prevailed amongst this people right up to the coming of Christ, Romans 3:2. Christ and his apostles were famously endowed with the same spirit, and left behind them far-reaching prophecies of that which was to come, up to the end of time, or as John expresses it, until 'the mystery of God should be finished,' Rev. 10:7 …

We discern, therefore, the spirit of prophecy, pervading all the ages of time, attesting to one Person of the greatest excellence and majesty, and proclaiming the fulfilment of the most godly and gracious purpose, design and intention of which the mind can conceive. This is the scriptural delineation of the function of prophecy.

The one area of scholarly accuracy in which Charles had been a degree uncertain was, ironically, that of his own native language. When he returned to Wales after his years in Oxford and Somerset, the standard of Charles's written Welsh was deficient. The few sentences of Welsh inserted in his English letters of the late 1770s to Sally reveal a natural, idiomatic knowledge of the oral language, but atrocious spelling. By this time, however, there was no need for such diffidence. His natural grasp of Welsh syntax had always been sound and after his years of study of the idiomatic, accurately-written Welsh of the Bibles of William Morgan, Dr John Davies, and others, he had become as proficient a writer as any of his period. John Morris-Jones (1864–1929), professor of Welsh at Bangor University, wrote of him, 'Thomas Charles's Welsh is strong and natural. The Bible was his pattern, and it is his Welsh that has been followed by the best writers after him.'[16]

---

[16] From *Y Gwyddionadur*, quoted by Jones, R. M. (1977), 533.

Thomas Charles in middle age.

The centrality of the teaching of the Bible

Although Charles provided his readers with a wealth of extra-biblical information to broaden their knowledge and understanding of the topographical and historical background of the Scriptures, his main aim was to convey the doctrines and teachings of the word. It is no surprise therefore that when any page of the dictionary is scanned, the first thing that strikes the eye is the large number of biblical references. Thus, for example, if two or three entries under the letter 'A' are scanned we find that:

In the six columns discussing the word 'regeneration' (*'aden-edigaeth'*) he gives 114 scriptural references. In the five columns discussing the word 'resurrection' ('*adgyfodiad*') he gives 116 scriptural references. Under the word 'promise' ('*addaw*') Charles writes, 'Perhaps it would be useful to note a few of the promises which refer to the main points of Christianity.' He then lists references to 129 scriptural promises, under such headings as 'Forgiveness,' 'Justification,' 'Comfort,' Eternal life,' etc. These numbers suggest that the volume contains somewhere in the region of 30,000 to 35,000 biblical references.

The contents of the *Geiriadur Ysgrythyrol*

The *Dictionary* is a book of 960 (*royal octavo*) pages, each page comprising two columns of small print (equivalent to a digital font of size 7 or 8). Its approximately 5,600 entries contain about 1.2 million words. This is the equivalent of writing a volume of more than 150,000 words in each of the eight years during which the book was being written, during which time, of course, Charles was continuing with all his other responsibilities. Its contents reveal etymological, topographical, biographical, historical, typological, theological, and experiential elements. Examples of these elements may be found interwoven in the various entries but some of them may be considered separately:

(1) *The etymological element*

Nearly all the entries of the *Geiriadur* which are longer than a few sentences begin with a study of the meaning of the word, based on the derivation of the original Hebrew or Greek. Charles's high view of Scripture required that its message be interpreted only by a strict adherence to the meaning of its words. His understanding of the inspiration of Scripture was that 'the doctrines were presented to their [the biblical writers'] minds, clothed in their appropriate words. The words and phrases are divine, as well as the doctrines.'[17] This conviction was his basic standard for all engaged in biblical exegesis and preaching:

---

[17] *Geiriadur*, on the word 'Scripture,' ('*Ysgrythur*'), 923.

I cannot but consider it no small fault in any who have the opportunity, for them to neglect the learning of the languages in which the Old and New Testaments were written, and [not] to make a habit of reading them in the original languages. There is a remarkable glory and excellence in them in the language of the Holy Spirit, greater than may be found in any translation of them, and the labour is but small compared to the incomparably valuable and useful gain obtained.[18]

One unique aspect of Charles's *Geiriadur* is that it was the first dictionary to define and explain the meaning of words through the medium of Welsh alone. Many other Welsh dictionaries, from the first Welsh-English dictionary of William Salesbury in 1546 and the Welsh-Latin dictionary of John Davies in 1632, up to the English-Welsh dictionaries of William Evans (1771) and Thomas Jones, Denbigh (1800), were of great usefulness to Charles in providing Welsh synonyms and phrases in order for him to accomplish his own purpose. But that purpose was not now the linguistic one of supplying equivalent words in order to understand or to write a second language but the discussion and explanation of concepts and themes in one's own tongue. Here again is seen Charles's underlying motivation of educating the Welsh people in biblical truths. Dafydd Johnston suggests that Thomas Jones's *English-Welsh Dictionary* and Charles's *Geiriadur* were two parts of a literary programme that the two friends had agreed between them in their endeavours to provide what was necessary for educating the Welsh Methodists. Johnston demonstrates also the use Charles made of his friend's work. Thus, the synonyms he provides for the word 'burden' ('*baich*') are exactly the five synonyms that Jones gives for the English word 'burden' in his dictionary; similarly, Charles's four synonyms for '*addfwyn*' are the same as those given by Jones for the English equivalent, 'meek.' Charles noted in his preface that the work was intended

[18] *Ibid.* Both these references are cited in Geraint Lloyd, 'Thomas Charles a'r Ysgrythur,' in DDM (2014), 65; 63-64.

for monolingual Welsh people thirsting for knowledge of God's word, yet there was a clear intention also to develop the minds of all Welshmen by providing in their own language the words for them to discuss and interpret the Scriptures in Sunday schools, societies, and sermons.[19] Although entirely unintended by Thomas Charles, his dictionary was a pioneering effort in the production of Welsh dictionaries generally.[20]

(2) *The topographical and personal references*

The entries for place-names and for personal names demonstrate the comprehensive nature of the *Geiriadur*. Although, as a Bible dictionary, it would not be expected to include as many word entries as a concordance, yet it may be favourably compared to many of these in this respect. The famous concordance of Alexander Cruden (1701–70) published in 1737 may be taken as an example. In its section on proper names, a twentieth-century edition of Cruden's *A Complete Concordance to the Holy Scriptures* has eighty-five references to place and personal names beginning with the letter 'A.' Charles's work, however, has 107 entries in this category. Similarly, Cruden's has 114 entries under the letters 'I/J,' where the *Geiriadur* has 232 entries.

The vast majority of the entries for these proper names are necessarily very brief, comprising generally the meaning of the Hebrew or Greek name, a short explanation, and a few Bible references. If, however, the name occurs in the Bible on more than a few occasions and carries some degree of significance, Charles adds further comment and explanation. For the more significant names Charles provides a full historical account, giving biographies of individuals and histories of cities and countries. Thus there is a 4,000 word essay on Abraham; 8,000 words on Moses; 8,600 on David and 4,000 on Solomon. Jerusalem's history and significance is described in about 4,000 words; Egypt's in 2,000; Babylon in

---

[19] Dafydd Johnston, '"Nid baich ond y baich o bechod": *Geiriadur Ysgrythyrol* Thomas Charles,' in DDM (2014), 78-79; 80-81.
[20] *Ibid.*, 77.

3,300; Rome in 2,000. In this way an extensive history of Old and New Testament times is provided.

At other times, when the necessary information has been provided elsewhere, Charles can be remarkably brief. The full entry for 'Israel,' for example, reads:

> (*one who has prevailed with God, or, a prince with God*) See
> JACOB. The name signifies, sometimes Jacob himself; sometimes his descendants; sometimes the kingdom of Israel
> – the ten tribes, as contrasted with the kingdom of Judah;
> and sometimes the church of God, called by him from the
> world.

(3) *Typological references*

Throughout the volume Charles is always to be found writing with most feeling and warmth in those passages that have any reference to Jesus Christ. Such passages occur often in the *Geiriadur* because he sees the need to explain and illustrate the person and work of Christ, not only in those entries which deal directly with these topics – Atonement, Cross, Incarnation, Jesus, Mediator, Messiah, Ransom, for example – but also in entries where the reference to Christ is more indirect, such as Alpha, Amen, Beloved, Body, Bread, Burden, Flesh, Heir, Lamb, Wonderful, etc. A third category is that of the very many entries involving the types and shadows of Christ in the Old Testament. Charles is a careful and balanced guide in this respect, being very aware of the extremes both of speculative allegorizing and of unbelieving blindness.[21] Typical entries in this category (in the order that they appear in the *Geiriadur*) are: Open, Altar, Heifer, High-Priest, Savour, Incense, First-Fruit, Branch, King, Shepherd, Ram, Meat Offering, Song of Songs, Beget, Dove, Rock, Cloud, First-Born, Blood, Sun, Melchizedek, Priest, Passover, Prophet, Serpent, Mercy-Seat.[22]

[21] DEJ, II, 474.
[22] Corresponding to the Welsh words: *Agor, Allor, Anner, Archoffeiriad, Arogl, Arogldarth, Blaenffrwyth, Blaguryn, Brenin, Bugail, Bwch, Bwydoffrwm, Cân y Caniadau, Cenhedlu, Colomen, Craig, Cwmwl, Cyntaf-anedig, Gwaed, Haul, Melchisedec, Offeiriad, Pasg, Proffwyd, Sarff, Trugareddfa.*

The content of such entries might be the usual etymological treatment, followed by descriptions of the various significances of the use of the word in Scripture. Charles will then point out the typological element, sometimes with only a short sentence or two. The following extract is from his entry for 'sun' (*haul*):

> ... there is no other object, known to us within the sphere of nature, more appropriate for illustrating what Christ is to his people: that which he is as he enlightens, revives, comforts them and makes them fruitful.
>
> 'The sun of righteousness shall arise with healing in his wings' or 'the *light* of righteousness, or, of *justification*, shall be shed abroad, with healing in its beams.' Not a fire burning but a gentle, reviving, healing light, expounding righteousness. Christ is the righteousness, and Christ is the light that expounds it, and by the preaching of the gospel he is shed abroad and declared to darkened sinners, Mal. 4:2; 2 Sam. 23:4; Isa. 49:6, 60:1; Ps. 84:11; Luke 1:78; 2:32 ...
>
> It is said of the continuation of any excellent object of bright glory that it shall 'endure as the sun.' Such is the throne and kingdom of the Messiah. Ps. 89:36; 72:17. 'His throne as the sun before me,' that is, everlasting, in its glorious radiance. See LIGHT.

(4) *The theological entries*

The *Geiriadur* has many articles on more directly theological subjects such as 'anathema,' 'blasphemy,' 'decree,' 'devil,' 'eternity,' 'faith,' 'God,' 'grace,' 'justification,' 'light,' 'regeneration,' 'resurrection,' 'sanctification,' 'Scripture,' 'surety,' etc. These together provide the best source for understanding Charles's theology. They reveal a thorough commitment to the evangelical Calvinism of the Reformation and Post-Reformation confessions and catechisms. The longest entry (some 6,600 words) is that on the word 'covenant' ('*cyfamod*').

The wide distribution of *Y Geiriadur Ysgrythyrol* resulted in its becoming the means of establishing classical reformed theology throughout Wales. This had been the predominant theology of most of the Protestant leaders in the country from the Reformation onwards but now, for the first time, by means of the preaching of the Methodists, Williams's hymns, and the *Geiriadur*, it became the theology of the common people. This was no unforeseen consequence but, as demonstrated by so many of Charles's long-term projects, was just one more example of an achieved objective of his persevering labours for the Christian education of the people of Wales. The dictionary form was helpful in that the various topics, with few exceptions, were presented in relatively short sections, making the material easily digestible and memorable. As each article proceeds from word-study to biblical references and examples, to exposition of verses, to theological commentary and to personal application, the style of writing varies. At times it may include an abrupt style, almost in note form or with brief paragraphs of short sentences, while at other times there are longer meditative passages. The variety of content and style keeps the reader's interest as the article proceeds. Dafydd Johnston comments:

> 'The changes of tempo and tone that appear in some of the outstanding entries of the *Geiriadur* are similar to the movements found in a piece of music. This, perhaps, is what R. Tudur Jones had in mind when he described the entry on "grace" as an "elegant symphony" … it is carefully structured in order to deal with the varied aspects of this key theological concept … One of his favourite techniques, seen at its most effective in this entry, is the way in which he weaves phrases from the Scriptures into his explanations, interweaving the whole into a praise of God's grace.[23]

This, indeed, was the heart and purpose of all theology to Charles: 'a praise of God's grace.' In all of these theological entries of the *Geiriadur* he glories in the being, the attributes and the work of God. It may be worth including a few longer passages from these entries in order to demonstrate his method. In each passage Charles glories in God and in his ways.

[23] Dafydd Johnston, in DDM (2014), 89–90.

God's holiness: 'He is called THE HOLY ONE (Job 6:10), HOLY
IS HIS NAME (Luke 1:49), he is GLORIOUS IN HOLINESS (Ex. 15:11).
His holiness indicates his essential purity and his innate opposition to all immorality. He is completely free from all imperfection,
opposed to impurity of every degree, of every type, and as found in
every one; he is full of every virtue and moral perfection. "There is
none holy as the Lord" (1 Sam. 2:2). His holiness is of his essence;
it is not only that God is holy, but that holiness is God. He can no
more fail to be holy than he can fail to be. Angels and wicked men
exist without holiness, but God cannot exist without holiness, for
holiness is his essence. His holiness is as infinite as his being; he is
holy in his majesty, in his immensity, and in his divine being. His
majesty is immeasurable and it is all of holy beauty. His majesty
consists of holiness, and his holiness of divine majesty. He glories
in his own holiness and beauty, with a delight and felicity corresponding to that holiness. He sees nothing but beauty in himself,
and he is infinitely pleased in that view of his own beauty. He is
his own bliss, and there is nothing in him to diminish that bliss;
in himself he meets his own standard of perfection. Of no other
of his attributes may it be said that it is his beauty and his bliss.'[24]

The Persons of the Godhead: '"Thou art my Son; this day have
I begotten thee." (Psa. 2:7). Words spoken by the Father of the
Son, and by the Son of himself. This generation is a property of
the Christ as a divine person, by which the Father is Father to the
Son, and the Son is Son to the Father, as Divine Persons in the
one infinite being … This is what distinguishes [the Son] from
the Father and from the Holy Spirit. And the property of the
Holy Spirit, as a Divine Person, is that he *proceeds*, or is *breathed
out*. This is what distinguishes him from the Father and from the
Son … There is no other reason that can ever be given to explain
why the name "Father" is attributed to the Father and not to the
Son and the Holy Spirit also. As far as creation, providence, the
adoption and regeneration of his people are concerned, the name

[24] From the entry on 'holy, holiness' ('*sanctaidd, sancteiddrwydd*').

"Father" is as appropriate to the Son and the Spirit as to the Father, in that they co-operate fully with the Father in all these activities. But the First Person would still be the Father had no creation or redemption ever occurred; so also would the Son have been the Son. Without this the doctrine of the Trinity could never be defended. If the eternal generation of the Son be denied, it can never be proved that he is a separate person within the Godhead, and therefore his Deity cannot be proved. There is nothing within the Godhead but that which is eternal, therefore the generation is eternal. Hence the Father is eternal, the Son is eternal, and the Spirit is eternal.

'It was not his office that made Christ the Son of God; it was not his ordination to the office that constituted his generation. How can an office produce a person or generate a relationship? It was rather the Eternal Son who took the offices upon himself, by the eternal predestination of the Trinity. It was not his incarnation in the womb of the Virgin by the power of the Spirit that made him the Son of God, rather, the Godhead, in the Person of the Son, became incarnate … "*Today*, have I begotten thee" – God's '*today*' is eternity. There is no yesterday or tomorrow for God, only one *eternal today*, and God's today contains our yesterday, today and tomorrow. This is therefore an eternal generation: complete, perfect, eternal, *essential* and *personal*, within the infinite Godhead, in the beginning of his way, before his works of old.'[25]

The Saviour of sinners: 'This wonderful Person lived among us here on earth and was, for thirty years, subject to his parents, in poor circumstances, unknown to all but a very few on earth … He was born in Bethlehem in a stable; he spent most of his life in Nazareth, Galilee, before beginning his public ministry. Little if any history is given of this period in his life. He received no education or upbringing, except, most probably, that which his parents were able to give him as required by the law, Deut. 4:9-10; 6:7; John 7:15 … As he grew, he was remarkable both in wisdom

[25] From the entry on 'generate' ('*cenedlu*').

and in stature, increasing in the one as in the other. His whole attitude and behaviour in those early years were most appropriate, sensible and attractive. This may be deduced from those words: that he increased "in favour with God and man" and that "the child grew and waxed strong in spirit, filled with wisdom; and the grace of God was upon him." A more beautiful and pleasant plant never grew on earth! ... He remained subject to his parents and lived with them in poor and obscure circumstances until he began his public ministry at the age of thirty ... In this, he manifested a remarkable example of obedience to parents, and of faithful diligence ... Throughout this time the majesty and pre-eminences of his divine Person were predominantly veiled; in the likeness of men and in the form of a servant, the form of God was hidden. But it must be remembered:

'1. That throughout this time he was representing his people; he was the Chief-covenanter and representative in every place and in all things, throughout his life from when he was first formed in the womb. As a representative he lived on behalf of, and in place of, his people. For their sake he became poor and of low estate.

'2. That he was obedient and fulfilled all righteousness for his people throughout his life. His whole life, in every part and situation and circumstance, was a perfect obedience, "he was obedient unto death." He obeyed in the whole man: in body and every physical member; in spirit and every faculty. And in that he was a representative throughout his life, his perfect obedience fulfilled all righteousness for his people. He had no need of a public life to accomplish this, and in that this was his greatest priority while on earth, he spent the greater part of his life in obscurity. Others, authorized and equipped by him, preached the gospel with power and to great effect, but none but he fulfilled all righteousness for his people ...

'As the sacrifice for his people it was necessary for him to suffer and die; not to die only, but to suffer. And not to suffer only, but also to die, giving his life as a ransom for many. And as it was necessary that every aspect of cruelty, contempt and shame should be involved in his suffering and death, he had to suffer and die in the public eye, outside the walls of Jerusalem, Heb. 13:11-13. Yet, in that this did not require a long period, Jesus ministered publicly, according to general opinion, for only a little over three years. These three years of his public life revealed what had been the nature of his life previously – it was all of great wonder!

'Though he lived in poverty, with no place to lay down his head; afflicted, without a comforter; persecuted, without a defender, yet, he went about doing good to others. In every circumstance, without wearying or weakening, he had one object constantly before him, namely the glory of God and the good of mankind. We see power, but it is power to protect and not to terrify; power moderated by tenderness, satisfying and comforting, while yet drawing forth reverent fear. Every gentleness is gathered together wonderfully in him; every divine greatness and excellence, every human ability and gift, everything sacred and gracious, meet together in him. He is seen having fellowship with prophets, law-givers and angels; he reveals himself as omniscient, probing and discerning the very depths of men's hearts; he claims his right to the keys of death and hell; he predicts his coming as judge on the last day, with divine majesty and pre-eminence. Yet he is also seen embracing little children; meek, gentle and humble, he will not lift his voice in the street, nor break the bruised reed, nor quench the smoking flax. He does not call his disciples servants but friends and brothers. Tenderly and lovingly, in kindness and friendship, he heals the sick, has compassion upon those in trouble, and restores the backslidden. In all the afflictions of his disciples, he is afflicted; he courteously answers his enemies, patiently and thoughtfully, and overcomes their cunning by his superior wisdom. He, "when he was reviled, reviled not again; when he suffered, he threatened not." He is altogether lovely! As a teacher he is incomparable; his illustrations are inexhaustible; he makes use of every-day incidents to great effect and embodies deepest wisdom in crystal-clear parables. He proclaims the deepest truths with an easy, informal and intimate dignity; he convicts hypocrites with a sacred majesty, strictness and wrath. As we read the evangelists' testimony of him, we see him with the mind's eye as he was here on earth, as if we were seeing him in the flesh and conversing with him. The mirror which reveals him is divine, as is the object it reveals. Blessed are those who have seen his glory in this mirror.'[26]

The gospel by which Christ saves: 'In the gospel Jesus Christ is offered as a *surety* for sinners. A surety is one who commits himself on behalf of others to serve, to pay debts, to be a refuge, for them: "By so much was Jesus made a surety of a better testament," (Heb. 7:22). We note: (i) That Jesus was made a surety by God's appointment. Jesus is what he is *for us* by counsel, by covenant, and by appointment. All the effectiveness of his work for us is founded upon his ordination to his offices by God, (Rom. 3:25). (ii) That Jesus is not only appointed in the Covenant of Grace as Mediator and Intercessor, but also as Surety. There was no Mediator, Intercessor or Surety in the Covenant of Works, but in the Covenant of Grace Christ is all of these. That he is a Surety is more than his being a Mediator and Intercessor, in that he is answerable for those for whom he is a Surety. There is a difference between the suretyship of Christ and suretyship between men. Amongst men the debtor and the surety are both bound; the surety must pay only if the debtor fails to do so. But here, Christ alone is bound over for the whole debt. This covenant involves a bond that has no name on it but that of Christ, so that *he* is called a "covenant of the people" (Isa. 42:6; 49:8).

'"I have laid help upon one who is mighty" (Psa. 89:19). *He* (and *he* alone) was made sin (or a sin-offering) for us, and "God was in Christ, reconciling the (elect) world unto himself, not imputing their trespasses unto them" (2 Cor. 5:19-21). He committed himself in his own Person to fulfil all righteousness and suffer every curse, as a Surety for his people. There was sufficient fullness in him to answer for all their indebtedness, and he and his people are forever free.'[27]

[26] From the entry on 'Jesus' ('*Iesu*').
[27] From the entry on 'surety' ('*mechnïydd*').

(5) *The Christian life*

Just as helpful to nineteenth-century Calvinistic Methodists as Charles's theological entries in the *Geiriadur* were his practical articles on aspects of Christian life and experience. As with the theological entries, there is an abundance of references in this category; topics such as: 'assurance,' 'betrothal,' 'conscience,' 'contentment,' 'fellowship,' 'guidance,' 'jealousy,' 'lust,' 'mortification,' 'pride,' 'shame,' 'thanksgiving,' 'unbelief,' 'worship,' etc. Years of preaching to the common people and, possibly of even greater relevance, years of leading the society meetings, had taught Charles the need for pinpointing key pastoral issues and listing the elements involved concisely and logically. Many who are in a position to judge believe that it is in this area of his writing that Charles excels and is most helpful. His point-by-point explanatory method may be seen in his entry on 'conviction' (*'argyhoeddiad'*). It is included in full (apart from the entymological element) as an illustration of the abiding benefit to be obtained from reading the *Geiriadur*.

'The word *conviction*, in its usual meaning, is given to the work of the Holy Spirit convicting of sin, or revealing sin. Sin is everywhere in the world and in every man in the world, but no one sees it except as the Holy Spirit reveals it. Sin cannot reveal sin: only a straight path can disclose a deviation. The holy Law is the straight rule by which we may recognize our deviations. The Holy Spirit applies this Law to the mind of the sinner with light and divine authority. He holds the sinner before this pure mirror and keeps him there until his conscience finds him guilty, and his trespasses and filthiness appear as gross sinfulness. At this solemn sight, the Holy Spirit produces appropriate feelings and states of mind, namely: lively feelings of danger; a recognition that one is completely lost, bereft of that righteousness called for by the Law; and repentance for sin, which involves godly distress, self-abhorrence because of sin, and serious searching for relief from it and from the wrath it merits.

'There are differences in the degree of conviction and its relative circumstances from person to person. Some feel more of the terrors that accompany it than others. But the degree of conviction and of terror are not always equivalent. There may be great terrors where the conviction is slight; lively fears of danger, yet with no acknowledgement of the trespass which provokes it. There may also be deep, true, enlightened conviction with little accompanying terror: the mind is aware and conscious more of the trespass, than of the punishment for it; it submits; it evinces godly sorrow; it abhors itself; it glorifies God; and wonders that it has been spared so long without being punished. Yet although it may not be of the same degree, it is of the same nature in all, and indispensably necessary for repentance of sin and for turning to God. For who can repent for sin without seeing its evil? And who will turn from it without first recognizing its danger and loathsomeness?

'If the conviction is thorough and saving it perceives the corrupt nature of each and every sin, and the continuation of this corruption throughout one's life on earth, and it responds accordingly, concluding with solemn pleas for a Saviour, John 16:8-9; 1 John 1:8-9; Mat. 11:28; Luke 5:31; Rom. 5:12; Ps. 51:5; Gen. 6:5; Jer. 17:9; Gal. 3:10; Acts 2:37; 16:30; Rom. 3:20; 7:7,9-14; Zech. 12:10.

'A man may know to what degree he has been convicted of being a guilty sinner: 1. By his hesitation to draw near to God, other than by a Mediator. 2. By the value he sets on the blood of the Saviour. 3. By his readiness to wait before God for spiritual and temporal mercies. 4. By his thankfulness for everything. 5. By his happy submission under the almighty hand of God. 6. By his readiness to confess his sin, when there is need to do so. 7. By his meekness in receiving rebukes and warnings. 8. By his readiness to think better of others than of himself.

'We may judge to what degree we have been convicted of our ignorance: 1. By our lack of confidence in our own understanding. 2. By our readiness to ask for guidance. 3. By our readiness to hear the views of others. 4. By our work in looking to God's Word for instruction in all things. 5. By our solemn requests for the light of the Holy Spirit in order to understand the Scriptures, and our not depending on our own reasonings over it. 6. By our dependence upon the light of the Holy Spirit upon our prayers. 7. By our aversion to contentious arguments.

'We may know to what degree our conviction of our own weakness has arrived: 1. By our lack of confidence in our own power and ability in every circumstance. 2. By our importunity in seeking grace to help in time of need. 3. By our work in looking often for divine help in every duty and every temptation. 4. By our work in appropriating to the Holy Spirit our every good thought, desire, motivation and deed.'

(6) *Every-day words of the Bible*

The following are three extracts from entries, drawn almost at random, for some more common-place words.

For 'begin' ('*dechrau*') he includes: '"Then began men to call upon the name of the Lord," Gen. 4:26 … The words do not mean that the worship of God only began in the days of Enos … but that a particular renewal of true religion began at this time … This is the first example of a revival of true religion in the world, and it is here specifically noted and wondered at. Zeph. 3:9; Rom. 10:13; Ps. 116:17.'

Under 'garden' ('*gardd*') he writes: 'In a garden the first Adam sinned and fell; in a garden the bloody conflict of the second Adam took place, and in a garden he was buried.'

The comment for 'hoarfrost' ('*llwydrew*') includes: 'The great God in his works of wisdom brings forth the hoar frost. Therefore it is fit that he should be praised for this, as for all his works. Job 38:29; Ps. 147:16-17.'

Conclusions

On 16 January 1809, in a letter to Ebenezer Richard, Tregaron, Cardiganshire, the secretary of the South Wales Association, Charles noted:

> I have been a prisoner, bound by the leg during the last four months. I am now about to be released once more. I consider it a particular blessing that I was able to proceed with my work during the whole time, though often unable to

walk from my bed to the sofa. By this means I was enabled
at last to finish writing the *Geiriadur*, which has eased me of
a heavy burden. It was a Herculean task. The second part of
the third volume will be out soon, and we will proceed with
the printing as soon as possible.[28]

A few days later, he wrote to a friend at Chester, 'To my great
satisfaction and relief of mind, I have finished the *Geiriadur*. It
really had well nigh *finished* me. I think of dying now with more
satisfaction.'[29]

Many of the elements of a biblical dictionary are necessarily
superseded as the years pass, with further research and understanding rendering much of the content out of date. Yet even in
the twenty-first century, the *Geiriadur* remains essential reading
for Welsh Christians, though, admittedly, few appreciate this. R.
Tudur Jones notes the humanity of the book, with its frequent
gentle humour and its practical household advice,[30] but over and
above every other element, what gives it its enduring quality is
its clear, heart-warming expositions of the weighty truths of the
gospel. 'There is a sweet unction in the writings of Thomas Charles.
His essay on "Joseph" is a great sermon on Providence, and his
entry on "Jesus Christ" is one of great tenderness …'[31] While much
of the etymological, topographical, and historical information
Charles provides has been shown to be inaccurate and must be
corrected, the quality of his balanced, godly, scriptural exposition
of Christian doctrines and the pastoral wisdom displayed in entries

[28] DEJ, III, 211-12.

[29] *Ibid.*, III, 214.

[30] Thus, in an entry on the word 'new'('*newydd*'), Charles refers to Jeremiah 31:22, 'for the Lord hath created a new thing in the earth, A woman
shall compass a man.' He then tells us that the scholar Blayney had suggested
a better translation, namely, 'for the Lord hath created a new thing on the
earth, a woman shall overcome a man.' Charles's sly comment is, 'I would
ask him, What *new* thing is that, for a woman to overcome a man?' Tudur
Jones adds, 'One can almost hear Sally's laugh!' *Ysgrifau Beirniadol*, Vol IV
(1969), 112-13.

[31] In J. E. Caerwyn Williams (ed.) *Ysgrifau Beirniadol*, Vol. IV, 114.

on Christian life and experience are only rarely found elsewhere in Welsh Christian writings. It has often been observed that the reason why no book of systematic theology has been written in Welsh since 1800 was because it was not considered that the articles of the *Geiriadur* could be bettered.[32]

The *Geiriadur* was read throughout the land, not only by Calvinistic Methodists but by members of all the Nonconformist bodies. It was particularly useful for those many preachers at that time who had not received much education, who were obliged to labour in the world throughout the week, but were yet eager to obtain a measure of familiarity with the truths of the gospel, and that within a small compass, which they could memorize and use in their sermons. In the *Geiriadur* they found all that they could want.[33]

In 1888, Thomas Charles Edwards (1837–1900), Thomas Charles's great-grandson, noted the books most treasured by the Welsh Methodists of the early nineteenth century:

> The theological product and monument of the Methodist revival of the last century is Charles's Bible-Dictionary, *Y Geiriadur*. This book contains elaborate articles on all doctrinal subjects ... If you entered the house of a rustic elder or leader of 'the private societies' fifty years ago, you would find that he had a small and very select library. It would nearly always contain Peter Williams's *Annotations on the Bible*; Williams of Pantycelyn's *Hymns and Elegies*, which are essentially doctrinal; Charles's *Bible Dictionary*; with translations into Welsh of Boston's *Fourfold State of Man*; Bunyan's *Pilgrim's Progress*; Owen on the *Person of Christ*, and on the *Mortification of Sin in Believers*; Gurnal's *Christian in Complete Armour*, Foxe's *Martyrology*, and, perhaps, Elijah Cole on the *Divine Sovereignty*.[34]

[32] Lewis Edwards, *Traethodau Llenyddol* (Wrexham, 1867), 279.
[33] See Henry Hughes, *Trefecca, Llangeitho a'r Bala* (Caernarvon, 1896), 99-100.
[34] D. D. Williams, *Thomas Charles Edwards* (1921), 104-05.

R. Tudur Jones, in his paper on the nature of Charles's scholarship, contains the best analysis to date of the *Bible Dictionary* (*Y Geiriadur Ysgrythyrol*), and its final paragraph is worth repeating:

> The *Geiriadur Ysgrythyrol* is a work of special importance. By it the wide and varied culture of its author was passed on to thousands of people in Wales. It combined the classical with the modern, the theological with the scientific, the scholarly with the practical. And it did this because it had been formed by the influence of a complete vision of the meaning of man's destiny in the world. Everything fits into its proper place under the sovereignty of Christ – the world of nature and literature, morality and medicine, humour and unction, work and godliness. The only thing with which no compromise is permitted is human sin. Against this, war is declared. In a word, Charles laid down a clear pattern for very many of the people of Wales by which to fashion for themselves a new life.[35]

---

[35] In J. E. Caerwyn Williams (ed.), *Ysgrifau Beirniadol*, Vol. IV, 114-15.

14

THE ORDINATION OF 1811
(1809–12)

A new chapel

THE continuing increase in the congregation of the Calvinistic Methodist chapel in Bala meant that the 1792 enlargement of the building very soon proved inadequate, and the only solution was to build a new chapel. This was completed in 1809 and could hold a thousand worshippers. It was named Bethel Chapel and was a large, square building with the pulpit placed between the two entrance doors. It was lit by candles and three chandeliers and warmed by a large bell-shaped stove.[1]

The road to 1811

As an evangelical movement operating within the Church of England, the position of the Calvinistic Methodist Connexion in Wales was, from its very beginnings, very unstable. There were two reasons why it did not sever its connections with the Established Church during the first seventy years of its existence (1740 to 1810): the influence of Howel Harris in its early years, and the combined influence of the Methodist clergymen later in the eighteenth century. But it was caught in a no-man's land between the Church of England and the Dissenting churches. Had the Established Church been able to accommodate the Methodists in Wales, as it did the Evangelical Anglicans, to some extent, in England, future events might have been very different. In England, men such as

[1] The present chapel, Capel Tegid, was built on a site adjacent to Bethel Chapel in 1867. It originally had a tower with a spire, but this very soon began to lean and proved a financial drain on the congregation until it was eventually demolished in 2000.

Newton, Cecil, Venn, Scott, Simeon, and Pratt, together with a host of other lesser known individuals such as Charles's friends, Griffin, Mayor, and Wilkinson, found livings, established gospel churches and communities, and were linked together in the strong network of Evangelical clergy. Had the Welsh bishops possessed sufficient toleration to ordain Howel Harris, to keep Rowland, Williams, Pantycelyn, Howel Davies, and others, within the camp, and to find livings for men like Charles, Thomas Jones, Creaton, and the many others who departed Wales for parishes in England, a very different situation would have arisen in Wales. Instead of swelling the numbers of the thousands of worshippers meeting in societies, the many revivals of the periods might have produced great congregations of believers with their lives centred around the parish churches. On the other hand, it might be argued that the spirit that burned in men such as Harris, Robert Roberts, Clynnog, John Elias, and others would never have been contained within parish boundaries: that the new wine would inevitably have required new wine skins.

As it was, the two main factors that contributed to the tensions inherent in Welsh Methodism became evident very early on in its history: the lack of clergymen to administer the ordinances, and the ambiguous status of the exhorters. From 1785 until 1806, the only men in the north to administer the sacraments to Methodist believers were Thomas Charles and Simon Lloyd. Then, in 1806, William Lloyd of Nefyn joined them. In the south there were about ten Methodist clergymen to perform this office.

The Wesleyan Methodists in England were in precisely the same position and, despite his determination to remain in the Church of England until the day he died, John Wesley had more or less ensured that the movement would become a separate church. In 1784 he had appointed a Conference of a hundred men to act as his successor (holding the properties of the many Wesleyan societies) and had provided a constitution by which it was to operate. Soon after Wesley's death in 1791, the movement (already a separate church in practice) was formally separated from the Church of

England by law.[2] It is worth noting that this took place when the proportion of Methodists in England was considerably lower than that of the Calvinistic Methodists in Wales at the time.

In Wales, the issue had first been raised as early as 1744, when members of the societies expressed their unwillingness to attend communion at the Established Church. Howel Harris, whose adherence to the Church was as strong as Wesley's, put a stop to any further discussions on the topic. But grass-roots resistance remained. In 1756, the New Inn society in Monmouthshire consulted Daniel Rowland who advised them to call Morgan John Lewis, a local exhorter, as minister over them, with prayer and fasting, adding that 'The prayer of faith will do him more good than the hands of any bishop under the sun.' Other similar ordinations took place and many of the causes formed had little option but to register as independent churches and to be lost to Methodism.

By the time Charles became a significant figure in north Wales, the leadership of the movement was in the hands of the south Wales clergy: David Jones, Llan-gan; David Griffiths, Nevern; Nathaniel Rowland. All of these were firm Churchmen. However, the second factor involved, namely the ambiguous situation of the exhorters or preachers, began to increase in influence. None of these clergymen, except perhaps David Griffiths, could match the preaching powers of Rowland and Harris, their authority over the mob and the congregation alike, and the depth of conviction that attended their ministries. But among the exhorters many men of comparable preaching gifts were being raised up. Preachers such as John Jones (1761–1822), Edern, Robert Roberts (1762–1802), Clynnog, Ebenezer Morris (1769–1825), and John Elias (1774–1841), were masters of pulpit and open-air preaching, and also spiritual leaders of much grace and wisdom. In addition, the practice was increasing for some of these men, while continuing their itinerating, to be particularly associated with a single congregation or society. Ebenezer Morris, for example, was in all practical points the pastor of the Tŵr-gwyn society in Cardiganshire, as his father, Dafydd

---

[2] Rupert E. Davies, *Methodism* (Epworth Press, 1985), 109-12.

Morris, had been before him. Why, complained his congregation, did they have to wait months for a Methodist clergyman to pass by before they could celebrate the Lord's Supper, while their own much-loved pastor, through whose preaching so many of them had been brought to spiritual life, was not allowed to administer the elements to them?

Charles's emergence as leader at the end of the eighteenth century certainly delayed the divorce between the Methodists in Wales and the Established Church. From about 1790 onwards the self-governing order that he had established within Welsh Calvinistic Methodists, together with the strength of his ecclesiastical principles, were sufficient to keep them together.[3] The pressure of the reality of their 'denominational' situation, however, had already brought about practices that were pushing them ever closer to an inevitable separation. Harris's *Rule Book* of 1741, the gathering of congregations in the societies, the collecting boxes of the societies, the hierarchical organization of monthly and quarterly meetings, the chapel buildings raised, the hymn-book prepared for the societies by Robert Jones, Rhos-lan, in 1795: all of these proclaimed their independence from the parish church. Most influential of all were the steps that Charles himself, like Wesley before him, felt compelled to take: his *Rules for the Private Societies* (1801); the burgeoning 'denominational' literature that he and his friends were producing; even his own reputation in the land as a Methodist leader rather than an Established Church leader. These were all identifying steps in the emergence of a new church. 'It seemed as if the child had grown altogether too large for the mother's lap.'[4]

To separate from the Church of England was certainly completely contrary to Charles's inclinations. The comment in the *Preface* to the above *Rules* has already been noted:

> Whatever appears in our proceedings as in any degree tending towards a separation from the Established Church,

[3] Derec Ll. Morgan, *Pobl Pantycelyn* (1986), 76.

[4] Eryn Mant White, 'Gyrfa Thomas Charles yn ei chyd-destun hanesyddol,' in DDM (2014), 7.

takes place from *necessity* and not from *choice*. Making a sect
or forming a party is not the object we are aiming at – God
forbid!

In his entry for the word 'master' (*'meistr'*) in the *Geiriadur
Ysgrythyrol*, his comment on James 3:1 ('Be not many masters'),
reads, 'There are none that do more harm to the cause of true religion, nor any of greater guilt and condemnation, than the authors
of parties and schisms in the church.'

It remains difficult to trace the steps which led to his change of
heart. He had never believed in the apostolic succession, calling it
'the old Popish doctrine of succession' in his *Vindications* of 1802.
However, in that same year he must have expressed to Thomas
Jones, Creaton, his disapproval of anything other than clerical
ordination, for Jones, in reply, had written,

> I was gratified to find … that you are still in your views of
> ordination, such a high churchman. Doubtless, the ordi-
> nation of Priests in the house of God is as much a divine
> positive Institution as either of the two sacraments are.[5]

Thomas Jones, Denbigh, suggests that there was still no change
in his view by 1806, stating, with reference to that date, that, 'At
first the intention and attempt [of ordaining lay men] was not
acceptable to Mr C.'s mind. He continued to resist the suggestion
for many years.'[6]

In the summer of 1807, at the South Wales Association at Llangeitho, the issue of ordaining ministers was raised publicly for the
first time at an Association. Charles was not present. Evan Davies,
an elder from Pen-sarn, Cardiganshire, began to present the case
but he was interrupted by one of the clergymen: 'Who is that man
who is speaking? Turn him out. It is a disgrace to tolerate such a
man amongst us. Out he goes, without any more ado.'[7] No debate
on the issue was allowed at this time. In north Wales, the matter

[5] DEJ, II, 442.
[6] Thomas Jones, *Cofiant y Parch. Thomas Charles* (Bala, 1816), 211.
[7] Jones and Morgan, *Calvinistic Methodist Fathers*, Vol. 2 (2008), 391.

was first discussed at an association at Caernarfon in the autumn of 1808.

The role of Thomas Jones, Denbigh

Charles was absent from this meeting also, in this case suffering from a bad leg. The issue drew ever closer to him when it was discussed at the Rhuthun Association of December 1809. He was again absent, preaching at Stockport, but the main protagonist on the stage and, indeed, the leader for change in the whole of north Wales was his great friend, Thomas Jones, Denbigh. Many at Rhuthun were disappointed that Charles could not be present to hear and contribute to the discussion and Jones decided to write to him to express his views. The letter (4 January 1810) shows clearly the heartache involved for Jones, as he wrote what he knew would not be acceptable to his friend and mentor:

> He that searcheth the heart knoweth it is with extreme reluctance that I dissent from your judgement. I plainly see, and unfeignedly confess, the Lord has endowed you much more of natural, acquired and spiritual knowledge than myself. He has eminently advanced you: he has made you faithful and remarkably successful in his house and service. Much more I might here express, as the real and undisguised sentiments of my heart. And have I envied, or shall I envy, your advancement? God forbid ... What strikes my mind with great force is the import of the following considerations.
>
> 1. The Scriptures appear to me as clear and positive in commanding the use of *both* sacraments in the church of Christ – also plainly in favour of the celebration of the Lord's supper more frequently, if not more statedly, than is practised amongst us.
>
> 2. I do not recollect seeing a visible church described by any writer, but as a congregation etc. of people, having the word of God truly preached, and the sacraments duly administered among them.
>
> 3. I observe that baptism, generally speaking, is not administered amongst us.

4. That in several of our societies there are many people, who are unwilling to have their children baptized in the Church of England, and by her Ministers. This unwillingness, as well as the number of people inclined to it, seems to be continually increasing; and as to communicating in the Church of England, there are but a very few of our people who are so inclined.

5. That to all appearance there are many of our fellow-members who are verily hurt in their consciences by being pressed to have their children baptized in the Church of England, by her unawakened ministers, etc. etc.

6. That several seek the ordinance from Dissenting Ministers, though with a mind unwilling through more than one consideration.

That compelling any of our members to seek for either of the sacraments from without the pale of our own connection is a thing we ought not to be guilty of, as being contrary to the word of God and to the universal custom of the Churches of God, in every age and country.

… If I have dropped any expression, or done any action that has hurt your mind, as indeed I fear I have (though without any intentional disrespect) I beg you will forgive me, for his sake who forgiveth us all our offences.

And now I most earnestly intreat you to bear with us all, that have spoken, or acted, in this way, not by any combination, but from the free impulse of our hearts; also that you yield at least in some degree, to the request of your brethren, for the sake of God and his truth, and for the sake of the Churches' peace and edification; moreover that you use the weight and authority which the Lord has given you, in regulating, rather than resisting, our weak and unseemly, yet honest, endeavour. If your heart be but favourably inclined to a moderating way, I doubt not of your being the instrument in God's hand to direct, regulate, and settle the matter …[8]

[8] Jones, Idwal, JHS, 29 (1944), 116-19.

This sincere and honest letter proved, in the event, to be a remarkably prescient statement, in that all of Jones's hopes were fulfilled and by exactly the method he had prayed for. In the meantime, however, by his actions, he began to increase the pressure on Charles. On 9 March 1810, he baptized a child at its home; then, on 9 June, he baptized a child at the chapel in Denbigh for the first time. By June 1811 he had baptized thirteen babies at Denbigh and others also in the neighbouring towns. These steps were not motivated by any thought of provoking Charles to a decision. Rather, they were the results of a long process of conviction during which Jones had struggled against the knowledge that such actions would sadden many of his colleagues, and 'one brother and father in particular, whose memory was, and is today, held in greater respect than that of any other man whom I have known on the face of the earth.'[9] However, the conviction that he was not fulfilling his pastoral duty towards the congregation at Denbigh led him, soon after the first baptisms, to raise the matter at a Monthly Meeting, and 'a number of my brethren ... allowed or tolerated the congregation and myself to follow our consciences, with respect to the other ordinance, the Lord's Supper.'[10]

Coming to a decision

In the light of the two issues of the administration of the ordinances and the status of the preachers, what would have weighed most on Charles's mind during the months from January to June 1810 was the knowledge, hinted at by Jones in his letter, that there was a very real danger of a division in the ranks of the Welsh Methodists. The reality of their situation suggested strongly that the formal ordaining of ministers to serve the Connexion was inevitable. Sooner or later, it would occur, either as a result of a corporate decision by the Connexion or as a series of individual rebellions in societies or Monthly Meetings. Within the membership, however, there existed a wide spectrum of views with respect to church

[9] Idwal Jones (ed.), *Hunangofiant Thomas Jones* (Aberystwyth, 1937), 53.
[10] *Ibid.*, 54.

government, and Charles would have realized that the magnitude of the division which would inevitably occur would be decided, to a considerable extent, by the position which he himself adopted.

He had always believed in the settled order of the Established Church and its place as a national institution; he considered the status of a religion that received the acknowledgment and support of the law of the land as a more privileged position than that of a religion only tolerated by legal enactment. These were principles that he had learnt from his early mentor, John Newton.[11] When the Countess of Huntingdon's Connexion had ordained preachers in 1783 he had refused to take part, and had not subsequently preached in any of her chapels until 1790. Were he to follow his life-long inclination of loyalty to the Established Church and refuse to allow a process of ordination to be put in place, the respect and prestige in which he was held would result in a large number of Methodists being retained within the Church of England. The separate Calvinistic Methodist denomination that would emerge would inevitably be a much weakened body.

Were he, on the other hand, to bow to the pressures for separation from the Established Church, he would be leading Methodism into Dissent, he would sever innumerable ties of Christian fellowship and co-operation, he would quite possibly lose most of the financial help from England for the schools and other projects. Indeed, such a step would jeopardise all his connections with Evangelical clergymen who had been a major element of his life since his conversion.

His close friend, Thomas Jones, knew exactly the tensions and anxieties with which Charles was burdened at the time. He described how in these years leading up to 1811, 'the aim and object were not to the mind of Mr Charles ... He continued to oppose for several years, but in a kind way, and admitting that it might become a necessity, by the increase of demands, and the ripeness of the time.'[12] The truths which Charles had emphasized to Edward

[11] J. E. Wynne Davies, JHS, 38 (2014), 74.
[12] Thomas Jones, *Cofiant* (1816), 210-11.

Morgan, Syston, would now have been often in his own mind:

> Providence, I am fully convinced led me in the way in which
> I move; for I never thought of it. Unbiased by prejudice,
> self-interest, the love of ease, or the honour which comes
> from men, lift up your eyes to the hills from whence our
> help cometh, and the Lord will guide you safely; and in his
> own good time, you will see the way clearly before you.[13]

On many occasions in the past, providence had opened up
for him paths which he had long desired to tread. Providence had
arranged that his marriage with Sally could proceed; had provided
a ministry for him at Bala; had blessed his schools; enabled him
to provide the societies with Christian literature; had established
a world-wide Society, so that his own land might have Welsh
Bibles. In all these steps he had acknowledged the wise hand of
providence. Now, it would seem, the guidance of providence was
again equally clear, but in this case pointing in a direction that was
directly opposite to his prejudices and loyalties.

It was during an association at this time (possibly the Bala Association of June 1810), when Charles was present and was chairing
the private meeting, that a famous debate took place. There was
considerable anxiety and concern in the societies and Monthly
Meetings leading up to the Association, with many fearing that
this could be the occasion of a parting of the ways among them.
The scene was described by John Morgan Jones as follows:

> The argument had become quite heated, the meeting was
> a degree agitated, and Mr Charles, who was in the chair,
> seemed completely unwilling to allow any further develop-
> ment. Many feared for the consequences, sensing that the
> meeting might end in disruption. When the discussion was
> at its fiercest, Ebenezer Morris rose to his feet in the big seat
> and leant his weight on one of the pillars supporting the
> pulpit. Everything about him expressed dignity, solemnity,
> and the air of one who had a message and was himself aware
> of its importance. Soon, all discussion ceased and the eyes of

[13] See above, p. 255.

the whole assembly were upon him. For a moment he did not speak but remained standing, as dumb as an idol. At last, with perfect self-possession but with a masterly manner, he stated that he had a question to ask and that he wished to receive a truthful answer. The congregation, anticipating that the question would be crucial, strained to hear with every eye fixed upon the questioner. Mr Morris proceeded:

'I represent many hundreds of people in this congregation and other places and I call upon Mr Charles to answer me, charging him to provide a sincere, honest answer to my query. And this is it. Which is the greater, the preaching of the gospel or the administering of the sacraments?'

The Association immediately recognized the importance of the question and the attention of all was transferred from Mr Morris to Mr Charles. After a moment's consideration he also got to his feet. The expression on his face proved that he himself realized that he had been pushed into a corner and in the midst of a profound and painful silence he replied:

'The greater work is the preaching of the gospel.'

'We are one therefore,' responded Mr Morris. 'The Devil thought he would split us as an Association today, but thank heaven, we are one.'

With these words an indescribable emotion shot through all hearts like a bolt of lightning, and all breathed freely. It does not appear that any resolution was passed on the matter there and then, but all departed with the conviction that the battle was over and that the argument for ordination had been won. The news of the meeting spread quickly throughout Wales. It was the one topic of conversation everywhere – Mr Morris's question, and Mr Charles's reply. And the hearts of the people rejoiced at the thought that they would receive a regular administration of the sacraments, and that from the hands of those eloquent preachers from whose ministry they drew such benefit.[14]

[14] Jones and Morgan, *Calvinistic Methodist Fathers*, Vol. 2 (2008), 401-02; HMGC2, 302-03.

Very soon after this meeting, Charles not only realized that he would have to agree to the ordaining of ministers within the Calvinistic Methodist Connexion but also, for the good of the Connexion, that he himself would have to be seen to be the guiding and organizing hand behind any arrangements made. He put aside his own feelings and accepted providence's guidance. In the words of Simon Lloyd, writing in the *Evangelical Magazine* for 1815: 'Mr C. for several years opposed this measure, wishing them to remain in communion with the established church; but, at length, this appearing to be impracticable, he acquiesced in it as a matter of indispensable necessity.'

Having made his decision, Charles responded quickly. In a letter to Joseph Tarn, dated 12 July, he noted the actions he had taken:

> I brought forward at the private meeting several propositions respecting the admittance of what is called the lay preachers to administer the Sacraments in conjunction with the clergy, which passed unanimously, to the great satisfaction of the whole body. I never had so delicate a subject under my consideration as I had prejudices of an opposite nature to combat with. However, through the Lord's blessing upon my endeavours, I hope I have succeeded. To pass incensured by different parties I do not expect, but I am happy that the body of Welsh Calvinistic Methodists seem to have been, by the means adopted, by all appearances more firmly compacted than ever; and by that means likely to be more extensively useful in promoting knowledge and reformation through the whole country.[15]

It is interesting that he wrote this letter to London so soon after the June Association meeting. The delicate balance of mutual zeal, friendships, and diplomacies that maintained the evangelical, inter-denominational co-operation so necessary for the success of the Bible Society and other societies, had always to be nurtured, and Charles would not have wished that wild stories of separation

[15] DEJ, III, 264.

and schism should have reached London before he had paved the way as carefully as he could.

The ordination services

In April 1811 Charles wrote from Bala to his brother, David, in the south:

> I wish to have an interview with some of the South Wales brethren before the annual meeting at Bala. If I cannot meet with you at Cardigan, I think a few of those who take a lead in the concerns of the body ought to meet here at Llanfyllin Association April 23 and 24. Our plan of proceeding ought to be agreed upon, that everything may be done decently, respectably and peaceably. I find very little help from any here. After all their bustle and clamour, they are all now at a stand, and totally at a loss how to proceed farther. It is no pleasant work for me; but I am willing to sacrifice everything for the good of the cause. My inmost soul abhors the conduct of some of our hot-headed young men; however they are now silent, and in a great degree have lost their imaginary importance.[16]

The last months of 1810, and the spring of 1811 were taken up with arrangements. Charles wished above all things to avoid controversy over the choice of the men who would be ordained. These would be men who would serve their various localities but would also be representatives of the Connexion as a whole. Both Monthly Meetings and the Annual Association had to be involved in the choice therefore and the possibilities of rival geographical claims and personal disagreement were only too evident. All arrangements had to be passed on to the South Wales Association for it to agree and to proceed with its own ordinations afterwards. Charles used David, his brother, as the go-between:

> Though I was not an ostensible agent, yet behind the curtain (*between us*) I was obliged to influence the whole, or else they

---

[16] *Ibid.*, III, 274.

would have been much at a loss how to proceed, and likely to create disputes and confusion. I wished the brethren in the different counties to know each other's minds, and to be sensible that they were not choosing the persons to act only for their respective districts, but for the whole body at large, and therefore, it was proper that they should be approved of by the body as collectively considered in their Association. But to have any proposed at the Association and *rejected*, I thought would be attended with a variety of bad disputes. Those who have been nominated at Bala are to be announced to the respective monthly meetings in each county, subject to animadversion there, and alterations if judged advisable.[17]

Such was Charles's sensitivity to the impression that their radical actions would make on all the many observers – friendly and otherwise – who watched with interest the developments in Wales, that he drew up strict restraints concerning who should be considered eligible to be ordained. He was very fearful of any failure of discernment that might result in the denomination being brought to shame and ridicule by scandal or backsliding amongst its ordained men. His draft document (which was subsequently adopted by the North and South Assemblies) therefore contained the following rule:

Inasmuch as the Apostle charges Timothy to lay hands hastily on no man, and thereby be a partner of other men's sins, and not to choose a novice in the faith, we are of the opinion that no one should be chosen unless the connexion has had proof of his ministry for at least five years.[18]

In the same letter to his brother, Charles described the form that the Ordination Service should take:

Lastly, their names are to be announced at the Bala Association and to be approved of by lifting up of hands before they

[17] DEJ, III, 277-78.
[18] *Ibid.*, III, 280.

are solemnly separated to the work by the prayers of three of
our oldest and most venerable brethren, viz. old John Evans,
Robert Jones [Rhos-lan], and John Jones, Bodynolwyn, in
Anglesey. I shall previously prepare everything ready for that
meeting, write down the questions to be asked, and order
the whole proceeding that everything may be conducted
with proper solemnity and decorum; but I do not choose to
take an *open* active part in the business.[19]

No clergyman was to take part in the proceedings, therefore,
and the candidates were to be ordained not by the laying on of
hands but by a show of hands of the gathered elders and clergymen. Both of these steps were in order to ensure that not a vestige
of apostolic succession might be read into the proceedings.

He had no concept, as in John Wesley's case when he
ordained men for America in September 1784, of continuing within the Episcopal Church … [nor did he] follow the
Form of Ordination of the Church. He ploughed his own
furrow, refusing a laying on of hands and instead proffering
the right hand of fellowship. He did not present a Bible
to those being ordained and the sacrament of the Lord's
Supper was not part of the service. He was fully aware that
there was now a new denomination, the Calvinistic Methodist Church of Wales.[20]

The Bala Association of 1811 was held on 19-20 June, where the
first eight Welsh Methodists were ordained to the ministry by their
own Connexion. Charles was not to have his own way of avoiding
taking 'an *open*, active part,' probably because the aged John Jones
of Anglesey was unable to make the journey, and he was pressed
to officiate alongside John Evans and Robert Jones. The following
description of the ceremony, and of the subsequent occasion at
the South Wales Association on 7-8 August (at Llandeilo, Carmarthenshire) has been included in every edition of the *Confession
of Faith of the Calvinistic Methodists* since it was published in 1823:

[19] *Ibid.*, III, 278.
[20] J. E. Wynne Davies, JHS, 38 (2014), 76.

First, the oldest and most revered member of the Connexion, John Evans of Bala, read 1 Tim. 3, making, as he read, simple and appropriate remarks on the qualifications required in ministers of the Gospel; and when he had read the chapter, he led in prayer, in language simple and appropriate to the occasion. Second, the Rev. T. Charles, of Bala, read, in the hearing of all, the names of those who had been chosen by the Monthly Meetings: Thomas Jones and John Davies, from Denbighshire; John Elias and Richard Lloyd, from Anglesey; Evan Richards, from Caernarvonshire; John Roberts, from Merioneth; Evan Griffiths and William Jones, from Montgomeryshire ...

When he had read their names to the representatives of the Connexion, about three hundred being present, the Rev. Thomas Charles requested them to signify, by show of hands if they wished him to ask the brethren a few questions, in their hearing, concerning the fundamental doctrines of the Christian religion. This being the unanimous wish of the assembly, he asked the following questions ...[21]

There followed nineteen questions on basic truths: the being and attributes of God; the Trinity; the word of God; God's decree and election; the person of Christ; the offices of Christ; the sacrifice of Christ and redemption; the work of the Holy Ghost in the plan of salvation; the call of the gospel; the ordinances, etc. The next two questions were:

20. Do you sincerely approve of the present form of church government of the Calvinistic Methodists of Wales?

21. Do you intend, as far as lies in your power, and with the Lord's help, to maintain the unity of the Connexion in the form in which the Lord has hitherto so greatly blessed it, and set your faces against all unprofitable and contentious disputes that tend to engender strife?

When he had asked these questions and received simple and intelligent answers, he requested the Connexion to

[21] *Confession of Faith of the Calvinistic Methodists* (Caernarfon, 1900), 20.

declare, by show of hands, if they chose these brethren to administer the ordinances of Baptism and the Lord's Supper among them. They did so unanimously.

After this the Rev. Thomas Charles asked the brethren:

22. Do you, with full consent of mind, accept the call of the Connexion to administer the ordinances of Baptism and the Lord's Supper, and are you resolved to labour faithfully and diligently, to feed the flock of God by administering to them the divine ordinances with all earnestness, according to the help that God may give you?

They answered humbly and simply, 'We do,' and earnestly desired the prayers of the whole Connexion.[22]

Robert Jones, Rhos-lan, then delivered a general exhortation to both ordinands and Connexion, and closed the meeting with prayer.

The South Wales Association ordained thirteen men: John Evans, David Rees, Arthur Evans and David Charles from Carmarthenshire; James James, David Parry and Evan Evans from Breconshire; Ebenezer Morris, John Thomas and Ebenezer Richard from Cardiganshire; Evan Harris from Pembrokeshire; Hopcin Bevan from Glamorgan, and John Rees from Monmouthshire. It was, of course, the prerogative of the south Wales brethren to appoint those whom they wished to conduct the service. In contrast to the service at Bala, they chose three clergymen: John Williams, Lledrod, to offer prayer; Thomas Charles to put the questions; John Williams, Pantycelyn, to close with prayer. Of all those involved in planning these meetings, Charles was by far the one with the strongest attachment to the Church of England, but it was he who had most realized that in their actions as a new denomination there should be no thoughtless repetition of the ceremonies and practices of the past but a new start based on their understanding of scriptural principles. 'It was not an Episcopal [ordination], for no bishop was present; nor was it an Independent or Presbyterian [ordination] for it was not the call of individual churches that

[22] *Ibid.*, 21.

appointed the men to be ordained.'[23] Eryn Mant White comments: 'As the last Anglican clergyman to lead the movement, he was in the strange situation of ensuring the disappearance of his type, as he chaired the meetings for ordaining ministers.'[24]

The aftermath

In the months following the ordinations various groups expressed their disapproval in different ways. The responses of four particular groups are worth noting:

(1) *The clergymen who left the movement*

Of the thirteen clergymen who had been attached to the Methodist Connexion, seven withdrew, all of them from south Wales. The six who remained were the three north Wales clergymen, Charles, Simon Lloyd, and William Lloyd, together with John Williams, Pantycelyn, John Williams, Lledrod, and Howel Howells, St Nicholas. This meant that after 1811 the total number of ordained Methodists in Wales was still only twenty-seven men; eleven serving in the north and sixteen in the south.[25] The greatest loss to the ranks of the Methodists was, by far, that of David Griffiths, Nevern. So many of the Methodist societies in Pembrokeshire retained their loyalty to him, breaking their connections with the new denomination, that the Calvinistic Methodist Church remained weaker in northern Pembrokeshire than in other parts of the country for much of the nineteenth century.

[23] Jonathan Jones, *Cofiant y Parch. Thomas Jones o Ddinbych* (1897), 248.

[24] Eryn Mant White, 'Gyrfa Thomas Charles yn ei chyd-destun hanesyddol,' in DDM (2014), 16.

[25] The example of Charles's self-imposed restraint on the numbers of men being ordained was followed over many years. During the next ten years, for example, out of the two to three hundred preachers serving the denomination, only a further thirty-four were ordained: eighteen in the north and sixteen in the south. This meant that by 1820 the movement had still less than sixty men eligible to administer the sacraments to the hundreds of societies throughout the land. Edward Jones, *Y Gymdeithasfa* (1891), 121-22; 146-47.

(2) *Remaining reservations within the new denomination*

The South Wales Association meeting in August was always held at Llangeitho but the elders there refused to host the 1811 Association. This is why the first ordinations in the south took place at Llandeilo. The probable reason for this refusal was that there was considerable feeling in Llangeitho against ordaining laymen. Why this was the case is not known. For very many years they had received communion monthly at the hands of Daniel Rowland and William Williams. After the death of Rowland in 1790, the Rev. John Williams, whose home was only eight miles away at Lledrod, visited them to administer communion. It may be that their privileged position in this respect had spoilt them and prejudiced them against receiving the elements from the denominationally-ordained ministers.

In 1812, however, John Williams was unwell and could not leave home. The society at Llangeitho took advantage of the fact that Charles was travelling to an association in Pembrokeshire and asked him to preach on the Sunday and to serve at the Lord's Supper. Their chapel was being enlarged at the time and so the tables with the elements were laid out in the village square. Travelling with Charles was John Roberts, Llangwm, Denbighshire, brother of Robert Roberts, Clynnog. He had been ordained at Bala the previous year, had ministered among the Methodists for thirty-two years, and had been a frequent preacher in their associations, both in the north and in the south. Both men preached in the morning and Charles then approached the table and called Roberts to his side to help distribute the bread and wine. When the Llangeitho elders saw this they stood up and refused to allow Roberts to participate. Charles was almost ruthless in response. Although between nine hundred and a thousand people were present expecting to receive communion, he refused to take the service. The people had to return to their homes, many in tears, and Charles then called the elders together. He rebuked them and demanded that they present themselves at the Pembrokeshire Association, at which he testified against them. They were required by their brethren to repent and to promise that they would not repeat the offence.

Charles's response is significant in that it reveals how firmly he supported the ordained men, once the decision had been taken. He was determined that no two-tier system of ministry should be contemplated. Whether episcopally-ordained or denomination-ally-ordained, all the ministers of the movement were of equal status, and he would not accept any undermining of that position.

(3) The Evangelicals of the Church in England

One immediate result of the ordination was the end of the long-standing friendship and correspondence between Charles and Thomas Jones, Creaton. Thomas Jones (1752–1845) was born in the village of Hafod, Cardiganshire, and was a fellow Welsh-speaker and fellow evangelical clergyman. Charles first met him in Lup-pington, twelve miles north of Shrewsbury, where he was a curate. In 1783 Jones moved to Creaton in Northamptonshire where he remained as curate, and then rector, for forty-three years. It is as Thomas Jones, Creaton, that he is generally known. He cor-responded with Charles about the foundation of Sunday schools and established one in Creaton in 1789. Apart from the first five years, his fifty-nine years of ministry were all in England, though he maintained a keen interest in and concern for his homeland, and longed at times to return.

In Jones, Creaton, we see, perhaps, a mirror of what Charles's life might have been had he not fallen in love with Sally: an evangelical clergyman who, failing to get a permanent curacy in Wales, had to accept a curacy in England in order to fulfil his calling; a successful preaching and writing career (amongst many other works, Jones translated Baxter's *Saints' Everlasting Rest* into Welsh); as vicar over his own church and parish, establishing a centre of evangelical influence, but always with an eye on his bishop to ensure that he kept on his right side. The example of Philip Oliver had warned him of the consequences of not doing so, namely, being forbidden to preach in the diocese.[26]

[26] Phillips, Sybil, JHS, 32 (2008), 90-93.

Towards the end of 1811, Jones made a journey through north Wales and subsequently published a forty-eight-page booklet based on what he had observed, entitled '*The Welsh Looking-Glass, or Thoughts on the State of Religion in North Wales.*' The quotation on the title-page revealed his view of events: 'The anger of the Lord hath divided them,' (Lam. 4:16). The work included four short sections: 'On the Manner of Some Preachers'; 'On the Sin of Schism'; 'On Spurious Ordination'; 'On Clerical Misconduct.' Jones was furious with the Methodists for their 'unscriptural' division of 'a Christian Church,' and furious with Charles (although not naming him) for allowing it.[27]

It would not have surprised Charles therefore, though no doubt it greatly saddened him, to receive eventually a letter (7 July 1813) from his old friend and fellow-labourer, ending any further correspondence between them. The following extracts convey the tone of the letter:

> … I once fondly hoped that the Calvinistic Welsh Methodists would have continued in existence, as such, during your days at least. But they are no more, no such body of men now exists in Wales, no, no, they are no more, and this I most deeply lament. You probably will attribute this to mistaken high Church principles, but surely not very high when I so highly esteem Methodism such as had existed long in Wales; and which I ardently wished to exist till the whole church had been illuminated and renovated; and things were bidding fair for such a glorious event, and could you have lived to better purpose? But lo! The bright prospect was clouded in a day. Methodism was annihilated, and in lieu of which a mischievous plan was introduced …
>
> … I pity your case from my very heart. I pity your awful mistake in yielding at all to a torrent of iniquity, when your influence was sufficient to prevent it, and it is still sufficient to overturn the whole of it, that is at all material to do away

---

[27] DEJ, III, 308; Sybil Philips, 'Thomas Jones of Creaton and *The Welsh Looking Glass,*' JHS, 32 (2008), 102-03.

... Should you plead that you listen to the voice of the people, I answer, no, but to the voice of the wicked spirits through a small part of the people. The thing is done. It is not of God. It will not end well ...[28]

There is very little evidence to judge how many of Charles's other Church of England friends and financial supporters in England responded in like manner.

(4) The Established Church in Wales

The damage done to the Established Church in Wales by the ordination of 1811 was enormous. Up to that point many thousands of believers who belonged to the Methodist Connexion also acknowledged some degree of affiliation to the Church (though in innumerable cases that affiliation was nominal at best). After 1811 any semblance of the Connexion being a wing or party within the Church disappeared. The returns of the religious census carried out by the Government in 1851 revealed the stark nature of the change that had occurred in the denominational profile of the country within forty years of the ordination. Of the total worshippers in Wales recorded for the service that drew the largest attendance on the day of the census, 79% attended Nonconformist chapels and 21% attended the Church. The percentages of the various denominations were made up as follows: Calvinistic Methodists, 25; Independents, 23; Church of England, 21; Baptists, 18; Wesleyans, 13.[29]

Eliezer Williams (1754–1820), the vicar of Lampeter, Cardiganshire, and son of the commentator, Peter Williams, complained:

Had our spiritual rulers given more encouragement to pious ministers, and had they pursued more conciliatory measures toward these men ... we should not now have to mourn over the prevalence of schism, & the emptiness of our venerable churches.[30]

[28] DEJ, III, 312-14.
[29] John Davies, *A History of Wales* (Penguin, 2007), 412.
[30] J. E. Wynne Davies, JHS, 38 (2014), 79.

Too late, the bishops realized their mistakes. In 1810, three months after the decision by the Methodists to ordain their own men, Bishop Cleaver of St Asaph, known as an 'Anti-Methodist,' ordained Thomas Richards and, later, John Lloyd, John Owen[31] and Lewis Hughes from amongst the laity. These were 'evangelicals given the liberty to deepen and nurture personal religion in the manner of the Methodists without fear of their being judged.'[32] These men, and other Evangelicals appointed later, could do little to repair the breach that had been made but, together with others of the same spirit, they ensured that the evangelical testimony within the Church did not die out entirely.

'I had prejudices … to combat with'

It needs to be remembered that sorrow over the parting of the ways was not alone the experience of men such as Jones, Creaton, and Eliezer Williams. It was acutely felt by Charles himself. This is well-expressed in one of the concluding paragraphs of a paper on Charles by a present-day Calvinistic Methodist historian:

> On reviewing the life of Thomas Charles, it is seen that he was deeply hurt when he failed to obtain a position in which to serve the Church which he loved, but he was more deeply pained still when he failed to keep the Methodist flock within it. He was an Evangelical Anglican to the end …'[33]

It is an ironic element in Charles's career that his strong Churchmanship and his position as a clergyman were crucial to the success of the Methodist cause. He could never have won over the London philanthropists to his schemes of circulating schools

---

[31] John Owen became vicar of Thrussington, Leicestershire, in 1845 and wrote brief biographies of Thomas Jones, Creaton, and Daniel Rowland. The latter was republished in the *Banner of Truth* magazine, issues 215-16 (1981). He also translated Calvin's commentaries on Jeremiah, Lamentations, and the Minor Prophets for the Calvin Translation Society.

[32] J. E. Wynne Davies, JHS, 38 (2014), 79, quoting from Roger Brown, *The Welsh Evangelicals* (Tongwynlais, 1986).

[33] J. E. Wynne Davies, JHS, 38 (2014), 79.

and Welsh Bible production, nor raised sufficient interest and support for them in Wales, had he been only a Methodist exhorter such as Howel Harris or John Elias. Nor could he have been in a position to learn of the national movements of his times – the missionary activities, the philanthropic societies, the powerful London evangelical lobby – had he not been made so familiar with the religious developments in the capital by his frequent visits to Spa Fields Chapel.

Furthermore, it was his reluctance to secede that delayed the divorce between the Methodists in Wales and the Established Church, thus ensuring that all the crucial institutions and educational means that he had set in place (schools, catechisms, Bible editions, the *Geiriadur*, etc.) had completely won their place in the nation before the break occurred. They would hardly have come into existence or, at the very most, their influence would have been fragmentary, had they been the products of the more disordered, uncoordinated Methodist denomination that would probably have resulted from a much earlier separation. In January 1813, eighteen months after the ordination and the formal separation of the Methodists from the Church of England, Charles could still affirm at a meeting held at Bala Town Hall for the purpose of forming an Auxiliary Bible Society and attended mainly by the Church of England gentry of Merioneth:

> I always use the prayers of the Church in publicly administering the Sacraments of the Lord's Supper, and in our Chapels, the Bible, with the Prayer Book bound with it, is in general on all our pulpits.[34]

It must, nevertheless, be considered a weakness in Charles that he had, for so long, failed to respond to the pressures building up within the Calvinistic Methodist ranks because of the scarcity of ministers. This may seem to contradict what is argued above

---

[34] DEJ, III, 454. It is surprising to learn that, in 1831, twenty years after the 1811 ordination, Charles's grand-daughter, Jane Charles, was still attending the Bala Anglican Church service on Sunday mornings, after having first worshipped at the Methodist meeting. DDM (2014), 203-04.

that his reticence to allow ordination rescued the movement from a premature separation from the Established Church. However, had Charles been allowed to continue to have his own way, it is possible, or likely even, that no action would have been taken until some catastrophic, disorganized revolt had broken out. It needed the courage and pastoral concern of Thomas Jones, as manifested by his unilateral actions of baptizing infants and his challenging of Charles by letter, and the persistence of men such as Ebenezer Morris in raising the issue repeatedly at the associations, to force Charles to a decision. And that decision was not the one that he would have come to of himself. When he wrote to Joseph Tarn, 'I never had so delicate a subject under my consideration as I had prejudices of an opposite nature to combat with,'[35] it would have been his own prejudices that he would have been most aware of. He was still unready to acknowledge fully the spiritual weaknesses of the Established Church in Wales, though he himself had suffered so much because of them. When the younger Methodist preachers called for separation in the associations he tended to dismiss their arguments as the opinions of 'hot-headed young men.'[36] Perhaps the situation at Bala might also have shielded him from the common experiences of most societies. Like the Llangeitho society in Cardiganshire, the Bala society had a clergyman near at hand, and knew nothing of the deprivation of the communion table, or of the humiliation of having to resort to unwelcoming parish churches when a child needed to be baptized. Thomas Jones, on the other hand, as the unordained pastor of Denbighshire societies depending on Charles's infrequent visits for their communion feasts, shared the situation of the vast majority of the Methodist preachers. He had a much clearer appreciation of the growing unrest and the critical state of the movement. It was this that eventually compelled him to write to Charles:

> I most earnestly intreat you to bear with us all … also that
> you yield at least to some extent, to the request of your

[35] See p. 298 above.
[36] See p. 299 above.

brethren, for the sake of God and his truth, and for the sake of the Church's peace and edification.[37]

The Methodist Revival continues unchecked

Nevertheless, the subsequent progress of the new denomination after the events of 1811 would have brought Charles considerable comfort. Far from 'sealing their own death warrant,' as prophesied by Thomas Jones, Creaton, the ordination ushered in a further period of quickening among the Methodists. As in the awakening of 1806 the greater numbers of those affected were the products of the Sunday schools. Now in his late fifties, Charles's health had so much improved that he was able to undertake preaching journeys of many weeks' duration, and he reported what he had experienced in a letter (March 1812) he wrote to a friend in London:

> The prospect in South Wales, in a religious point of view, is most delightful. In some parts was truly presented to us a faithful representation of the Day of Pentecost; there was a mighty rushing wind that bore down all before it. Into one Society, above 140 were received in the space of about two months. All the young people in a *large* district were under religious impressions. The Associations at Aberystwyth and Haverfordwest were very pleasing and profitable. The congregation at the former amounted to about 20,000 people, and great order and solemnity prevailed during the whole of the meetings. I have seen something similar in former days, but nothing like it for years past. Preaching was as easy as opening the lips. Without being in the work, and partakers of the influences, no one can form any conception of it. For my own part, whilst I have any memory, I shall never forget it! It is the more delightful to me as I view it, in a great measure, as the happy fruit of our Sunday Schools. I pray the Lord it may spread wider and wider, till it cover the land! More had been done in a few weeks since the work began, than was done before in many years painful labour,

---

[37] See p. 293 above.

although perhaps it is the produce of those years of faithful labour.

The Lord hath done great things for us, whereof we are glad! Our mouths are filled with laughter! Excuse my warmth in writing on the subject. When I think of it my whole soul is kindled in a flame.[38]

Three months later, in the June 1812 issue of the '*Trysorfa*,' he described the beginning of the revival in more detail:

The Sunday schools are in a more flourishing state in many places in the south and in Gwynedd than ever before. The efforts of the faithful and godly teachers are being crowned by that success which they long for, namely the awakening and conversion, it is hoped, of hundreds of the children and youth under their instruction. In my journey through parts of the south this last spring the scenes were very pleasant in many places, and were a particular proof of the labour and faithfulness of the teachers. In some areas all the youth of the place were under their tuition, and most of them under discipline also, having joined the private societies in their neighbourhoods. They were under strong influences, with very satisfactory indications of the reformation of their lives. It was pleasing to see the old mother church of Llangeitho, once more renewed in her youth, rising up as the eagle. The present revival began in Lledrod, from there it spread to Swyddffynnon, Tregaron and Llangeitho. I now hear that the church at Morfa, and the Sunday school associated have received refreshing showers. In the regions around Bala a hopeful awakening has begun among the youth in the schools, and I hear that there is a similar work among the children and youth of Denbigh. Go forth, heavenly fire, until you have overcome the whole of Wales!

[38] DEJ, III, 419-20.

Top: The two Charles brothers, Thomas and David.
Bottom: Thomas Jones, Creaton.

15

THE LAST YEARS
(1812–14)

Thomas Rice Charles had been in partnership with his mother in the shop at Bala since 1808, and in May 1810 Sally eventually retired from the business. At this time, she and Charles moved house, but only as far as next door (the house to the right when facing the shop). Thomas Rice had married Maria Jones of Wrexham in 1806 and they were to have five children: Sarah (1807–33), Maria (1809–36), Thomas (1810–73), David (1812–78), and Jane (1813–92). Thomas Charles lived to see all these, his five grand-children. Living next door to the shop, he and Sally would have known the pleasure of their company around them for the last seven years of their lives. Sally was by now fifty-six years old and during her remaining years her health deteriorated rapidly. She suffered her first stroke early in 1810. 'I am hardly a moment from her through the whole of the day,' wrote Charles to a friend in March.[1] In the last week of November 1811, she experienced a second stroke during a mid-week society meeting. The following extracts from two letters Charles wrote to Lydia Foulks at this time, show further evidence of the love between these two Christian pilgrims as they neared the end of their days. They also reveal that Sally had never completely freed herself from periods of lack of assurance:

> … We can do but little for her but commit her to the Lord, whose she is, and will be forever. Her mind is in some degree stayed upon the Lord, who is precious to her as the God of her salvation. Though I am able to commit her to the Lord, yet I am very loath to part with her, who has afforded me so

[1] DEJ, III, 257.

A late nineteenth-century photograph of the Charles home.
(After Sally retired from the shop the couple moved into the house to
the right of the shop.)

much comfort for the eight and twenty years we have lived
together. But sooner or later we must part for a time, though
not without hope of meeting again in a better world. This is
a blessed hope indeed!

I have not the least doubt of the safety of her state. I
have had such satisfactory and repeated proofs of her sincerity and piety towards God. The Saviour is precious to her,
though seldom through her whole life without her doubts
and anxious fears ...

I am happy to inform you that my dear partner's health
is much improved since my last ... She is able to read a little
now and then in the Bible and in Caryl on Job. You would
think her very courageous, were you to see her with a tre-
mendously large folio, such as Caryl is, before her; but that
is the sight she presents us with often ... She finds profit in
Caryl.[2]

[2] DEJ, III, 410-11.

Whenever Charles was away for any length of time on his preaching itineraries, he ensured that someone stayed with Sally to care for her. Often this companion was Mary Foulks, Lydia and Thomas Foulks's daughter, who would come over from Machynlleth and spend the required week or fortnight at Bala. Sally became very attached to her.

Charles's youngest child, David Jones Charles, was by now nineteen years old and had served an apprenticeship with a local apothecary. Charles wrote to Joseph Tarn in London in the hope of obtaining work for him, describing him as 'a good tempered man and fond of his profession' but 'not a spiritual man.' In the same letter, Charles wrote,

> Mrs Charles is still an invalid, though much improved in health. I venture to leave her for 5 to 6 weeks, though I tremble at the thought of it. At home and abroad I must commit her to the Lord, and leave her to his kind care and keeping.[3]

An occasion of great joy to Charles took place in the Town Hall, Bala, on 7 January 1813 when a public meeting agreed to form the Merioneth Auxiliary Bible Society. The chairman of the meeting was Sir Watkin Williams Wynn, Bart., Lord Lieutenant of the county, and several others of the gentry of Merioneth were present, who would all, of course, have been members of the Church of England. Wales was far behind England in the formation of such auxiliaries, and the main obstacle was the refusal of the clergy to co-operate. Their reticence held back influential Churchmen who would otherwise have willingly assisted. In Merioneth, however, the general respect and admiration for Charles's work overcame all opposition and lukewarmness, and not the least of Charles's rejoicings was the knowledge that this step in Bala would help to change the climate in other Welsh counties. He shared the good news with Tarn:

> The Bishops and the clergy raise up all the opposition they can against us; but however I hope we shall so far prevail as

[3] *Ibid.*, III, 444.

to do some good. We have gained a whole Army, by gaining Sir Watkin. It is God's doings and it is marvellous in our sight. His Grandfather was the greatest opposer of religion that our country ever knew[4] – but he is no more.[5]

Throughout this period there was no reduction in the amount of work that Charles undertook. It was in 1813 that he wrote up his mature thoughts on the nature of the Sunday schools in his *Rheolau Ffurfiaw a Threfnu Ysgolion Sabbothawl* (*Rules for Establishing and Organizing the Sunday Schools*).[6] The *Geiriadur* had been finished but he decided that a revised second edition was necessary. He therefore began to write articles on words that had been omitted from the first edition, and to expand on his comments on other words. He was also continuing to publish the second series of the periodical, *Trysorfa*, now under his sole editorship. His regular duties of itinerating, preaching, attending Associations, superintending the work of the circulating and Sunday schools, and his London visits, etc., were continuing, but all of these now carried with them the added burden that he fulfilled them, not as a Methodist cleric in a reforming movement within the Church of England, but as the leading statesman and spokesman of a new and hugely influential denomination.

A further continuing burden is revealed in a letter he wrote to Joseph Tarn on 27 February 1813:

> At Bangor on my way home from Anglesey a man met me informing me that my eldest son [Thomas Rice] was at the point of death. He was indeed very dangerously ill of a brain fever. Through the Lord's mercy it has abated and he is now composed. O that the Lord would bless the affliction to him, and that a real change may take place in his future life. Pray for him and us.[7]

[4] Sir Watkin Williams Wynn (d. 1749), the grandfather, was a Jacobite and 'a hater of the Methodists' (DWB), the persecutor of Harris, Peter Williams, and any other exhorter who ventured within his jurisdiction.

[5] DEJ, III, 462-63.

[6] See above, pp. 147-48.

[7] *Ibid.*, III, 467.

In a letter, a fortnight later, he could add, 'Always suppose Mrs Ch. sends kind respects, when I omit to mention it. She is tolerable – and my son recovers.'[8] Thomas and Sally were not to know if either of their surviving children was to become a believer. Neither Thomas Rice nor David Jones, who were twenty-nine and twenty at the time of Charles's death, had shown any signs of coming to faith by that time.

The 1814 Welsh Bible

By Sunday, 11 April 1813, Charles had arrived in London and he occupied the pulpit at Spa Fields until 9 May. On the 19 April the minute book of the BFBS noted a resolution to print 10,000 copies of a new edition of the Welsh Bible in a larger type than their previous edition. The minute continued, 'The Rev. Mr Charles having kindly offered his service to prepare the copy for the same, and to superintend the Correction of the Press, the said offer was thankfully accepted.'[9]

When eventually he had completed editing the text, Charles could find no one willing or competent enough, to carry out the proof-reading, and he had to shoulder this task also. Memories of the delays and embarrassments caused by the mistakes of William Owen Pughe were still with him. 'I never will commit myself a second time to those who are careless or ignorant or both,' he wrote to Robert Saunderson.[10] He prevailed upon Saunderson to release one of his promising assistants to work for a year at the London printers so that a Welsh-speaker could help set the type and avoid very many of the errors that would otherwise have to be addressed by himself at the proof-reading stage.

On its publication in October 1814, the Bible was particularly well received in Wales as it had a larger type than the previous Bible Society edition. In the judgement of D. E. Jenkins this is one of the best editions of the Welsh Bible as far as the accuracy of the editing is concerned. 'And no wonder!' comments R. Tudur Jones.

[8] *Ibid.*, III, 468.
[9] *Ibid.*, III, 470.
[10] *Ibid.*, III, 473.

It was the fruit of ten years of detailed concentration on the various editions of the Welsh Bible by Thomas Charles. No one of his generation knew of the details of the various texts as thoroughly as he did, and it is a question as to whether anyone after him has been as great an authority in this field.[11]

Some of the knowledge imparted to this edition may be gleaned from comments he had included in his *Geiriadur Ysgrythyrol* (*Scriptural Dictionary*). In referring, for example, to the correct spelling of the word '*hysiant*' (KJV 'hiss'), Job 27:23, he provided a footnote, 'It is therefore better not to print this word as *hyssant*, as in the 1690, 1717, 1727, 1746, 1752, 1769, and 1790 editions. This is not how it should be printed, and it was not so in the 1620, 1630, 1654 and 1678 editions.'

From its publication onwards, this edition would become the standard text for the Welsh Bible for a hundred and fifty years. Its orthography was modernized in 1955,[12] but it remained the only text of the Welsh Bible until the *Beibl Cymraeg Newydd* (*New Welsh Bible*) of 1988.

In the light of these ongoing labours it is no great surprise to meet with the following letter which Charles wrote to his London friends, the Astles, in September 1813:

> I have been for these two months past and more in a state of great bodily debility; supposed by the doctors to be the effect of over-exertion of body and mind. I had frequent pains and was confined to the house, and I was frequently on the bed. I was not fit for anything that required exertion either of body or mind, and was recommended to indulge myself in rest and cessation from all work, as the most likely way to restore my strength. Through mercy I am now much better, free from pain, though still languid.[13]

---

[11] RTJ (1979), 33.
[12] By Henry Lewis (1888–1968), professor of Welsh, Swansea University. See Owen, Goronwy Prys, *Thomas Charles a'r Bala* (Y Bala: Cantref, 2016), 74.
[13] DEJ, III, 487.

Such attacks were to be his experience periodically for the remaining twelve months of his life.

Entering his last year

Charles had two priorities at the beginning of 1814: the first was to ensure that the increasing care required for Sally was maintained; the second was the work on the new edition of the Bible. A letter to Tarn, in February 1814, included the words, 'I am overtaken with a degree of my debility last summer, and not able to do much.'[14] But what Charles meant by 'not doing much' must not be measured by normal standards, as is seen in a letter to Edward Morgan, written the following day:

> I am nearly finishing the Bible, comparing the Welsh translation with the originals ... This is always my morning work before breakfast, which I mean to follow as long as I live. I buy every new publication on *Biblical* criticism I hear of ...[15]

By March, Charles was a little better, but this was not true of Sally. He tells Tarn:

> My poor dear invalid continues feeble and is entirely confined to the house, though not to bed. She is too feeble to walk hardly any – only from the parlour to the kitchen ... All these little concerns of health are in the Lord's hands, and it cannot be better. It is well when we are able to acquiesce in his disposal of us in all things. He has a right to dispose of us and he will do us no injury in the end. He died to do us eternal good ...[16]

Thomas Jones, Denbigh, wrote to him in May, inviting him to an Association of the Methodists of Denbighshire and Flintshire, but he had to decline:

---

[14] *Ibid.*, III, 512.
[15] *Ibid.*, III, 512-13.
[16] *Ibid.*, III. 514.

Mrs C. is weak, and she can hardly endure a short journey … She and I feel very much obliged to you and Mrs J. for your kind invitations, and your efforts to extend them on our behalf; but I am afraid she will never see Denbigh. We are both on the hill's descent, though our descent is easy and gradual.[17]

The 1814 Bala Association

Sally was well enough for Charles to leave her and be present at the meetings of the Bala Association of 14-15 June, 1814. His description of it in a letter to London friends emphasizes the changes that had been witnessed in Bala during his years there, arising predominantly from his ministry and organization:

We had last week our great annual (Association) here. The congregation, though always large, was more numerous, by some thousands, than we have ever witnessed before. The meeting lasted part of four days. There were fourteen discourses delivered, and four private meetings held. Great harmony prevailed in the private meetings, and love which is the 'bond of perfectness.' The public discourses were edifying and powerful, and commanded the attention of between 15,000 and 20,000 people without intermission. The order and decorum, which prevailed among such a large concourse of people, was great and pleasing. No signs of intemperance or disorder were perceived among them. Nothing but the hand of God could preserve so much order among so many corrupted sinners so long together. It was the Lord's doing, and it is marvellous, surpassing marvellous in our eyes …

Through mercy my strength is considerably improved, though it is not what it has formerly been. Mrs C. continues still feeble, and it is doubtful whether she can bear a journey to the sea this year as heretofore. Thus it pleases the good Lord at present to order his Providence towards us. To be thankful in all things is our duty and privilege, and I hope

[17] DEJ, III, 523.

we are so in some small degree. Thankful! Surely it becomes those to be so, who have by free grace been saved from hell – and saved in such a way, what a wonder! None but God could show such wonderful things. Pray for us, my dear friends.[18]

During these meetings, the second ordination service of ministers for the north Association took place. There is no doubt that Charles would have officiated in some way during the service. Seven ministers were ordained, in their midst some of the most notable of the denomination. When John Jones, Edern, Caernarfonshire, was asked of his views of the being of God the question so affected him that he failed to speak a word. He began to tremble, broke out in tears and had to sit down. The majesty of God and his attributes had caused the old warrior to break down, and the whole congregation was greatly affected.[19]

The death of Thomas Charles

For years Charles had been overtaxing his constitution. He had never fully recovered his remarkable physical stamina after the frostbite in his hand in 1799 and the severe illness that followed. Nevertheless, after some years of curtailing his frequent and extensive preaching tours, he had been able to return to these again and his ceaseless agenda of evangelistic work continued with very little change. Inevitably, this took its toll. On the Sunday night, 24 July, Charles was returning on horseback from a preaching engagement, eight miles from Bala, when he suddenly collapsed and fell unconscious on to the road. He was carried to a nearby cottage, about three miles from his house. After a few weeks at home his doctor sent him and Sally to Barmouth to rest and they both enjoyed a degree of rejuvenation of mind and body. Indeed, Charles could not refuse an invitation to preach there. He was overheard telling his wife, 'Well, Sally, the fifteen years are nearly

---

[18] *Ibid.*, III, 530-31.
[19] HMGC2, 342-43.

completed.'[20] After a fortnight they moved on to Machynlleth and on Sunday, 4 September, Charles preached twice in the Calvinistic Methodist chapel there. These were the last occasions for him to preach. After a lifetime of preaching, his final text in the morning was, 'I say unto you, that likewise joy shall be in heaven over one sinner that repenteth, more than over ninety and nine just persons, which need no repentance' (Luke 15:7). In the evening the text was, 'If any man love not the Lord Jesus Christ, let him be Anathema Maranatha' (1 Cor. 16:22).

He was troubled by physical weakness and weariness greater than he had ever known, and periods of much pain, and he longed to be back in Bala. They arrived there on 10 September only to find that further sorrows awaited them. Firstly, their son Thomas Rice was again taken gravely ill and was close to death. Within a few days, however, they were assured that he would recover, but then their much-loved maid-servant, Peggy (Margaret Edwards), who had been with them for nine years, was suddenly taken ill with typhus and died within three days aged twenty-seven. During this period, Charles continued in pain and weakness and was frequently heard repeating the words of 2 Kings 13:14, 'Now Elisha was fallen sick of the sickness whereof he died.' His final corrections to the Welsh Bible had already been sent to Tarn and it was published on 3 October, but it is not known if Charles ever saw a copy.

On Monday, 3 October, Thomas Jones, Denbigh, returning from an association at Caernarfon, paid him a visit. He found Charles as affable as ever and lively in conversation. He did not stay long, in order not to overtire him, but left much encouraged at his more hopeful appearance. Jones saw him again on the Tuesday, learning that he had had a difficult night. He then had to leave him to return home to Denbigh. The next morning, Wednesday, 5 October 1814, at about six o'clock, Charles's condition began to deteriorate rapidly. He experienced much pain and was evidently weakening. He died at ten o'clock that morning, nine days short of his fifty-ninth birthday; almost his last words were, 'There is a refuge.'

[20] See above, p. 184.

Michael Roberts (1780–1849), one of the outstanding preachers of the time, heard of his death and wrote in his diary:

> October 5th. Our dear brother and father, the Rev. Thomas Charles of Bala, has passed away. This death is the darkest cloud that has ever hung above our heads as a Connexion in Gwynedd. I hope that I and my brethren may consider, submit, and cry that the Lord might have mercy upon us.[21]

On the afternoon of Friday, 7 October, a 'vast concourse' of people gathered in the open air at Bala. The service was led by John Roberts, Llangwm, and a sermon preached by Thomas Jones, Denbigh. Both these men had been his close friends and fellow-labourers for thirty years, since the very beginning of his association with the north Wales Methodists. Jones preached on Hebrews 11:4, 'And by it he, being dead, yet speaketh.' As he described the fruits of faith of the loyal servant of Christ whose body they were about to bury, and the eloquent witness that he had left behind him in the great variety of his labours for the souls of so many, of every degree and all ages, throughout the country, both preacher and congregation could not keep back their tears. The crowd then walked in procession from Bala, along the side of the lake, to the parish church at Llanycil, about a mile away, where he and Sally had been married and where the burial service was conducted.[22]

Sally's death

Sally did not have long to wait before she followed her husband. The circumstances of her death are given in a letter of Lydia Lloyd (November 1814), her closest friend since childhood, who had then (as Lydia Foulks) become her step-mother. She would have learnt

---

[21] John Jones, *Cofiant y Parch. Michael Roberts, Pwllheli* (Pwllheli, 1883), 26-27.

[22] A marble monument to Thomas Charles was erected in front of Capel Tegid, the Calvinistic Methodist Chapel in Bala, in 1875. The seven-foot-high statue shows him in a Geneva preaching gown, with one hand on his heart and the other offering a copy of the Bible. See picture p. 332.

of the events of the last days from her daughter, Mary, who had
again been helping to care for Sally:

> ... Poor Mrs Charles's health was much impaired in con-
> sequence of losing her dear Mr Charles. Sometimes her
> recollection failed her so much that she had no idea of his
> death. When she was convinced how things were, she would
> weep and wonder how he was taken before her. It was in
> much love and tender mercy that her sorrows were put an
> end to so suddenly after his removal; he dying on October
> the 5th, and she on October 24th, 1814.
>
> The day before she died, she and her youngest son, Dr
> David Charles, were in the tea room, the family were gone
> to chapel. She said, 'Let us go a little to prayer.' Her ideas
> were collected, clear and spiritual, both for herself and for
> her son. The following night she was put to bed as usual
> about seven o'clock. The maid stopped in her room till she
> slept, and had been upstairs several times, and finding her
> in a comfortable and sound sleep, gave Mary a hint, lest
> she should disturb her, by going to bed, as they both slept
> together. As Mary was raising the clothes to go to bed, she
> perceived that Mrs Charles was paler than usual, and cried
> out, 'O! I am afraid she is dead!' It was a sudden shock to
> her feelings; as it was to the family.[23]

According to R. Tudur Jones: 'Theirs was one of the great Welsh
courtships. He fell in love with her when he first saw her on his
visit to Bala in the summer of 1778 and he was still in love with
her after she had her second stroke in November 1811 when her
graceful body was paralysed and her memory failing.'[24]

Postscripts

(1) *First biographies*

When he heard of the death of his friend Thomas Jones laid aside
the autobiography which he was writing (never to return to it)[25]

[23] DEJ, III, 553-54.
[24] RTJ (1979), 17.
[25] The autobiography ends with Jones's description of his last visit to

and began a memoir of Charles's life. He accomplished the work in about fifteen months, and the subsequent *Cofiant* (*Memoir*) was published early in 1816.[26] Its core is a translation into Welsh of the diary that Charles kept for the period from January 1773 to August 1785, that is, from his conversion to the time he took up an itinerant ministry among the Methodists. The contents of the diary amount to about one hundred and fifty pages of the 252-page book, and the remaining pages include many of his letters. On the title-page the book is described as 'translated and collected by the Rev. Thomas Jones.' The two men had been the closest of friends; each had influenced the other considerably, and their constant conferring and loving co-operation over whatever either of them took in hand had lasted for twenty-nine years.

Once he had completed a translation of the diary, Jones sent it to Simon Lloyd of Bala who used it as the basis for a short English biography published in the November and December numbers of the *Evangelical Magazine* for 1815. Charles's various papers, including the *Diary*, were then passed on to Edward Morgan, Syston, who eventually published *A Brief Memoir of the Life and Labours of the Rev. Thomas Charles* (1828, 394 pages) and a second, enlarged, edition (1831, 440 pages). In 1836, he produced *Essays, Letters, and Interesting Papers of the late Rev. Thomas Charles*, a book of 478 pages.

(2) The development of the Sunday school in Wales

For twenty years from 1790 the increase in the number of schools was slow but steady. Thereafter, as the other Nonconformist bodies and even the Established Church took up the idea, a significant percentage of the population became involved. By the Religious Census of 1851 the numbers attending a Sunday school in England and Wales had risen to two and a half million, nearly 13% of the population. But for Wales alone, the proportion was much higher

---

Charles, and its last words are some of Charles's last words, 'There is a refuge.' Idwal Jones (ed.), *Hunangofiant Thomas Jones, Dinbych* (Aberystwyth, 1937), 58.

[26] Thomas Jones, *Cofiant y Parch. Thomas Charles* (Bala, 1816). It is thought to be the first Welsh biography to be published in book form.

so that by 1881 it was calculated that over half a million out of a total population for Wales of one and a half million (34.1%) attended the Sunday schools. In Bala, Thomas Charles's home-town, the proportion was 61.4%.

The enormous effect and significance of Thomas Charles's movement will be best appreciated by considering the statistics when it was at its highest point of influence. In 1905 there were in Wales 5,375 Sunday schools. At the time the population of the country was 2,012,876. Of these, 836,343 were members of a Sunday school, and 69,936 were teachers. This meant that about 41% of the total population of Wales attended the schools. The county with by far the highest percentage (Merioneth with 67.5%) was Thomas Charles's county, with Bala at its centre.[27]

There can hardly have been such a moral and intellectual transformation achieved so rapidly and thoroughly in any other country than that which occurred in Wales at this time. It was brought about by the influence of the Sunday schools operating in a period of spiritual awakening. The effect of the change could be viewed almost as that of a revolution. God's blessing upon the circulating schools and then the Sunday schools ensured that, by the middle of the nineteenth century, Wales had become one of the most literate nations in Europe.

(3) The spread of the Welsh Bible

Between 1567, the date of the publication by William Salesbury of the first Welsh New Testament, and 1799, there were only twenty editions of New Testaments or complete Bibles produced in Welsh – an average of eight editions every hundred years. The next century was to be the golden age of Bible production in Wales. In the ninety-nine years between 1800 and 1899 there were 351 different editions.[28] Without doubt the explanation for this great demand

---

[27] R. Tudur Jones, 'Dylanwad y Beibl ar Feddwl Cymru,' in R. Geraint Gruffydd (ed.), *Y Gair ar Waith* (Cardiff: University of Wales Press, 1988), 126.

[28] *Ibid.*, 114.

is found in the effects, during the first half of the century, of the continuing spiritual awakening in the land and of the increasing literacy resulting from the Circulating schools and Sunday schools.

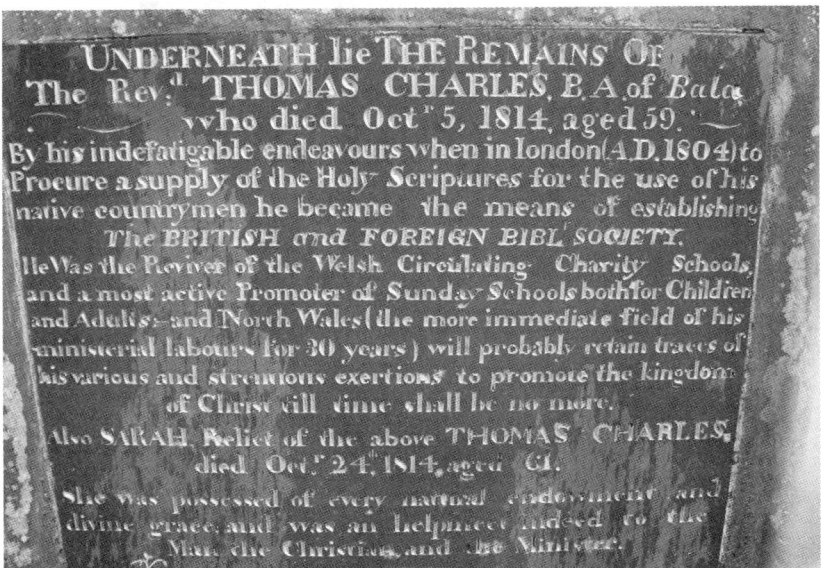

UNDERNEATH lie THE REMAINS OF
The Revd THOMAS CHARLES, B.A. of *Bala*
who died Octr 5, 1814, aged 59.
By his indefatigable endeavours when in London(A.D.1804) to
Procure a supply of the Holy Scriptures for the use of his
native countrymen he became the means of establishing
The BRITISH and FOREIGN BIBL SOCIETY.
He Was the Reviver of the Welsh Circulating Charity Schools,
and a most active Promoter of Sunday Schools both for Children
and Adults;—and North Wales (the more immediate field of his
ministerial labours for 30 years) will probably retain traces of
his various and strenuous exertions to promote the kingdom
of Christ till time shall be no more.
Also SARAH Relict of the above THOMAS CHARLES,
died Octr 24, 1814, aged 61.
She was possessed of every natural endowment and
divine grace, and was an helpmeet indeed to
the Man, the Christian, and the Minister,

Thomas and Sally Charles's grave and headstone.

The grave of Charles's three children (Sarah, Thomas Rice and David Jones) and a grandchild (Maria).

Top: An early print of Llanycil church at the side of Llyn Tegid.
Bottom: The Charles's home in Bala as it is today.

The statue of Thomas Charles outside Capel Tegid, Bala.

16

'AS A PRINCE OF GOD IN OUR MIDST'

Thomas Charles as a preacher

E. Wyn James notes that during the golden age of the itinerant preacher in Wales, open-air preaching was predominantly a means of evangelizing unbelievers rather than of building up the saints. It was in the society, rather than under the sermon, that the work of nurturing believers took place.[1] The Methodist exhorters of the eighteenth century were therefore predominantly evangelists, and not until the beginning of the nineteenth century, with the gathering of large congregations within large chapel buildings under men who were, to all intents and purposes, their pastors, was the sermon developed for a fuller teaching ministry. Thomas Charles's ministry bridged these two periods and it should be remembered therefore that, for all his organizational and literary work, he was, essentially, a preacher; and as a preacher, he was, firstly, an evangelist. All his other ministries developed from his work as an evangelist.[2] It is no surprise therefore to find the following words in the *Geiriadur* under the entry 'sermon' ('*pregeth*'):

> The preaching of the gospel by men called [by God] is the chief means ordained by God to save the souls of men, by the extension of the knowledge of the Saviour amongst sinners. No one has been of greater blessing to mankind than such preachers ...

But not every evangelist has the same style of, and approach to, preaching. There is a tendency to think of all the Welsh Methodist

---

[1] E. Wyn James, 'John Hughes, Pontrobert, a'i gefndir,' JHS, 37 (2013), 84.
[2] E. Wyn James, 'Pererinion ar y Ffordd, JHS, 29-30 (2005-06), 79.

preachers as being fiery, dramatic orators who overcame congregations with the power and strength of their ministry. Certainly this was true, to varying degrees, of Howel Harris, Robert Roberts, Clynnog and John Elias, but not of David Jones, Llan-gan, or John Evans, Bala; nor, indeed, of Thomas Charles.

To Charles, the importance of words and the meaning of words, and especially the importance of the meaning of each individual word of Scripture, was as foundational for his approach to preaching as it was for writing the *Geiriadur*. He would not allow himself such use of the imagination and drama as was employed to great effect by others. He spoke in his natural voice, calmly and cogently, communicating as clearly as possible the meaning of Scripture. Edward Morgan comments:

> He never aimed at what might lead people to think him deep in his knowledge, or profound in his researches. He might, with more reason than many, have undertaken to speak of the mysterious parts of truth in a way that seemed learned. But this was never his practice: and on this account, perhaps, in some measure it was, that he was not generally deemed a great preacher; and he did not indeed appear to have at all cultivated those gifts which commonly attract public admiration.[3]

But far more important than volume, passion, drama, or imagination, was the divine unction that accompanied his words on so many occasions. Often in his letters he expressed the conviction, first written in a letter to Watts Wilkinson, before he had even begun preaching, when he was only twenty-two years old: 'One may speak a great deal, and that very orthodox, but unless he has a little of the unction of the Holy Spirit, he might, for aught I know, *as well be silent.*'[4] That he knew much of that divine help is evidenced by the fact that he would always be asked to preach at any Association that he attended away from home, and is attested to by the almost universal affection, respect, and love in which he

[3] *Memoir*, 399.
[4] See above, p. 34.

was held within the Connexion. This was certainly how Williams Williams, Pantycelyn, viewed him. As he wrote in his final letter to Charles:

> A visit from some of your preachers is much needed in south Wales ... the north Wales preachers most in favour with the people have not visited us for some time. You yourself are one of them, because your services are called for from every part of south Wales, and the Lord will reward you if you come.[5]

There were occasions when his ministry gripped and touched all who were listening.

No copies of any of Charles's sermons have survived in published form. In this he was typical of most of his Methodist predecessors. As itinerant gospel evangelists, the sermon was to them a spoken word, a message from God, to be delivered to that congregation, gathered at that particular time and place, in front of them. It is possible that the nature and style of Charles's preaching may be dimly discerned from some of the more informal, exhortative paragraphs of his *Geiriadur*. For instance, from his entry on the word 'covenant' ('*cyfamod*'):

> If these observations concerning the great God are true and scriptural, we see, without doubt, that it is impossible to rescue man from the threats of this broken covenant, without righteousness. Do you believe this, O man? If you do, from where do you think you will obtain it? If you turn to the law, there you find true righteousness *demanded*, but no righteousness *provided*. If you turn to yourself, and look within, there is not the slightest grain of comfort to be found. Unrighteousness alone is what you will find there. Behold therefore, unrighteous man in the grip of a righteous law, which is itself upheld by an infinite righteous God. I ask, and let any who can provide an answer, 'Shall the prey be taken from the mighty, or the lawful captive delivered?' If a righteousness may be found to answer for them, they may be delivered; otherwise, they shall be forever captive. To

[5] See above, p. 155.

possess that righteousness that delivers from death, we must turn our eyes away from ourselves, and from the law also, to some other place: to him, indeed, who 'is the end of the law for righteousness to everyone that believeth …

Charles passed on much of his thoughts and views on preaching and on preparation for preaching in the series of letters which he wrote to the young curate, Edward Morgan, Syston, and extracts from these letters have been given above.[6]

Thomas Charles as a correspondent

No one familiar with the letters of John Newton and Thomas Charles could fail to notice the similarity between them. The two men, of course, were of the same era and culture, as also of the same denominational and religious milieu. They had spent much time in one another's company and we would therefore expect similarities of style and syntax, of greetings and courtesies, and of theological understanding and emphases. Furthermore, Charles had read Newton's letters (had even helped to prepare some of them for the press[7]) and because of his admiration of them and of their author, they could not have failed to provide a pattern to follow. But there is more to this similarity than merely coincidence of style and subject matter. C. H. Spurgeon noted of Newton's work: 'In few writers are Christian doctrine, experience and practice more happily balanced than in the author of these letters, and few write with more simplicity, piety and force.' Such words are exactly what one would wish to state of Charles's letters also. When writing to a friend, John Elias commented, 'As for printing a volume of Mr Charles' Letters, that also would be most acceptable. Whatever proceeded from him is excellent.'[8]

---

[6] See above, pp. 255-57.

[7] John Mayor, in a letter to a daughter-in-law (1871), wrote: 'Newton's *Cardiphonia* would be pleasant reading. Mr Charles of Bala and I copied out many of those letters for the press, and I can tell you almost all the parties to whom they were addressed.' (DEJ, I, 53-54.)

[8] Morgan (ed.), *John Elias* (1973), 329.

Edward Morgan published a selection of these and in his preface commented on them:

> What [Charles] seems to excel in, is on the subject of Christian experience; and on this he does greatly excel ... The tried, the doubting, and the tempted, will find in this volume what may by God's blessing be of great service to them. The self-deceived, the formal, the self-righteous, may also learn here what may be of vital consequence for them to know ... If there be a peculiarity in this good man's writing, it is this – he speaks as one *really acquainted* with what he has in hand, and *deeply impressed* with its importance ... When he speaks of God, he does so like one who has *seen* him who is invisible. When he describes the deceitfulness of the heart and the evil of sin, he does so as one who had known both by sad experience, and had found how injurious they are and what misery they bring. When again he delineates the glory and sufficiency of the Saviour, and the value of his word, he does so as one who had seen his glory, experienced his sufficiency, and found how precious he is.[9]

Thomas Charles as a theologian

In 1801, in their introduction to the *Rules for the Private Societies*, Charles and Thomas Jones, Denbigh, wrote:

> In doctrine we exactly agree with the Articles of the Church of England; and preach no other doctrines but what are contained and fully and clearly expressed in them.[10] Since we are altogether of the same judgement as the Doctrinal Articles of the Established Church ... we see no need for a special publication of our convictions and doctrines.[11]

It would be of interest to discover by what path Charles arrived at his theological views. These were certainly in a comparatively complete form by the time he joined the Methodists in 1785. His

[9] *Spiritual Counsels*, xxxviii-xxxix [xxxi-xxxii].
[10] DEJ, III, 299.
[11] *Rules and Designs* (Chester, 1802), viii.

almost immediate acceptance by able theologians such as Robert
Jones, Daniel Rowland, and William Williams proves that he
must have held to the orthodox Calvinism of the Methodists at
that time. He would not however have received that Reformed
theology from any course taught at Oxford University, nor, as has
been shown, from his tuition at Carmarthen Academy. Much of
his understanding of the biblical revelation must have been formed
by discussion and fellowship with other believers, particularly his
evangelical student friends: fellowship conducted face-to-face
during the years at Oxford, and then by letter as they entered into
ministerial ranks. But for one whose choice of reading as a fourteen-
year-old was Bunyan on the Covenants, and Luther on Galatians
when eighteen, the foundation of the beliefs which informed his
mind and soul would have been discovered by means of his own
extensive private reading of theology and commentaries.

Although this was the case, while drawing up his *Hyfforddwr*
and other catechisms, and writing his detailed theological entries
in the *Geiriadur*, he himself would have considered that he was
doing no more than expanding on the theological foundation of
the *Thirty-nine Articles*. And in so doing, he would have viewed
himself as merely expressing the orthodox, catholic belief of the
Christian church throughout the centuries.[12] From this body of
divinity, however, he often emphasized certain themes which he
presumably considered were particularly necessary truths for his
own day and age. Both in the *Geiriadur* and in his letters, the
topics of Scripture, the Trinity, and the Reformation doctrines of
grace, are frequently encountered, and always with that 'happy
balance' of doctrine, experience, and practice. These emphases may
be illustrated by quotations from his writings.

(1) *Scripture*

Charles saw the Bible as an inerrant, infallible revelation from
God:

[12] This is demonstrated by D. Densil Morgan in his descriptions of the
Hyfforddwr and the *Geiriadur*, HMGC3, 112-124.

The Holy Scriptures are a treasury of all profitable and necessary information. As they have all been given by the inspiration of God they must all partake of his perfection and be worthy of him. Because of the perfection of his knowledge, they cannot fail: and because of the integrity of his nature, he would not deceive us in anything.[13]

Such a high view of Scripture required a correspondingly high view of the method of divine inspiration:

The doctrines were presented to their minds clothed in their appropriate phrases. The words and the phrases are divine, as well as the doctrines. This is the *form* of sound words of which the apostle speaks, 2 Tim. 1:13.[14]

In order to emphasize the role of the Holy Spirit while avoiding the conclusion that inspiration involved a form of 'verbal dictation,' Charles added that, 'Although each writer had his own appropriate idiom of writing, yet, in all this variety, it was the Holy Spirit that taught each one of them, in that idiom.'

With such a view of the Scriptures, Charles naturally placed a high priority on the importance of understanding them in their original language. As he wrote to Edward Morgan,

I cannot but consider it no small fault on the part of any who, having the opportunity, neglect to learn the languages in which the Old and New Testaments were written, and fail to read them in those languages.[15]

(2) *The Trinity*

When reading comments by Charles on differing subjects, one will often come across a passage of praise to Almighty God, especially in his essential being as the triune God, the three persons in one – Father, Son and Spirit. The following passage is a diary entry of

---

[13] *Geiriadur*, v.

[14] Entry on 'Scripture' ('*Ysgrythur*'), *Geiriadur*, 923.

[15] *Ibid.*, and see pp. 270-71 and the discussion by Geraint Lloyd in DDM (2014), 63-66.

his (11 September 1783), in which he had been meditating on the verse, 'Without me ye can do nothing' (John 15:5), and on our dependence upon the Holy Spirit:

> How incontestably do the foregoing considerations prove the divinity of the Holy Spirit! Would it not be blasphemy to say of any creature that 'he searcheth all things, yea the deep things of God'? Is it possible that any Antitrinitarian can enjoy any of the blessings or consolations of the gospel? Let others believe and say what they please, the doctrine of the Trinity is the foundation of all my hopes, the life and soul of all my comforts. The more I study it and meditate on it, in connection with the gospel-scheme, the more of heaven I find in my soul. I can freely and heartily join with the great and pious divine who says: 'It is much to be lamented, that believers in general take so little pains to get a clear knowledge of the doctrine of the ever-blessed Trinity. For want of which their faith is unsettled, and they are liable to many errors, both in judgement and in practice. I would therefore most earnestly recommend it to all who are weak in faith, to be diligent in hearing and reading what in Scripture is revealed concerning the Trinity in Unity, looking always up for the inward teaching of the Holy Spirit.'[16]

(3) *Calvinism*

D. Densil Morgan describes Charles accurately as 'a disciple of the high Reformed orthodoxy.'[17] Some church historians in the twentieth and twenty-first centuries, however, have sought to paint the Calvinism of the first and second generation of Welsh Methodists as being more moderate and less extreme (as they perceive it) than that of the generation associated with the theological controversies of 1810 to 1840. One motive for this was the wish to disassociate these men, the founders of the denomination, from what was judged to be the ultra High Calvinism of John Elias (1774–1841) and of the denomination's *Confession of Faith* written in 1823. Thus,

[16] *Memoir*, 211.
[17] D. Densil Morgan in HMGC3, 124.

Charles's theology has been described as 'a Moderate Calvinism tempered by evangelicalism,'[18] and the following is a typical twenty-first-century comment on the situation in 1823:

> Sadly, despite the moderating influence of Thomas Charles of Bala (1755–1814), Thomas Jones of Denbigh (1756–1820), Edward Williams of Rotherham (1750–1857) and John Jones, Talsarn (1796–1857), Welsh Calvinistic Methodism became more 'ultra' in the 1823 *Confession of Faith*.[19]

No one has ever alleged that Charles did not believe the Calvinistic understanding of human sinfulness, of election, of effectual calling, and the perseverance of the saints. However, it has been suggested, specifically, that the emphasis on particular redemption found in the 1823 *Confession* was not part of the early Welsh Methodist tradition, and would not have been supported by Charles. This is demonstrably untrue, as the following quotations show:

From *Yr Hyfforddwr* (1807)

> Question 130. *For whom did Christ die?*
> For his elect people given to him by the Father. 'I lay down my life for the sheep,' John 10:15, 28-29; 17:6.[20]

From the entry on 'redemption' ('*prynedigaeth*'), *Y Geiriadur Ysgrythyrol* (c. 1808)

> Three things are involved in the redemption which is in Christ:
>
> 1. The election and appointment of his Person in place of those persons to be redeemed. This was according to the order and decree of the eternal counsel …
>
> 2. A reckoning of their sins to his account. 'The Lord hath laid on him the iniquity of us all.' …

---

[18] H. J. Hughes, 'Thomas Charles, llythrennedd a'r Ysgol Sul,' in DDM (2014), 22.

[19] Alan C. Clifford, *John Jones Talsarn* (Norwich: Charenton Reformed Publishing, 2013), 283.

[20] *Yr Hyfforddwr* (78th edition, n.d.) 21.

3. He suffered in his own Person the due punishment for those sins so reckoned to him …[21]

When we consider the nature of redemption, we must realize that Christ did not suffer *for* his people, in the sense that he suffered *on their behalf*, and *for their benefit*, but he suffered *instead* of his people and *in their place*. Many hold to a kind of redemption, though hardly worthy of the name, but deny it vehemently when it is given its proper meaning. They are willing to speak of Christ dying *for us* or *on our behalf*, and that we receive many blessings through him, but for him to suffer *instead of us*, and *in our place*, the punishment that we deserved, that they will not acknowledge. But I see no cause or reason why he should suffer at all, were it not that he suffered instead of and in the place of his people …

When considering the extent and measure of the atonement, it cannot be understood in its full significance unless viewed as relating only to those who will be saved. Therefore, those who hold that he redeemed all, deny the innate nature of redemption. On the basis of their view, it could never be proved that Christ died for anybody, and therefore, this being so, no one would be saved. Their sacrifice *for all* is completely insufficient to save *one*. It is not a sacrifice, or an atonement, or a redemption, but an empty name having no substance. But not so our Christ; he purchased the redeemed, those elected and given to him by the Father, with the intention of saving them, and saved they will be forever. Election, redemption, intercession, calling, justification, and glorification all flow from the same eternal love, all pertain to the same objects, and are in full harmony with one another.[22]

Charles directed those who wished to read further on the subject to 'Turretin's *Institutio Theol. Elenct.*, Vol. II, *Locus Decimus*

---

[21] Entry on 'Redemption' ('*Prynedigaeth*'), *Geiriadur Ysgrythyrol*, 751.
[22] *Ibid.*, 751-52.

Quartus; John Brine on *The Christian Efficacy of the Death of Christ*; Dr Owen on *The Death of Christ*; Gill's *Cause of God and Truth*.'[23]

When, in 1823, nine years after Charles's death, the Calvinistic Methodists drew up their *Confession of Faith*, criticism was made by some (and by others later in the twentieth century) of the phrase '*and those only*' as it occurs in Section 18, 'Of Redemption,' of the *Confession*:

> In an eternal decree and counsel between the Father, the Son, and the Holy Ghost, for the redemption of sinners, the Son was chosen to be the Redeemer, and it was ordained that he should assume human nature, in order to be our kinsman, with the right to redeem his brethren. It was ordained that his Person should stand in the stead of those persons (and those only) who had been given him to redeem.[24]

It was argued by some in 1823 that the phrase emphasised the doctrine of limited atonement, or particular redemption, to an extent greater than generally held by the earlier Methodists, that is during the period of Daniel Rowland and Thomas Charles. John Elias defended the phrase strongly, as did David Charles, Thomas Charles's brother, and it was agreed to retain it. There should not really have been any debate on this basis in that there is nothing in the whole of Section 18 of the *Confession* that is not found in the above quotations from Thomas Charles's works. Furthermore, the very wording of the disputed phrase was taken from (or, at the very least, echoed) Charles's own words in his *Minutes* of a discussion at the Bala Association of 1809 (an association in which all would have looked to Charles for theological guidance), which he had published in the second *Trysorfa* of 1813,[25] and which read:

> Three things are involved in the redemption which is in Christ, according to the language by which it is expressed in the Bible, namely:

[23] *Ibid.*

[24] *Confession of Faith of the Calvinistic Methodists* (1900), 73-74.

[25] See above, p. 232.

1. The election and appointment of the Person of Christ in place of those persons (and they only) to be redeemed. This was according to the order and decree of the eternal counsel ...

2. A reckoning of their sins (and theirs only) to his account. 'The Lord hath laid on him the iniquity of us all.' ...

3. He suffered in his own Person the due punishment for those sins (and those only) reckoned to him ...

We judge, also, that it is invidious to assert, or to argue, whether Christ's death is, or is not, sufficient atonement for the whole world, or, whether it would not have been necessary for him to have suffered more if all men were saved; in that none are considered in the redemption, any more than in the election, other than those who are truly saved. None will perish because of insufficiency in the atonement, but all because they will not come unto Christ to be saved; and these men will have no excuse to make for their neglect of Christ. We do not know what would have been necessary had God's order and decrees been different; and we do not need to know.[26]

It is interesting to note that the first section of this passage from the 1809 *Minutes* is more or less identical with the first quotation above taken from the *Geiriadur*, except for the addition, three times, of the phrase '*and they only*,' or its equivalent, in the former. Charles had finished writing the *Geiriadur* some time before January 1809.[27] His entry on 'redemption' ('*prynedigaeth*') would have been completed in late 1807, or early 1808 perhaps, but certainly more than a year before the discussion on redemption in the Private Society at the 1809 Bala Association. It must be assumed therefore that during that discussion Charles read out his *Geiriadur* entry, or parts of his entry, on the topic, to the general agreement of the Connexion. In addition, however, he, or some other brother, must have felt the need to add the relevant phrase

---

[26] *Trysorfa,* Book 2 (1813), 72-76.
[27] See above, pp. 283-84.

to each of the three points, again, to the general satisfaction of the body. In this way, it found its way into his *Minutes,* and from there into the *Confession.*

There are three further aspects of Charles's Calvinism that should be noted:

(a) *Covenant theology*

Thomas Charles's theology lies centrally within the Reformed tradition in that it is evident that he understood his Calvinistic belief within the parameters of a federal, covenant theology. On 16 September 1813, he wrote to Edward Morgan:

> A Salvation in covenant, made by Jehovah, and therefore 'well ordered and sure,' appeared to me glorious. Every thing is *well ordered and sure* – '*rhagderfynedig gyngor*' (pre-determined counsel). A salvation in covenant is but little known in these days, and therefore but little preached, but scouted and laughed at. Hence arise the prevailing notions about universal redemption, etc. etc., and a thousand other concomitant errors, which leave every thing at random and in uncertainty. I hope the Lord will enable you and me more clearly to view a salvation in covenant ...[28]

Charles's entry on the word 'covenant' ('*cyfamod*') is by far the longest in his *Geiriadur.* He explains that the covenant is 'the gracious revelation of God's will, with respect to the salvation of sinners through the great Mediator, Jesus Christ.' The message of the covenant is therefore the heart of the Bible. Though he developed his understanding of the covenant from Reformed continental writers,[29] he did not follow them slavishly. While Cocceius and Witsius, for instance, argued for a 'covenant of redemption' made between Father and Son in eternity past, in addition to the covenants of works and of grace,[30] Charles preferred the simpler

---

[28] *Spiritual Counsels*, 392 [291-92].

[29] See above, p. 266.

[30] Peter Golding, *Covenant Theology* (Fearn, Ross-shire: Mentor CFP, 2004), 138.

two-covenant idea: [31]

> The Scriptures speak of various covenants: such as that made
> with Noah, with Abraham, the Sinaitic covenant, etc., but
> all may be incorporated in two covenants only, called by
> theologians the COVENANT OF WORKS, and the COVENANT
> OF GRACE. This is because all the other covenants mentioned
> are but various dispensations of the Covenant of Grace. [32]

The article continues with a full description of the contrasting
elements of each covenant, culminating in the glory of the covenant of grace:

> There is no refuge or hiding place of any degree for the con-
> dition of the sinner in any place other than in this covenant.
> God rejects everything that man may call 'wisdom, right-
> eousness, sanctification and redemption' unless it derives
> from this covenant, through union with Christ. Whatever
> they may be, they do not in the least relate to the salvation
> of a sinner. These privileges and blessings that are in Christ
> are of a different nature and are infinitely higher and more
> excellent than anything that may be similar to them of
> human manufacture. The righteousness of this covenant is
> a divine righteousness: there is nothing in created nature
> that resembles it; nothing comparable to it may be seen in
> heaven. It is not appropriate for anyone other than a sinner.
> For transgressors *alone* is it suitable, and to them *alone* is it
> revealed. The holiness of this covenant is also of a different
> nature, and derives from a different fountain. Christ is both
> its author and fountain. Sinners washed in the blood of
> Jesus Christ and receiving life in him as members of him,
> are a wonder to behold. 'What are these? And whence came
> they?' are appropriate questions, on seeing their radiant

---

[31] See also Geraint Lloyd, 'Geiriau, Gair a Gwerin,' in Eryl Davies (ed.),
Diwinydda Ddoe a Heddiw (Bridgend: Bryntirion Press, 2012), 68-69. This
was also the approach of John Bunyan in his *The Doctrine of Law and Grace
Unfolded*, which Charles read as a youth.

[32] Entry on 'Covenant' ('*Cyfamod*'), *Geiriadur Ysgrythyrol*.

appearance (Rev. 7:13-14). Their love will be for one who died for them; and their songs will forever be of praise to one who washed them from their sins by his own blood. This is a new song, even in heaven itself.[33]

The doctrine of the covenants had been presented by various authors in Wales before Charles's time. The Puritan, Vavasor Powell, wrote a treatise on the two covenants, *Christ and Moses Excellency*, in 1650; Welsh Presbyterians and Baptists who could read English would have learnt of it from their *Confessions of Faith* of 1646 and 1689 respectively. The first discussion of it in Welsh was in a translation of the famous *Marrow of Modern Divinity* by Edward Fisher (*Madruddyn y Difinyddiaeth Diweddaraf*) in 1651.[34] But the comparatively small influence of the early Nonconformists in Wales meant that there was little consciousness of this doctrine among the people generally. The concepts involved in the doctrine of the covenants had indeed been often expressed in the sermons and writings of other Puritans such as Walter Cradock, Morgan Llwyd, and later Dissenters, and in the hymns and poetry of William Williams and other early Methodists, but they were not generally presented in covenant theology terms. It was left to Thomas Charles to introduce this terminology to the Welsh people in a more popular form. Through his catechism, *Yr Hyfforddwr*, thousands of Welsh children memorized its tenets, and from his articles in the *Geiriadur* they assimilated its teaching in their later years. From the publication of the *Geiriadur* onwards, right up to the end of the nineteenth century, there are innumerable references to the covenants to be found in Welsh sermons and hymns.

(b) *An emphasis on the union of the believer with Christ*

Arising, perhaps, from his delight in the doctrine of the covenants, Charles always insisted on the believer's union with Christ as being the source of so much of the blessedness of the spiritual life. This

---

[33] *Ibid.*

[34] A remarkably early translation in that the *Marrow* was not published in its complete form until 1645.

is an emphasis which may often be seen in his various writings. We find an example in the case of Edward Morgan, Syston, who, at the beginning of his ministry, was for some time confused in his mind concerning the sequence of events in the conversion of a sinner, and the experiential connections between faith, repentance, regeneration, union with Christ, etc. He wrote long detailed letters to Charles on these points. It is significant that Charles chose consistently not to answer him in kind, with multiple arguments. Instead he replied relatively shortly and simply, emphasizing that the various experiences of the Christian arise as a result of life in Christ:

> You seem to have puzzled yourself about the point you have written to me about, but I apprehend your perplexity arises from wrong ideas of cause and effect. The light in the understanding, and the holy bent of the will, are the effects of regeneration, and not regeneration itself. Faith is not regeneration, but the fruit and effect by which it is proved. By Christ *apprehending* our souls, by his word, through his Spirit, we are united to Christ. The effect of that act of Christ is the communication of the divine nature to the soul, which is regeneration. Then by faith we apprehend him by whom we are apprehended, Phil. 3:12-13.
>
> These are my simple ideas of this mysterious work; but fully to comprehend it we cannot ... But I still venture humbly to assert, that it is by uniting the soul to Christ – ingrafting it into that true vine; and the consequence will be the receiving out of his fullness all grace and all divine privileges to all eternity. There can be no change, no holiness, no comfort, without that. Everything will forever wither and decay but what is one with Christ and proceeds from him.[35]

As with repentance and faith, so also with justification by faith and sanctification: Charles understood these as consequences of our initial union with Christ:

---

[35] DEJ, III, 519-20; *Spiritual Counsels*, 398-99 [296-97].

We have considered briefly the love and goodness of God towards his people, giving them in his eternal purpose to Christ, as their head and representative. We have considered also the way in which the Son of God gave himself, of his own free will, to stand in their place and engaged himself to fulfil the conditions of the covenant on their behalf. We now consider further the way in which they are brought to possess, in their own persons, the gifts and privileges of this covenant, namely, through spiritual and personal union with Christ, their exalted Head within the covenant.[36]

This point has been discussed when dealing with his catechism, *Yr Hyfforddwr*.[37]

(c) *Evangelical emphasis*

There is a spirit that treats Calvinism, or any other system for that matter, as an opportunity merely for rational, dogmatic, and dialectical argument. Some of the later Reformed continental thought exhibited a tendency to descend into such a sterile and scholastic approach. No trace of this was ever present in Charles's mind. The strength of his evangelical convictions and experience meant that whatever truth or doctrine was contemplated, it was viewed through the lens of gospel grace. In a letter of 1811 to Edward Morgan, he writes:

> I am sorry to hear of your dejection of mind. Look up, look up, all is well *there*. Come as a sinner, and you will find all in your favour – all; the door open, and every face smiling upon you. But if you attempt to come as a saint, and you are dubious whether you are so or not, you will come as an imposter and a hypocrite; and you will be detested. There can be no doubt that you are a sinner. Well, then, come in your real character, and you will be welcome. Everything in the councils of heaven favours a returning sinner – election, particular redemption, vocation, justification, etc. – all, all

[36] Entry on 'Covenant' ('*Cyfamod*'), *Geiriadur Ysgrythyrol*.
[37] See above, pp. 245-56.

are in his favour and give him every encouragement he can want and God can give. But imposters are abhorred. And such is everyone who assumes a character which he is not sure belongs to him.[38]

A letter to Watts Wilkinson on the love of God (8 June 1803) confirms his general approach:

I do not trouble myself about his love to me in particular. I know he has loved sinners; and I am one of them. This consideration endears me to him; so that I cannot help loving and praising him, and cleaving to him without any great doubt or hesitation. Everything in Jesus seems to suit me. I know that all his blessings were intended for such as I am. Who else could make use of them? And why not for me? He is altogether lovely – altogether such a one as I could wish him to be; and I see everything that I want in him. Where else can I go, or should I go? I see so little holiness in me, that I can hardly persuade myself that I am a saint. But I know that I am a sinner; and as such I seldom fail of having a free access and a favourable audience. I wonder at him, and wonder at myself too. I wonder how he admits me into his presence; and I wonder how I can venture, being so vile and unworthy. But when I look towards the throne, everything seems to favour me – a throne of grace – a great High Priest, touched with the feeling of our infirmities – mercy and grace to be obtained and received; the very things I want, and which alone can help me. What blessings! ... all the wonders of love to a poor sinner![39]

(4) The Last Things

The great fact of the Christian's eternal inheritance and glory in heaven is one of Charles's most constant subjects. He did not dwell to any great extent, however, on eschatological details. But he held definite views on the nature of the last days and we need only

[38] DEJ, III, 397; *Spiritual Counsels* 387-88 [288].
[39] DEJ, II, 449-50.

turn to the word '*mil*' ('thousand') in the *Geiriadur* to find that he was postmillennial in his eschatological beliefs.[40] In this he was typical of the evangelical belief of the period as seen in the writings of Jonathan Edwards in America, Thomas Boston in Scotland, George Whitefield in England or William Williams, Pantycelyn, in Wales, and many others. His understanding of the Scriptures and of Revelation 20, in particular, led him to believe:

> 1. The Church of Christ, which has been for long ages under severe oppression, and cruel persecution, will be successful and will blossom exceedingly on earth before the end of time …
>
> 2. A general return of the Jews and Gentiles, from all over the world, to the Church and to the religion of Christ …
>
> 3. That it will not be an external profession only of Christ's religion that will be present, amongst Jews and Gentiles, but the true saving faith of the Holy Spirit will abide in the souls of men and the power of godliness will flourish gloriously in the Church …
>
> 4. The Church will have rest from all heresies and persecutions …
>
> 5. Clearly, this time of gladness for the Church has not yet begun …
>
> 6. This great success of the Church will last for a thousand years … Most probably the period will begin gradually; one obstacle after another will be removed, and the efforts of the Church will increase gradually until the gospel will have spread throughout the world …[41]

The many revivals and the phenomenal growth in the numbers of believers added to the church during the Evangelical Awakening of the eighteenth century contributed to the general optimism.[42] Charles not only believed that the thousand years would precede

---

[40] See also pp. 178-79.

[41] Entry on 'Thousand,' ('*Mil*'), in the *Geiriadur Ysgrythyrol*, 645-47.

[42] See E. Wyn James, 'David Charles (1762–1834), Caerfyrddin: Diwinydd, Pregethwr, Emynydd,' JHS, 36 (2012), 34-35.

Christ's second coming but considered that it might well be at hand. Writing to a friend in London while in the midst of the Bala Revival of 1791, Charles stated:

> It is an easy and delightful work to preach the glorious Gospel here, in these days ... I bless God for these days ... And I am not without hopes, but these are dawnings of the promised millennium, and showers that precede the storm which will entirely overturn the kingdom of darkness.[43]

The balance between doctrine and experience in Charles's theology

In all of Charles's writing there is a constant warning note that doctrine and experience go hand in hand, that they cannot be separated in the believer's life:

> Human, speculative knowledge, even of divine truths, freeze[s] and starve[s] the soul; whilst divine, experimental knowledge, warms, enlivens, and invigorates those, who are blessed with it from above. They then become not truths to *talk* of only, but to *feed* and live upon; and when we *live* on this *living* bread, we cannot but be *lively* and *strong* ourselves.[44]

The balance between the word and the Spirit is an even greater necessity for the preacher of the word and the pastor of the flock, and Charles never lost sight of this truth for himself. In a letter to Watts Wilkinson dated 29 September 1783 he emphasized this need:

> My dear friend, who is sufficient for these things? Unless continually taught by God, we are no more fit or able to preach the gospel than a blind man to be a guide, or a dumb man to teach languages. St Paul was sent forth to bear witness to these things which he had seen, and to those things in which the Lord would appear to him. It was not

[43] DEJ, II, 90-91.
[44] DEJ, II, 94; *Christian Magazine*, iii, (1792).

sufficient that the Lord had appeared to him; but it was necessary that the Lord should appear daily in those things which he was to testify to others. When the Lord appears to our souls in divine truths, he teaches us more in one quarter of an hour than ten thousand years' study without his teaching. None teach like him. When the Spirit teaches us divine truths, then we can see them as they are, in their own glory and excellency; and we are changed into the same image from glory to glory. This keeps life in our souls, and prevents the power of godliness from dwindling into a mere lifeless, inanimate form. May the Lord keep me in this school while I live.[45]

* * *

Seeking the Measure of the Man

(1) *Thomas Charles's Character*

A close friend of Charles described him as

> of moderate height, somewhat stout, with a well-formed physique, comely, good-looking, lively of movement, with gentlemanly expression ... a man full of thought, discernment and judgement ... His first appearance, perhaps, might repel one with a certain awe of reverence, but his geniality and gentleness soon drew one towards him with confidence.[46]

All who have written on him agree that leadership came naturally to him. There had been examples among the Calvinistic Methodists, as with every gathering of leaders in whatever context, of tensions and divisions because of striving after power and influence. Harris and Rowland struggled for supremacy in the early years of Methodism. But Charles's experience was of a gradual enlarging of his sphere of leadership as the circumstances around

[45] DEJ, I, 427-28.
[46] DEJ, III, 609.

him required it, and of a general acknowledgement by others that this was his natural position. The mantle of leadership settled comfortably upon his shoulders.

Qualities often mentioned by his contemporaries and acquaintances were his kindness and generosity. His and Sally's hospitality knew no bounds; his correspondence frequently reveals invitations for others to stay at his house for long periods. Thus, in 1803, when he was hoping to obtain Robert Saunderson's help with the new press, but still waiting for its delivery, he wrote to him,

> If you should find any difficulty in getting employment for a month, I shall be glad to see you here immediately; and you shall live at our house free of all expense to you. If you should want a little money, show this letter to Mr Lloyd and I dare say he will be so kind as to advance what you may want for me, and place it to my account.[47]

Nine years later, when he and Sally were in poor health, his generosity was unabated, and he pressed Mary Hughes, a friend from Liverpool: 'Should your journey ever take you through Bala, we shall be very happy to receive any of your family who happen to come under our roof. We always have four beds to spare.'[48]

Those who knew him well also furnish plenty of evidence of his humble character. Thus, on a Sunday morning at Llansannan, Denbighshire, early in his ministry he was about to preach to a vast crowd in the open air when the church bell began to toll, calling the people to the service. Charles immediately postponed his meeting and attended at the church, taking the people with him. The service over, Charles stood outside the churchyard wall, and prepared again to preach. The clergyman now interfered, objecting that he stood too near the sacred enclosure of the church. Without the least protest Charles deferred to his authority and led the crowd about a quarter of a mile away from that spot. The meeting then proceeded without further interruption.

[47] DEJ, II, 446.
[48] DEJ, III, 443.

Reflecting upon his gentlemanly conduct and Christian bearing, the clergyman was moved to desire an interview with the itinerant … Owing to an engagement to preach elsewhere, Mr Charles was unable to accept the invitation; but the clergyman never again interfered with the Methodist gatherings.[49]

John Campbell of Edinburgh, writing to John Scott, Thomas Scott's son, recalled a conversation with Thomas Charles:

On a visit to London I was expressing a great desire to see the late Mr Charles of Bala, with whom I had corresponded for three years, concerning a remarkable revival which had taken place under his ministry. Mr Charles happening to be in town at the time, your father kindly took me to Lady Ann Erskine's, where he resided. We spent there two happy hours. Your father requested Mr C. to favour us with a brief outline of the circumstances which led to the remarkable revival at Bala, and the surrounding region, its progress, etc. He did so, for upwards of an hour. On our leaving, your father said, Did you not observe the singular humility of Mr Charles, in the narrative he gave? Never to have once mentioned himself, though he was the chief actor and instrument in the whole matter.[50]

But of all his attributes, those mentioned most often by his contemporaries and biographers alike were his spiritual wisdom and balance. One of the warmest of such expressions was that of his closest friend and collaborator, Thomas Jones, Denbigh. In the preface to his *Memoir* to Charles he wrote, 'By grace, he was made an experienced, discerning, warm-hearted, true Christian at the very onset of his career; he was, as it were, old in learning and spiritual experience when still only a boy.'[51]

* * *

[49] DEJ, III, 603-04.

[50] DEJ, II, 241, quoting from *Letters and Papers of the Rev. Thomas Scott* (1824), 112-13.

[51] Thomas Jones, *Cofiant y Parch. Thomas Charles* (Bala, 1816), iv.

In July 1781, two years before they married, Thomas Charles, late at night, wrote one of his regular letters to Sally. He had no particular news or message of importance to share but in the ordinariness of the letter he revealed a great deal of himself:

8 July 1781

My Dearest Heart

There is nothing more difficult to distinguish than the precise difference between hypocritical, unsound professors and the real Christian. And there are few things with which the mind of the real Christian – who is apt to be very suspicious of himself – is more perplexed…

Sometimes I think there is nothing within me but sin and misery, darkness and confusion; at other times I verily believe myself the completest hypocrite that ever existed. I may well adopt the appellations the pious martyr John Bradford gives himself in some of his letters: 'The most miserable sinner, hard-hearted, unthankful' Thomas Charles; 'the painted hypocrite' Thomas Charles…

Well it is late, my eyes ache and I must go to bed – good night, my dearest Sally.

Then, the next morning, he added:

… Don't forget my kindest love as usual to dear Mr and Mrs Foulks – write *very* soon. J. Bradford's letters which I alluded to above, you will find in Fox's *Book of Martyrs* which I believe you have. I read them about two years ago. Some of them are very excellent indeed. The apricots are ripe, but dearest Sally is not here to partake. Alas, no! How much better would they be if she were! *O na bawn yn y Bala gyda Sally fach!*[52]

In this night-time/early morning note may be seen glimpses of many aspects of the man: his understanding of the Christian life; his humility before God; the degree to which his conversation was always 'seasoned with salt'; his ever-present eagerness to encourage

[52] 'O that I were at Bala with *Sally fach*!' DEJ, I, 292.

others (for, certainly, his exposure of his own, sometimes down-
cast, thoughts was motivated by the hope of comforting Sally in
her own lack of assurance); his wide reading; his delight in social
and spiritual friendships; his enjoyment of all God's good gifts; his
abiding love for Sally.

(2) *His capacity for work*

Charles believed firmly that God guides his people into that work
which he has for them, and that in most cases the main instruments
that he uses for that guidance are the providential circumstances
of life. He was not, therefore, a man to rush into activity. Often,
when giving advice to a correspondent, he would quote verses such
as, 'He that believeth shall not make haste,' Isa. 28:16; 'Rest in the
Lord, and wait patiently for him,' Psa. 37:7. According to R. Tudur
Jones, '[Charles] was not a man of preconceived plans, determin-
ing his career and work by programme. A pragmatic man rather;
one who responded to circumstances, in that he believed deeply
that they were the indicators of divine providence.'[53] However,
once he was assured of what had to be done and of his role in it,
he responded with amazing vigour, perseverance and unrelenting
labours. Whether preaching, itinerating, catechizing, organizing,
administering, fund-raising, writing, editing, leading the Association, or whatever else in which he was engaged, he fulfilled the
commandment, 'Whatsoever thy hand findeth to do, do it with
thy might,' Eccles. 9:10. His early-rising habit meant that he had
accomplished two or three hours of work before most men were
beginning their breakfasts, and he had the physical strength and
mental stamina to fit in up to ten hours or more a day in his study,
day after day, on top of his more public duties. In the years when
he first worked on preparing the text of the Welsh Bible, or on
his *Geiriadur*, or in later years when he did not wish to leave Bala
because of Sally's illness, this was generally his pattern of work.
Without this determination and commitment he would never
have accomplished so much.

[53] RTJ (1979), 41.

R. Tudur Jones has a second perceptive comment on this aspect of Charles's character:

> When considering the inordinate amount of work which passed through his hands, it is natural to wonder how his nerves held up. The answer is that he was supported by the quiet certainty that Christ carries the burdens of his servants. This is clear from his lucid *Dictionary* entry on 'Care.' 'To care (that is, being anxious),' he writes, 'is to take God's work upon ourselves; "he cares for us"; believing, loving, and obeying is our work.' Care 'weighs heavily on the mind,' and 'the great work of faith is to release the mind from it, by loading it upon him to whom it belongs, namely, the Lord, our heavenly Father.' Such daring words! But this is the very fountain-head of the joy that overtook Thomas Charles in Llangeitho, and that breathes a gracious serenity throughout his Calvinism and through all his years of hard labour. To work unsparingly, therefore, is part of our faith. 'No man has any sufficient proof that his faith is true and healthy, if he does not *work* by love ...' Furthermore, we are not 'generous in any work, if we set bounds to it other than those set by God for us; there are no bounds set by God to good works, other than "as we have opportunity," Gal. 6:10, and "as we have prospered," 1 Cor. 16:2.'[54]

He wrote in a similar vein in his *Diary* as a twenty-six year old:

> 'In spiritual as well as temporal things, we are to take no thought for the morrow; for the morrow, when it comes, will take thought for the things of itself. To think for the morrow is to anticipate its evils; as if the evils of today were not sufficient, and as much as we could bear. We must remember the promise, "As the day is, so shall thy strength be." If therefore we anticipate today the evils of tomorrow we must grapple with them in our own strength; for God has promised only strength sufficient for the evils of today.

[54] *Ibid.*, 15-16. The last two short quotations are from the entry on 'Work' ('*Gwaith*') in *Geiriadur Ysgrythyrol*.

For bread and strength for today, we have the sure word of promise to depend on, even sufficient for our greatest need. That is enough for our peace and comfort.'[55]

The joy of the Lord was Charles's strength. Whenever one chances upon him, in his writings or in more personal letters, there is always a sense of great optimism and expectation about him.

(3) *Raised 'for such a time as this'*

There is agreement, again, among all writers on Thomas Charles that his life and work was of strategic significance for Methodism in Wales. David Williams is typical in describing him as 'an organizer of genius … the architect of his denomination.'[56] But the nature of that significance is not understood in the same way by all. He belonged to the second generation of Welsh Methodists. The days of Harris, Rowland and Williams had passed by the time Charles assumed leadership. Some historians of the twentieth century have depicted his work as leader as a battening down the hatches on the fires of revival and of making respectable the offence of the Methodist message; a man 'who appeared late upon the stage when the most thrilling episodes of the play were over. Instead of the prophet came the organizer. After the fiery experience had passed, the defender of orthodoxy filled the breach. Instead of the ecstatic societies, the schools appeared, and where there was once the sharing of spiritual experiences, there was now the memorizing by rote of catechisms.'[57] He was 'a new kind of Methodist … a more doctrinal man than the warm preachers who preceded him.'[58] 'Charles was not, first and foremost, a charismatic preacher, but an organized teacher.'[59] 'The Pantycelyn emphasis on psychology has turned into an emphasis on morality. It is not Dr Aletheius, the

[55] *Memoir*, 183.

[56] David Williams, *A History of Modern Wales* (London: John Murray, 1950), 150, 156.

[57] But R. Tudor Jones then adds: 'This is the picture presented. But in truth it is a caricature.' RTJ (1979), 35.

[58] John Roberts, in *Y Bywgraffiadur Cymreig hyd 1940* (London, 1953), 69.

[59] Derec Ll. Morgan, *Pobl Pantycelyn* (1986), 78.

steward of Theomemphus's society,[60] that speaks for 1799 but the superintendent of the new Sunday schools.'[61]

It is true that there were differences between the Methodism of 1735–85 and that of 1815 onwards. The explosive, dramatic beginnings of the awakening in Wales were such that about three hundred and fifty societies in the south and eighty-two in the north had been formed between 1735 and 1750, whereas the phenomenal growth in Nonconformity from 1815 onwards was more in the form of a continually incoming tide (though still interspersed with regular local and widespread awakenings). Charles's ministry was the main factor in achieving this consolidation. The result of his leadership was the establishing of a stable, enduring witness to the gospel of Jesus Christ. Even at the height of the early Methodist Revival a discord between two individuals, Harris and Rowland, had resulted in a complete division of the work. The exhorters took sides, many criticizing the leaders of the other party. Over a period of twelve years, from 1750 onwards, the work regressed. Many societies were wound up and hundreds of their members were scattered and lost to the movement. Not until the sudden outbreak of the Llangeitho Revival of 1762 did the spiritual powers and blessings return. After 1815, it is not very probable that any discord between two men, however senior in the ranks of the movement, would have resulted in such a devastating division. Indeed, when, a few years after Charles's death, the great theological controversies over the nature of the atonement arose in the denomination, it was the mutual regard for the work and principles of the one who himself had not wished to form a new denomination, that kept them together.

Charles's genius lay in his ability to consolidate, build up and regularize the movement, and to lay down a structure of government. By 1814 he had guided the movement in a Presbyterian direction by licensing their meeting-places, arranging that every congregation had the right to call its own elders, ensuring that

---

[60] The reference is to William Williams's *Theomemphus* (1764), a poetic narrative of the spiritual progress of a typical Methodist convert.

[61] Morgan, *Pobl Pantycelyn* (1986), 82.

those elders were members of the association (the governing body of the denomination), and that the association had the right to ordain its ministers. Within a further eight years, based on the doctrinal foundation laid by Charles in his *Hyfforddwr* and *Geiriadur*, and by Thomas Jones in his historical writings, the denomination had its own *Confession of Faith*.

Thomas Charles was called to preside over the Welsh Calvinistic Methodists during the period which became a watershed in their history. The outward appearance and practice of the eighteenth-century Methodist were very different from those of his nineteenth-century counterpart, yet they were one and the same in their nature and experience. Charles was the bridge between the two periods, the guide and leader who successfully steered a movement vulnerable to doctrinal and organizational hazards into the comparative stability and social acceptability of an established Nonconformist denomination. In 1700, before the Methodist revival, Nonconformity in Wales (predominantly Presbyterians, Baptists and Congregationalists) amounted to less than five percent of the Welsh population. By 1750, after the initial pioneering labours of Harris, Rowland, Williams and others, the Methodist movement consisted of about eight to ten thousand members in a land whose population was approaching half a million (i.e. an addition of a further 2 percent to the Nonconformist percentage). Forty years after the Methodists had ordained their own ministers, the 1851 Religious Census revealed that a total of 480,000 people worshipped in the services of the five main denominations on the Sunday morning of the census, over 40 percent of a population of 1.2 million. Of these the largest grouping was the Calvinistic Methodists with 120,000 in attendance; the Church of England congregations numbered 100,800.[62]

All this is, indeed, testament to Charles's organizational genius, but it must be strongly emphasised that the picture of Charles as only an organizer and administrator, a legalistic douser of the spiritual flames, expert at moulding eighteenth-century

---

[62] John Davies, *A History of Wales* (2007), 412.

enthusiasm into nineteenth-century respectability, is a complete caricature. His own conversion was sudden and dramatic. He engaged in the work of an evangelist throughout his life, cutting back on his extensive preaching itineraries only during periods of ill-health. He rejoiced in days of revival and on more than one occasion was the instrument of revival. At times some of the movements and events which he had set in motion – the meetings of the Sunday schools Associations, for example, or the arrival of despatches of Bibles to an area – proved to be occasions for the onset of local awakenings. His sharing of spiritual experience was as warm and exuberant as any eighteenth-century exhorter. If there was a difference between them it was that Charles had the spiritual and theological education – the words and the wisdom – to interpret and present those experiences in balanced, scriptural terms so as to enable the young converts to understand the spiritual changes that were taking place within them. It must also be remembered that as far as north Wales was concerned, the situation when Charles settled there in the 1780s was still that of 'first generation' Methodism. And throughout his thirty-year ministry there he lived in a time of considerable religious change and development. Hugh Hughes goes so far as to describe the period 1785–1815 as 'the most successful period of [revival] religion in our country.'[63]

The historical statistics of the period also testify to Charles's genius as a nation's teacher and educator. But here again the general agreement is that the one motivation behind all of Charles's educational labours was his concern for the salvation of souls. His cultural and educational achievements must not be emphasized to the extent that this key to all his work is lost sight of. The overwhelming need for every man, woman and child was to read God's Word, the Bible, in order that they might be saved.

'Above all,' wrote R. Tudur Jones,

[63] E. Wyn James, JHS, 36 (2012), 16; quoting Hugh Hughes (1841–1924), the historian of Welsh revivals, *Hanes Diwygiadau Crefyddol Cymru* (Caernarfon, 1907), 170.

he was a servant. He was at the service of all at all times. He was a servant of the people of Wales in his generation. He was concerned for them and laboured to give of his best to them. This is what made him a friend to the nation. But a friend to the nation only in so much as he was a servant of the Word. It was the strength of his longing to share the riches of the Covenant of Christ with his generation that spurred on his service to Wales – and to the world. Part of the uniqueness of Thomas Charles is that in seeking to serve Wales he served the whole world through the Bible Society.[64]

(4) *The Guidance of Providence*

In seeking the measure of the man, it is necessary to remember that to which he himself paid so much attention, namely the various steps of providence which married the man to the work given him to do, and which secured success and blessing upon that work. The following are examples of 'concurring providences,' as he called them, as they arose in his life:

(i) His family background, upbringing and education prepared him for leadership and provided him with the linguistic and theological skills that enabled him to provide such a rich literary heritage for the converts of the Methodist Revival.

(ii) His conversion under the preaching of Daniel Rowland ensured that, however strong might be his commitment to the Church of England, the gospel came to him in the demonstration of the Spirit and power of the Methodist Revival, so that his evangelical convictions were thereafter always stronger by far than any ecclesiastical preferences.

(iii) His period in Oxford introduced him to the society of the leading English evangelical clergy who were to be his main support for so many of his endeavours. The annual requests that he minister for some months at Spa Fields Chapel, London, enabled him to

[64] RTJ (1979), 41. By 1900 the BFBS had distributed more than 160 million portions of Scripture. In the year 2014 a total of 34 million Bibles, and a total of 428.2 million portions of Scripture, were distributed by Bible societies world-wide.

maintain these connections for most of his life.

(iv) His love for Sally Jones, with her strong Methodist links and her unwillingness to move from Bala, settled him in north Wales at exactly the time when the Methodists of the region required a strong leader. Her commercial skills enabled him to give all his time, for the remaining thirty years of his life, to the ministry. He had written to her in April 1782, sixteen months before they were married: 'When I look back upon the commencement of our correspondence, and also its continuance, I cannot but see the hand of Providence in it from the beginning to end. You asked me more than once why I wrote to you at that time more than any other. I really know of no other reason but that it was impressed upon my mind, but now I see the reason, and also see the hand of God in it, to my great joy and comfort.'[65] This conviction only increased within him throughout their life together.

(v) His early meeting and friendship with Thomas Jones, Denbigh, resulted in a very effective and powerful partnership. With statesmanlike wisdom, they foresaw the needs of the Methodist societies, and together led the movement: planning, cooperating, publishing, 'pull[ing] together very peaceably under the yoke,' and laying a solid foundation for the future denomination.

* * *

In 1841, in the last year of his life, John Elias wrote a brief autobiography. In it he discussed the servants of God whom he had admired and worked with in the gospel for many years. He noted:

> I was more conversant with the work in North Wales during my life. There were very notable men taking the lead in the work when I was young. Although not many of them were learned, the Lord gave one very learned man to North Wales, the late Reverend Thomas Charles of Bala, who was as a Prince of God in our midst. The late Reverend Thomas Jones of Denbigh was a learned man, laborious and very

[65] DEJ, I, 342-43.

useful, although not ordained a minister of the Established Church. He and Mr Charles pulled together very peaceably under the yoke ...

Concerning the Quarterly Associations in North Wales, the cloud of God's glory was often upon them. The trumpet-blast of the King was heard among the assemblies. There were evident signs of God's gracious presence in the private meetings as well as in the public preaching. The Reverend Thomas Charles was a wise Moderator in these meetings – fatherly, very tender, yea, a Moderator set by God on us. None of us coveted his position, or wished to take his chair. He was at all times ready to place profitable things before the brethren, in points of doctrine and of discipline; he used to state them in a wise and proper order. He would encourage the brethren to speak their minds on the matters under consideration: he would assist the weak and guide the disorderly. At the end of the discussion, he would sum everything up into a systematic order; and he would exhort the brethren to take everything home to their congregations. Oh what heavenly dew descended in these meetings![66]

[66] Morgan, *John Elias* (1973), 177-78.

BIBLIOGRAPHIES

Thomas Charles's Major Literary Works, by Date of Publication[1]

1789   *Crynodeb o Egwyddorion Crefydd: neu Catecism Byrr i Blant, ac eraill, i'w ddysgu* (*A Summary of the Principles of Religion: or a Short Catechism to be learnt by Children and others*); 3rd ed. in 1794.

1797   *An Evangelical Catechism.*

1799   *Crynodeb o Egwyddorion Crefydd: neu Catecism Byrr i Blant, ac eraill, i'w dysgu* (*A Summary of the Principles of Religion: or, a Short Catechism for Children, and others, to learn*), the same title but a different work to the above; 6th ed. in 1808.

1799   *Trysorfa Ysbrydol* (*A Spiritual Treasury*), Series 1, co-edited with Thomas Jones, Denbigh; 2nd ed. in 1809.

1800   *The Works of Walter Cradock*, co-edited with Philip Oliver.

1801   *A Short Evangelical Catechism; containing the first Principles of Christianity*; 8th ed. in 1859.

---

[1] DEJ, III, 651-65; Goronwy Prys Owen, *Thomas Charles a'r Bala* (Bala: Cantref, 2016), 125-27.

1801   *Rheolau a Dybenion y Cymdeithasau Neillduol yn mlith y Bobl a elwir y Methodistiaid yn Nghymru* (*The Rules and Designs of the Religious Societies among the Welsh Methodists*); 2nd ed. in 1802.

1801   *Esboniad Byr ar y Deg Gorchymyn* (*A Short Commentary on the Ten Commandments*); 7th ed. in 1856.

1802   *The Rules and the Design of the Religious Societies among the Welsh Methodists.*

1802   *The Welsh Methodists Vindicated.*

1805   *An Exposition of the Ten Commandments.*

1805   *Geiriadur Ysgrythyrol*, Llyfr 1. (*Scriptural Dictionary*, Book 1); 3rd ed. in 1836.

1806   *Casgliad o Hymnau* (*A Collection of Hymns*); 3rd ed. with additions in 1809.

1806   *Testament Newydd* (*New Testament*), edited with the help of Robert Jones, Rhos-lan and Thomas Jones, Denbigh.

1807   *Hyfforddwr yn Egwyddorion y Grefydd Gristionogol* (*An Instructor in the Principles of the Christian Religion*); eighty editions before 1900.

1807   *Y Sillydd Cymraeg; neu arweinydd i'r Frutaniaith* (*The Welsh Primer: or a guide to the British Language*); 8th ed. in 1893.

1807   *Y Bible Cyssegr-Lan (The Sacred Bible)*, the first Bible produced by the BFBS.

1808   *Geiriadur Ysgrythyrol*, Llyfr 2. (*Scriptural Dictionary*, Book 2); 3rd ed. in 1829.

1810   *Geiriadur Ysgrythyrol*, Llyfr 3. (*Scriptural Dictionary*, Book 3); 2nd ed. in 1823.

1811   *Geiriadur Ysgrythyrol*, Llyfr 4. (*Scriptural Dictionary*, Book 4); 2nd ed. in 1825.

1813   *Rheolau Ffurfiaw a Threfnu Ysgolion Sabbothawl (Rules for Establishing and Organizing Sunday schools)*.

1813   *Trysorfa (A Treasury)*, Series 2.

1814   *Y Bible Cyssegr-Lan (The Sacred Bible)*.

1853   *Geiriadur Ysgrythyrol. (Scriptural Dictionary*, in one volume); 5th ed. in 1885.

English Biographies of Thomas Charles

1828   Morgan, Edward, *A Brief History of the Life and Labours of the Rev. T. Charles, A.B.* (London, 1828); 2nd edition, *A Brief Memoir of the Life …* (London, 1831).

1881   Hughes, William, *Life and Letters of the Rev. Thos. Charles, B.A., of Bala* (Rhyl, 1881).

1908   Jenkins, D. E., *The Rev. Thomas Charles of Bala*, Vols. I-III (Denbigh, 1908).

1955   Pritchard, R. A., *Thomas Charles, 1755-1814* (Cardiff, 1955).

Select Bibliography of English Titles

Cook, Faith, *Selina Countess of Huntingdon* (Edinburgh: Banner of Truth Trust, 2001).

Dictionary of Welsh Biography down to 1940 (Oxford: Blackwell, 1959).

Evans, Eifion, *Bread of Heaven: The Life and Work of William Williams* (Bridgend: Bryntirion Press, 2010).

Evans, Eifion, *Daniel Rowland and the Great Evangelical Awakening in Wales* (Edinburgh: Banner of Truth Trust, 1985).

Jones, John Morgan and Morgan, William, trans. by John Aaron, *The Calvinistic Methodist Fathers of Wales*, Vols 1 and 2 (Edinburgh: Banner of Truth Trust, 2008).

Morgan, Edward, *Memoir of John Elias* (1844); repub. as *John Elias: Life, Letters and Essays* (Edinburgh: Banner of Truth Trust, 1973)

Morgan, Edward (ed.), *Essays, Letters and Interesting Papers of Thomas Charles* (1836); repub. as *Thomas Charles' Spiritual Counsels* (Edinburgh: Banner of Truth Trust, 1993, 2021).

Murray, Iain H., *Heroes* (Edinburgh: Banner of Truth Trust, 2009).

Scott, Thomas, *The Force of Truth* (1779; repub. Edinburgh: Banner of Truth Trust, 1984).

Williams, William, *Welsh Calvinistic Methodism* (1872; repub. Bridgend: Bryntirion Press, 1998).

INDEX

Trefeca 9, 20, 30
Trysorfa, (1813), see Charles, Thomas:
  publications
Trysorfa Ysbrydol (1799), see Charles,
  Thomas: publications
Turkdean 27
Turretin, Francois 266, 342
'Twm o'r Nant', see Edwards, Thomas
Venema, Hermann 266
Venn, John 33, 288
Vitringa, Campegius 266
Warren, John 205
Watts, Isaac 19
Waugh, Alexander 176
Welsh Bible
  editions
    Stephen Hughes' Bible (1677/78)
      13
    SPCK (1746) 221
    SPCK (1752) 221
    SPCK (1769) 204
    Peter Williams (1770) 156
    Peter Williams (1790) 158, 205
    SPCK (1799) 206, 217
    BFBS (1807) 217-23
    BFBS (1814) 319
    Beibl Cymraeg Newydd (1988)
      320
  numbers produced in the nine-
    teenth century 328
  scarcity in Wales 204
Welsh Calvinistic Methodist Church
  (London) 182
Welsh counties, old 2
Welsh Looking-Glass, The (1812) 307
Welsh Methodists Vindicated, The
  (1802), see Charles, Thomas: publi-
  cations
'Welsh Not, the' 141
Welsh Trust, The 130, 136
Wesleyan Conference, the 235, 288
Wesley, John 3, 44, 142, 288, 301

Westminster Confession of Faith, The
  (1646) 18
Westminster Shorter Catechism (1648)
  243
Whitefield, George 3, 4, 5, 9, 15, 231,
  233, 351
Wilberforce, William 33, 137, 207, 213
Wilderness Row 182
Wilkinson, Watts 30, 38, 65, 81, 98,
  104, 288, 334, 350, 352
Wilks, Matthew 212
Williams, David 359
Williams, Edward (Rotherham) 341
Williams, Eliezer 308
Williams, John (Lledrod) 303, 304,
  305
Williams, John (Pantycelyn) 233, 303,
  304
Williams, Lewis 139
Williams, Peter 3, 6, 152, 173, 233, 308
  excommunication by Methodists
    156-63
Williams, William 3, 16, 17, 45, 68, 75,
  123, 152, 173, 176, 190, 233, 258, 275,
  288, 305, 335, 338, 347, 351
  excommunication of Peter
    Williams 156-60
Williams, William (Wern) 171
Wilson, James 177
Wilson, William 177
Witsius, Hermann 266
Wollaston, William 19
Wrexham 45
Wroth, William 233
Wynn, Sir Watkin Williams (d. 1749)
  6, 193, 318
Wynn, Sir Watkin Williams (1772-
  1840) 317
Ymddiddanion rhwng Scrutator a Senex
  232
Zanchius, Hieronymus 266

BANNER *of* TRUTH

The Banner of Truth Trust originated in 1957 in London. The founders believed that much of the best literature of historic Christianity had been allowed to fall into oblivion and that, under God, its recovery could well lead not only to a strengthening of the church, but to true revival.

Interdenominational in vision, this publishing work is now international, and our lists include a number of contemporary authors, together with classics from the past. The translation of these books into many languages is encouraged.

A monthly magazine, *The Banner of Truth*, is also published, and further information about this, and all our other publications, may be found on our website, banneroftruth.org, or by contacting the offices below:

Head Office:
3 Murrayfield Road
Edinburgh
EH12 6EL
United Kingdom
Email: info@banneroftruth.co.uk

North America Office:
PO Box 621
Carlisle, PA 17013
United States of America
Email: info@banneroftruth.org